The Power of Divine:

A Healer's Guide

Tapping into the Miracle

The Power of Divine:
A Healer's Guide

Tapping into the Miracle

Tiffany Snow D.D.

Spirit Journey Books

San Diego, California

The Power of Divine: A Healer's Guide
Tapping into the Miracle
Copyright © 2004 Tiffany Snow

Printed in the United States of America
First Edition

Unless otherwise identified, Scripture taken from the HOLY BIBLE, New International Version ®. Copyright © 1973, 1978, 1984 by International Bible Society. Used by permission of Zondervan Publishing House. All rights reserved.

Published by
Spirit Journey Books
P.O. Box 61
San Marcos, CA 92079

www.SpiritJourneyBooks.com

Toll-Free 1(800) 535-5474
SpiritJourneyBks@aol.com

For more information regarding Tiffany Snow's workshops, seminars and books, please visit:

www.TiffanySnow.com
or: emailtiffanysnow@aol.com

Edited by
Adrienne Adams
Cover Design by
Tiffany Snow, Sierra Neal
Cat Stevenson

Library of Congress Catalog Number: 2004102626
International Standard Book Number
ISBN 0-9729623-3-6

1. Health. 2. Spirituality.

DEDICATION

Most Gracious One,
Thank You for desiring to heal your people.
Your continued signs and wonders
Abundantly show your everlasting power and ability!
Thank You for letting me be there when you lovingly touch,
I can see your Spirit shine through the hearts of mankind!

Dear Father, when the lightning took me and my flesh expired,
When my spirit was before you in heaven,
I wanted more than anything else to stay.
To stay in your Awesome Wave
of Iridescent Love. To stay!

Yet, you asked me to go back, and you gave me work to do.
You said, "I am with you always," that people will see me,
but experience You.
How then, could I seek my own joy of your Presence,
When your desire is to manifest your Presence to all others?
It is a glorious work you have given your intimate lovers,
As we see Spirit unfurl, we passionately weep
for Deeper Connection all day long.

Now, you help me see people like you see them -
Your Divine Spark Within each one,
the aching part of the soul that calls you by Name.
I see the hunger, and I see how you offer to fill them,
and how they push away from the buffet of your love.

And I want to help them too,
And let them feel your comforting arms.
Now I can stay, Joyously Stay!
Yes, I will stay joyously.
Because Father now I love them too, and I will finish the work
You have graciously given me to do.
The colors of your love reach even to the far ends of heaven.
And I am Never alone in the Oneness.
Lord, I can feel your Iridescent Wave,
your Love, from here.

TIFFANY SNOW has been called a Modern-Day Mystic, along the spiritual paths of Teresa of Avila or Kathryn Kulhman. She is a Gifted Healer, Medical Intuitive, Minister, Public Speaker and Spiritual Communicator. Tiffany Snow simply calls herself, "A Worker for The Big Guy." Quite a difference from her previous life of producing records and writing songs in Nashville, Tennessee!

But, it took some persuasion. So, a lightning strike and incredible near-death-experience gave her a "push." Tiffany says, "The best thing that happened in my life, was almost losing it…"

Now, her "stage" is conducting workshops and motivating others as she offers a buffet of personal tools, techniques, and experiences, including ancient Biblical ones, to help accelerate each person's own spiritual development and healing gifts.

You won't find Tiffany Snow in white billowy dresses, separating and elevating herself above others and belting out a religious agenda – instead, you will find her wearing green or blue nurse "scrubs," while working and moving among people of all faiths, beliefs and non-belief systems, as she helps and inspires through words and demonstrations to all.

Tiffany Snow is a woman on a mission, "led by the Spirit," encouraging others with her stories, and actively sharing The Gifts. She is able to help people "fill their God-Spot" and see "Supernatural Gifts manifest in their own lives as they access the Divine Connection."

She draws people to her like moths to a flame. They come to feel her warmth, be healed by her hands, and bask in the glow of her simple communion with God. All the while, she teaches. She gently reminds people that she is not special or in any way different from them, and all can have the gifts she has. She tells them, "I am a child of God. Just like you! We are the same."

In New Mexico she was welcomed and accepted in a Pueblo Indian reservation to work side-by-side with their local medicine woman; in the hollows of Kentucky she was "adopted" by locals to heal their farms - all inclusive of people, horses, dogs and cats. In the "Bible Belt" of Tennessee, she was quietly brought into hospitals and churches to heal the sick and infirm. In Hawaii, she gave astonishing and validated information on Hawaiian history and archeology, as she also did in Tennessee and New Mexico. She has helped on missing person cases, and with the FBI on 9/11. As an ordained minister, for decades she has "released" ghosts, "bound" entities, and offered Deliverance (Exorcism). Tiffany Snow, D.D. is leading an interesting life!

Tiffany was born in Vista, California. As an only child, she grew up in a motor-home traveling the back roads of the American Dream. She is a "local girl makes good" to many hometowns. Tiffany started writing, playing musical instruments and painting as a child. She went on to produce instrumental and country albums, toured extensively, and received standing-ovations at the Grand 'Ole Opry. She has been published in several magazines, and in 2003 authored the spiritually motivating book, *Psychic Gifts in the Christian Life – Tools to Connect* to an appreciative audience.

Coming full circle, Tiffany now lives back in Southern California with her family and the sea, where she continues to work facilitated for Divine Healing at three clinics and many churches. She is a Licensed CE Provider for the California Board of Registered Nursing (Governed by the State of California Dept. of Consumer Affairs); Member of the International Holistic Healing Circle & Society; Missionary Pastor at Corner Stone Christian Fellowship; Usui Reiki Master Practitioner, 4th Degree; Founding Member of Bless This House, Deliverance & Exorcism Ministry; Member of the International Order of St. Luke the Physician (OSL); Doctorate of Divinity, World Christianship Ministries; Senior Pastor Hearts & Hands Outreach Ministry; Member IANDS (International Association of Near-Death Studies); Medically Documented Survivor of Lightning Strike/Electrical Shock (NDE), and president of Spirit Journey Books and SnowCat Music, independent music and book publishing companies.

"It's about learning to trust and surrender in Power beyond oneself, and learning to receive while giving. Unconditional Love manifests Miracles in the world. Let your natural spirit be touched by Divine Spirit, and every aspect of your life will be healed!"

CONTENTS

INTRODUCTION

Dr. Tiffany Snow's title for her new book is provocative in the fundamental sense of the word: *to call* faith, *to evoke* a personal response, from you the reader.

Do you want to be a healer, do you want to evoke the healing powers that you have and might not be aware of? Here is a guide based upon extensive experience.

Tiffany is not saying "do it my way." She is encouraging us to find *our* way. What she gives is a road map to assist us if we decide to undertake this journey, with all the arduous effort and risk that it entails.

The Greek philosopher Socrates stated "the unexamined life is not worth living." In this book Tiffany examines and reflects upon the meaning of her vocation - her calling - to be a healer, and insightfully describes what she has learned about herself and the healing process. How Socratic!

There is a strong unifying theme on what the preconditions are for engaging in the healing process. First of all, there is the need for *self healing* and a *love of self.*

This is why, as I see it, the fundamental importance of *self forgiveness* resonates throughout her experiential reflections. Indeed, all forgiveness begins in self forgiveness. That is to say, when we see and understand the importance of self acceptance, we find the ability to feel at home with ourselves, to overcome our insecurities. The Latin word *"securus"* means *safe, free from care*. In essence, it is the feeling of being at home with oneself. If we are not, we are insecure.

Importantly, Dr. Snow gives a new perspective of what "alternative" means in the context of "alternative medicine." She points out the variegated modalities that are possible. It's not about doing things differently; but understanding what differences work, and why, in a particular case. This, in turn, brings us back to reflect upon the first principle of self healing, where we have learned these lessons for ourselves. Once learned, we can let them overflow to those in need of healing with whom we come in contact.

But so that we do not make the mistake of assuming that what works for us will work for others, let us keep in mind that we, in the words of Henri Nouwen, are "wounded healers." Be that as it may, to paraphrase the scripture, "by our wounds others can be healed," because our wounds make us conscious that the pain and suffering of others - emotional, psychological and physical - must be approached in the basis of what they are experiencing.

Along with the need for self forgiveness and self love, there is another important principle for engaging in the healing process. And that is *not getting in God's way!* Philip Neri, the 16th century Roman priest, had a favorite morning prayer; "Lord, let me not do too much harm today." Another way of expressing this is: "Lord, help me keep out of your way today." This is living in God's presence, the source of our effectiveness in the healing ministry.

Tiffany raises an important theological question: "Why does God depend upon us to be his mediators?" The response, simply stated, is because it enables us, his creation, to exercise the power of the Divine. God is silent in the world unless we speak and act on His behalf. He has chosen us to be His partners in Divine love in giving to each other compassionate sharing and healing of the wounds that affect us. Remember Jesus said: *"You* are the salt of the earth...*You* are the light of the world." (Mt. 5:13-16)

As was her earlier book, *Psychic Gifts in the Christian Life - Tools to Connect*, this is also written from a Christian conviction and her own theological perspective. But accepting this perspective, based upon her personal experience, is in no way a *"sine qua now;"* a *pre-condition* for engaging in the journey she maps out for becoming a self healer and a healer of others.

At the core of what is required is a *God-centeredness* which has a universal application. "In God, with God and through God." This is the foundation, the fundamental perspective in order to become a healer of self and of others.

Also, Dr. Snow gives an excellent last-chapter summary, a mini-healer's guide that I could describe as "questions I never thought of."

How Socratic indeed! Have a productive read.

Rev. Francis J. Marcolongo
S.T.L., S.S.L., Ph.D., MFT
Escondido, California

AUTHOR'S NOTE

The Power of Divine: A Healer's Guide removes many of the fear-based and man-made traditions that have overshadowed modern teaching about hands-on-healing, while explaining the difference between spiritual healing and Divine Healing. As you step upon this path of activating your True Potential, my prayer for you is that you'll find yourself embracing an abundantly joyful life, full of purpose, health and happiness, *every minute of your day!*

As we slowly surrender to the spiritual journey of knowing ourselves, loving others and trusting the One who is invisible, we receive in equal measure all the blessings that we are created to hold, and abundantly overflow to others. Through this journey we discover the purpose for our life, as we discover the uniqueness of our own path and how this uniqueness heals and gifts not only our own self, but our family, friends, and the entire world.

Let this book be a helpful guide to break through the physical, emotional, and spiritual barriers that act as distractions to the true life. When we have balanced wholeness, it increases the greater good we are able to do in service for others. When we have balanced wholeness, we are never bored, but have daily stimulation that makes our spirit glow and life seem boundlessly joyful. Seeking wholeness and balance, we do not fear when our soul ascends and transforms through the Free Will journey; we learn to trust ourselves and the consequences and blessings of the choices we make, as we come closer to Him, our True Source.

Personal experience has been a factor, indeed, for writing this book, for I see my entire life as a classroom in preparation for this healing journey. Many have been the questions as struggle and blessings came across my path, each carrying their own specific burden and lessons. Some of these trappings, most of which were victim-based and religious in nature, I have stumbled on; I have found by tripping I've learned to lift my feet. Looking back, I realize that all the times of my brokenness were simply excellent opportunities for me to choose *love* over bitterness, *love* over fear, *love* over unforgiveness. By exercising the opportunity to use our Free Will to always choose *love,* we allow ourselves to become rebuilt into a better vessel; strong enough to be a flowing channel for Unconditional Love to all people, a true reflection of the nature of the Christ.

I wish you love! Enjoy your Journey into the miraculous and powerful world of Divine Healing, where anything can happen, and often does! *Health & Blessings to You!*

- A Fellow Worker for The Big Guy, Tiffany Snow

CHAPTER 1

Divine Healing & Physical Health
Research; Hands-on-Healing; Medical Intuitiveness

Can prayer heal? Do miracles happen? Can a person tap into a Supernatural Power so strong that the impossible becomes reality? Can ancestral curses and negativity manifest as illness in a descendant's body? Can the scaring of emotional trauma truly be healed? Could these things truly be possible in this day and age?

For more and more people, across every continent in the world, the answer is a resounding "Yes!" This is not a modern phenomena, the art of Divine Healing goes back to the beginning of time. People have long called upon God for the healing of their bodies, homes, families and fields. What is modern is that science is now becoming *developed enough* to back it up – giving the doubtful a logical reason to believe, and thus promoting more healings and more Supernatural events in our time, in more variety, thus creating a blessed ripple effect.

In a recent interview with David Larson, MD, MSPH, and president of the National Institute for Healthcare Research, Jeanie Lerche Davis of WebMD reported: "Research focusing on the power of prayer in healing has nearly doubled in the past 10 years. Even the NIH, which refused to even review a study with the word prayer in it four years ago, is now funding one prayer study through its Frontier Medicine Initiative. Today, we're seeing systematic investigations - clinical research - as well as position statements from professional societies supporting this research, federal subsidies from the NIH, funding from Congress…all of these studies, all the reports, are remarkably consistent in suggesting the potential measurable health benefit associated with prayer or spiritual interventions." Where is this ripple leading?

Change in the World of Healthcare

The American Medical Association (AMA) now considers many different methods of healing as Complementary Alternative Medicine, or *CAM.* This includes not only naturopathic and holistic medicine, but spiritual and prayer-based healing as well. Things are changing in the way we look at personal health and wellness. Even at this time, through the efforts of the Foundation for Integrative Healthcare and Alternative Link, over 4,000 ABC codes have been developed which are HIPAA-compliant, which makes the terminology for many alternative therapies billable to insurance companies. Many individuals, private parties, various organizations, and forward-thinking politicians are of the popular opinion that insurance companies should have to pay for *alternative methods of healing.* Why? Because they work! Many therapies shorten recuperation time, and may offer more affordable treatment with less medical contraindications. Utilizing complementary alternative medicine helps free up hospital beds and time and caseload for overwhelmed doctors and nurses. Also, studies show that patients feel more in control and are more apt to take a personal interest in their own health, follow through with it, and monitor the results more closely.

Also - and perhaps the major "unspoken" reason why U.S. health practitioners are looking at alternative medicine - is because they're *losing billions of dollars every year to alternative therapies!* It has come down to literally, "jumping on the band wagon or getting left behind." Is it any wonder that most medical colleges are now adding a variety of new alternative programs, however reluctantly, to their regime?

What about the cost? At the moment, in most cases the cost for alternative therapy is being paid out of the client's own pocket, and not by the insurance companies. Surveys show that most people who decide to use these therapies are not the poor and downtrodden, but actually the more educated and well-off. Also, many report having had previous experiences that were the catalyst for "opening them up" to new treatments. Most of these pioneering souls use both worlds - conventional medicine and CAM. They are to be applauded! We are on a new frontier of healthcare, with the inevitable blending of both, into a viable and exciting union. This pairing includes the wellness available through various forms of hands-on-healing, and prayer.

Prayer Changes Physical and Emotional Health Too

Science is setting out to prove what most of the faithful already know - *that prayer heals.* Everyday, more and more headlines are announcing the spiritual practices of celebrities and the average people who have escaped impossible situations. We want to know what others are doing about the Spiritual and Supernatural dimensions in their lives. For example, it's well-know that U.S. Attorney General John Ashcroft kicks off his morning Justice Department meetings with prayer and Bible readings. More magazines are abounding with stories of miracles and Divine interventions. And, whether you do research at a library, pick up a book at the bookstore, or access the internet, you are going to find numerous articles and studies that validate the link of prayer and spirituality to physical, emotional and spiritual health. Duke, Dartmouth, and Yale are just a few universities who conduct studies on prayer and health. Here are a few headlines from Duke University Medical Center:

"Religious attendance linked to lower mortality in elderly.
A study of nearly 4,000 elderly North Carolinians has found that those who attended

religious services every week were 46 percent less likely to die over a six-year period than people who attended less often or not at all, according to researchers at Duke University Medical Center." 07/22/1999

"Use of prayer or Noetic therapy may contribute to better outcomes.
Combining prayer with traditional treatments may offer the best medicine of all, say researchers who tested the power of spirituality to affect the outcome of heart patients undergoing coronary balloon angioplasty." 11/09/1998

"Religious elderly have lower blood pressure.
It could be the fellowship, the ceremonies, or the connection with a higher power, but whatever the reason, religious practices have a beneficial effect on physical and mental health." 08/10/1998

The Best Research Tool is Personal Experience

There are numerous studies being conducted and planned, hundreds already concluded, and many fine books already on the market citing double-blind studies, case histories, and years of careful observation and research on the subject of spirituality, religion, prayer, health, and their symbiotic relationship. I will not duplicate in this book the research findings, and I suspect that many readers are already a practitioner of some form of healing work, or have experienced it in their lives. But, in case you are new to this ancient/modern idea, let me encourage you to actively read up on the matter as much as possible, and talk to as many qualified practitioners as you can. I always let my clients know that I do not require them to come to me *already believing* in Divine Healing, but suggest only to be *open to the possibility* of its reality; and to believe from the end results of the treatment. *Let your own personal experience convince you!*

Through the intervention of Spirit, we humans can change the world with a message that never changes at all - the awareness that there is definitely something greater than ourselves, and that this Something Greater has the *ability and desire* to make an powerful difference in our individual lives! In our continued spiritual quest, we discover more about this Being, the one titled by many names: God, Divine, Yahweh (YHWH), Source, Spirit, The One, Jehovah, The Alpha & Omega, The Light, The LORD (all caps when referring to the Father, and "Lord" when referring to the Son, Jesus Christ). As healing evangelist Kathryn Kulhman once said; "I have decided that God doesn't have preferences in theology. We are the ones who try to put a fence around God."

As we develop a longing to draw closer to him and grasp the finer details of our Quest, we find out what "made is his image" means, as we also discover *ourselves,* our *true inner nature,* and our *true purpose* in life. We find that this multi-faceted God has a

3

winning personality and golden qualities, and loves his creation and desires to stay in constant communication with us. We find that no matter what nationality, race or religion, we are all his children, and as such we should be careful with ourselves and each other, always reflecting the mirrored image of Divine through love.

These personal, empirical spiritual discoveries actually make a difference in our physical bodies. It also makes a difference in our emotional health. By truly understanding this and letting Light work through us, we gain true sensitivity, peace and power that we have never experienced before. *We become greater than we are.* We understand that which is beyond the realm of reality. And then we see miracles unfold before our very eyes. *All kinds of them!*

What is the Difference between Spiritual & Divine Healing?

Spiritual healing can be Reiki, Therapeutic Touch®, Qigong, Quantum Healing, etc. Spiritual healing has come to mean a variety of methods which may employ some sort of spiritual aspect with the healing, but may or may not include prayer. Also, the person healing may or may not be including his *own* energy in with the healing. *Divine Healing always* includes prayer, cannot activate without it, and healing is *never* done by including any of the person's own energy. It often includes some version of hands-on-healing or "laying-on-of-hands."

A person may, such as I, be certified as a Reiki Practitioner, yet do Divine Healing. I always include Connection in prayer before I begin, cannot do a healing without it, and then I proceed to get myself out of the way so The Big Guy can work. Reiki allows me to easily work in the clinics under CAM, and prayer allows me to facilitate the best healings possible. These Supernatural healings tap into Power beyond our own capabilities, and are far beyond just speeding up the body's own natural recuperation times, as may be seen typically in spiritual healing. *Miracles* can and do occur. The invisible may become manifest in our physical world, beyond the scope of our known perception of reality. The difference might be compared to using a battery with stored energy, as compared to live current. AC versus DC. Both use energy; either their own or Someone else's. But which is more powerful? Which one would you choose to work on you?

By experience, I suggest that when you look for a healer, no matter what alternative medicine "title" they may fall under, be sure to ask if they use Godly prayer with their healing; if they recognize True Source. See if their spirit reflects the yielded glow of an active spiritual life. True humility which acknowledges the Lord as the source of all healing activates Supernatural Power. You will see a marked difference in the results

4

you receive!

Matter is Slowed-Down Energy

Modern Science has shown that everything in the universe is composed of energy, and that the apparent difference between solids, liquids, gases, sound and light is merely a difference in their vibratory rates. *Einstein stated, "All matter is slowed down energy."* Science has also eagerly shown that energy cannot be destroyed, but simply changes form.

Similarly, the world's great religions state that all created things originate in the cosmic vibratory energy of AUM, or Amen, the Word or the Holy Ghost. "In the beginning was the Word, and the Word was with God...all things were made by Him, and without Him was not anything made which was made." (Jn.1:1,3) We live in a cosmic soup of vibrating energy! Everything that *surrounds* us, is *IN* us, and *IS* us, is *FROM* our direct link to The Original Source. And we are made in the image, or likeness, of him. We are also taught, "God is Spirit," and "God's Spirit lives in you." *We* have to choose to be part of our healing process. (Ge.1:26; Jn.4:24; 1 Cor. 3:16) Divine Spirit touching natural spirit.

Here on this material plane of existence, many of the needs and yearnings of our heart need *physical manipulation of matter* to make things work out. This might come in the form of miraculous healings of the body; financial needs being met; new relationships brought into our lives, or beneficial situations opening up. These are only *some* examples of the physical manifestations of prayer, even though we might be surprised by how or when they occur! It's quite probable that you've already had some personal experience with Supernatural Intervention, Divine Coincidences, or are in need of it right now. Or perhaps you have a friend or relative who has experienced a wonderful event, or needs one. Or maybe you are simply curious because of the articles you've read or stories you've heard. There are many of them!

Then, again, there could be *another* reason why you've picked up this book...perhaps you are being *called to your purpose in life,* your true destiny! Called to be a healer!

Becoming Your True Potential

During your journey within this book and outside of it, you may find an undeniable "inner knowing" that healing is the work you are supposed to do in your life There may be an overwhelming sense of joy, excitement, and peacefulness of mind that pervades your consciousness whenever the opportunity for healing is near. Recognizing and becoming your true potential is one of the highest joys in life! And realizing what all your previous life experiences were training you for, all your periods of brokenness and rebuilding, and having the 20/20 hindsight vision of "everything being just the way it should be" lets you release the past and push on ahead to greener pastures. If you find healing is your true calling my friend, congratulations and welcome! Consider this book one of your friendly directional arrows along the twisting and turning roadmap!

Each person called into this work will experience the Gifts, Interventions and Coincidences needed to fully embrace their new abilities. There is much to learn, and it never (thankfully) ends. Now everyday can be a new adventure, as your consciousness is gradually shifted into your new employment, as a "Worker for The Big Guy." You will be tested for your ability to yield. You will be tested as to ego. You will be tested for your ability to withstand reproach under fire. There are many tests; similar to a mighty sword being folded, hammered, and folded again, which passes through water and through fire, until a perfect and strong tool stands ready and balanced in the hand of its Master. Life is a learning process. Being facilitated for healing accelerates personal growth at a knuckle-whitening speed. So, hang on, and enjoy! There is much work to be done - let's begin!

Becoming a Conduit of Change

Imagine yourself a lamp in a house - what has to occur for your bulb to light up? The cord has to reach to the outlet in the wall. The wall switch has to be turned on. The wiring from the house to the electrical pole has to be in order, as does the conduit from there to the city power supply. A lot has to happen for your bulb to allow your warm brightness to aid the children in their homework, the father to read his paper, and the mother to do handiwork. But, the effort is worth it. So much can be done to light up the darkness when you are plugged in! In this same way you allow yourself to be a live wire, a conduit for healing.

Healing is pure Energy work, connecting with the God of all Energy and allowing this Energy to shine through us, and to recognize that *we are but the tool,* and not the Energy itself. We do not need to *add* our own selves to the process, but we work to keep our own selves *out* of the process. The more we are able to fully "let go," the better the flow of Love though us to the client, the "good vibration" that heals physically, emotionally and spiritually. How can this be explained? Think of a fresh mountain lake with a cool stream splashing in on one side and another splashing out. The water is healthy, active and clear. Compare it to a lake with only an outlet - it will flow until it's dry, and be no longer a lake but simply a sea of grass or a rocky field. Worse yet, take a mountain lake that receives run-off now and then, and has no outlet. It becomes overrun with algae and sludge, is not fit to drink, is stagnate and smells. It

6

floods its shores and becomes a burden on the land. It's unhealthy. Don't try to keep Source to yourself - by letting it flow, you will be life to the forest of people around you. We were created to share good things, and be of service to one another.

The Basics

What happens if we take a magnifying glass outside and hold it above a piece of paper? The natural energy is concentrated to a spot that bursts into flames. This is an example of *directed energy*. Prayer directs Supernatural energy.

(1). Free Will desire to Help One Another and Show Unconditional Love.
(2). Ability to Get Yourself Out of the Way and Trust.
(3). Plugging into Source via Prayer and Active Stillness.

"Standing in the Gap"

Prayer is communication (a *two-way* dialog) with the Absolute. Interceding or supplicating prayer is where you are communicating in behalf of someone else - usually these prayers are in request of something. "Intercessory" comes from the Latin word *inter,* "between," and *cedere,* "to go." So intercessory prayer is "going in between," standing in the gap, as it were, mediation *between the two.* This is why the person receiving may not have the faith to be healed, and yet a miracle may still occur, because the intercessor *does!* We see the precedent set of human intercession in the scriptures, such as Moses praying for healing in behalf of his leprous sister Miriam, and praying to stop the venomous snakes from killing the Israelites. (Nu. 12:10-13; 21:7)

Prayer is *not* the "power of positive thinking" nor "wishful thinking." Prayer is not just for special occasions or illness. There are no ill effects or contraindications with prayer. Prayer cannot be overdosed - you never have to worry if you are sending too much! Is your mind of Self Will in touch with the God Will of the greater mind? Visualize the outcome you want (without telling the Almighty what to do), and consider this outcome as already having been accomplished. Only in this way are you truly out of the physical brain/mind-set, of "seeing is believing." Visualization helps bridge the gap. But, *believing* is the key. *Knowing* is even better! How strong do you believe/know God? See in your mind's eye that which you pray for already existing in spiritual form. Jesus said: "Have faith in God...therefore I tell you, whatever you ask for in prayer, believe that you have received it, *and it will be yours."* (Mk. 11:24) Powerful words indeed!

The Source of All Healing

So, petitionary prayer is for oneself - *intercessory* prayer is the connecting of the

Healing Force with the one who needs the healing. Just as you would not expect the lamp to light on its own without being connected to a main electrical facility, you should likewise not expect to have power on your own for healing. Those who do, always see their light glow dim in comparison, and they may be plagued with constant headaches, illnesses or pains of various kinds because they are tapping into their own energy, instead of the One who sustains all life and IS energy. Look around you and see if any of the self-based energy healers from even seven years ago are still practicing *in good health.* That will tell you the story! Your job is to get yourself out of the way, and let the healing come *around and through you.* You will also *receive* a healing as you give one! This is just one of the "perks" of working for a good and caring Boss.

"Praise the Lord…who heals all your diseases." (Ps.103:1-3)

See Them Well! The Visualization of Wholeness

See an image of the person whole, knowing that the Lord knows the DNA, the bones, the sinews, the trauma of emotions - everything. Pray for His Will to be done, which is always for the Highest Good for *all* concerned. But, in praying for this in true faith and without ego, also be open to the possibility that the Highest Good may include enduring the illness or problem a while longer. The timing is not yours. And healing may be occurring at *other* levels first – spiritual or emotional.

For example, I have seen cancer clients undergo tremendous emotional and spiritual healing simply from the fact that it was the first time in their lives that they have felt *love* – with all their relatives, friends, workmates and neighbors rallying around them as a caring support system. Also, severe illness tends to encourage us put our priorities straight, and can help us embrace the time and need for spiritual advancement. It often changes a hectic, angry life into a peaceful, fulfilling one - putting love and relationships above all material pursuits.

Sometimes a healing includes the slower steps toward improvement and wholeness, but you must also be prepared for the *other end* of the spectrum. Wondrous things! *Immediate and spontaneous healings!* Miracles can happen today, *right now,* even if you have worked with the same person a dozen times before, and previous progress seemed slow! Always expect the unexpected. Never give up hope - while there is breath there is life - and while there is life, there is opportunity for Divine to appear in a blaze of glory. *It is your job to faithfully expect* recuperation to be remarkably fast, scars to fade and disappear, brain tumors to shrink and go away, cancer to go into remission, and all the other events that Spirit can do! Look for miracles and immediate healings to happen before your very eyes, and they will! Be Realistic…*Expect*

Miracles!

So as you wait in expectation and see them well, do not allow your ego to dictate what is good or what is bad in their individual case. This even includes judgment about the *ultimate* healing, of releasing the final breath in death. Your job as one facilitated for healing is similar to waking up in the morning, and visualizing walking through the wildflowers on the fresh spring day. Instead, you may look outside and see it is raining. But, you know that the flowers need water to grow, and accept that this day is *also* good, while you look forward to the next time you can walk in the flowers, in the sunshine. It is just like that! Let go of your personal need for a decisive outcome *today.* This is what the surrendered soul is all about, true letting go and not governing the "how," "when," or "whys and why-nots." Just concentrate on the "Who." *Then he can use you for incredible things..*

See It as Being Already Accomplished

So…in your mind's eye see the coma victim opening his eyes for the first time, and watch how joyful his family is all around his bedside - see him sit up and wide-eyed, receiving hugs as all cry tears of joy and happiness!

See the little girl with burns all over her body start to heal, the skin reconstructing from the inside out, from the edges to the middle, turning pink and healthy, closing with no scar tissue at all, and the nurses exclaiming wildly as they tear off the gauze and bandages to reveal normal skin - whereby the girl jumps down off the bed and starts running around with no pain, in complete recuperation!

See the parents of the kidnapped boy grasping their dear child safe in their arms again, a family once more! So long they were emotionally traumatized and fearful that they may never see him again, that he had been injured or even killed. Now he is at home! Safe at last!

Let God use the abilities he gave you to make it more real for you; use your thoughts as a "touch-stone" for the Power to flow without restraint, as you see people the way God sees his children; as whole and totally protected and loved.

Walt Whitman said in *Leaves of Grass:* "I do not ask how the wounded one feels, I, myself, become the wounded one." Let me take that one step further, you do not have to ask how the wounded one feels, you become the empathetic intercessor and prayerfully *transcend* their painful experience with love. Then you, *and them,* are not the victim anymore. You add your heartfelt agreement for blessing and healing, and trust the Spirit will flow and that healing is occurring. Look in anticipation for a

9

metamorphosis to happen, and for changes to occur, at any or all levels (physically, emotionally, and spiritually).

Healing can also occur *without* any kind of visualization. But there are benefits to imaging; it helps keep us focused on what we are doing, and it can also lead into the gift of medical intuitiveness. Empathy (fellow-feeling) and unconditional, heart-felt desire to heal is necessary. Do you have the kind of strength to be absolutely vulnerable to Love?

Trust that the outcome *will be the best one.* Do you have enough knowledge of the Divine to trust? Can you tap into personal experience? If you have a history of walking with God, your conduit of faith is much wider and you are able to accomplish more. In your personal history of witnessing Godly Supernatural Intervention you will be more able to surrender, because you have already experienced some out-of-this-world things. Let me share with you a closely guarded secret: *the 10% of the brain acts as a bridge or a barrier to the possibilities of the mind.* This is why in "less-developed" areas (where Spirit is watched more than TV) such as some Indian Reservations and Third World countries, people respond very easily to healing - with many spontaneous miracles occurring, since Godly Energy can flow *without the restraint of the constantly skeptical mind.* They watch for Spirit to move in their lives. They expect it!

It is interesting that most people in poverty or dismal conditions have a high desire for spiritual life, and are always open to Divine Intervention for help, although they may not be living according to Loving principles that would favor this. Does this hinder them from healing? Must the thief turn around from thieving, the prostitute from adultery, the business man from greed? All of us have places of darkness in our soul. *It's not about us being good, but about Him being good.* That's where forgiveness of oneself comes in, the belief that we are truly lovable. If there is one thing that I have seen hamper a healing, is the feeling of one's own unworthiness. We feel we have to earn it. So, we think healing will happen for the other person, but not for us – we know our shortcomings, our sins, our selfish nature and all the bad choices we've made. But, breaking through our personal barriers and asking for God's forgiveness helps to us heal, and he *always* grants absolution. Now, we also need to forgive ourselves, others, and the painful memories our lives.

We will discuss this in further detail later. Forgiveness allows healing to occur at many levels. Feel worthy; you are a child of God! It's time to heal and be healed! For the faithful, belief may be their *only* lifeline in a world of drugs, poverty, sickness and abuse. No matter what situation a person or family finds themselves in, faith can powerfully sustain with the *spiritual* fortitude to keep strong and make it through whatever the *physical* situation brings, in whatever part of the world they live in. And besides all this, they will see Supernatural coincidences abound in their lives, and wholeness and wellness greet them in a variety of ways.

Agnes Sanford said: "We pray not only with the conscious mind. Nine-tenths of the thinking is in the subconscious, and the spirit uses the path of the subconscious in sending forth the power of prayer. Therefore if the subconscious retains the picture of the person sick, the spirit can send at best only a divided message, suggesting life and death, health and illness at the same time."- *The Healing Light* (Random House, 1972).

There are cases when "seeing it whole" creates an opportunity for medical intervention *and* faith, as the next story shows.

God Sees it Whole - Healing of a Ruptured Breast Implant
(As received by letter from Susan. J. Fisher)

I am writing this as a testimony for God's work in me through Tiffany Snow. I was fist referred to her by a pastor friend of mine and I've always believed in, and been blessed by the supernatural Spirit of God. What I experienced during a visit to Tiffany was something far beyond my expectations.

To make a long story short, I went to have a treatment with Tiffany because I thought I had a silicone breast implant rupture. When I visited Tiffany she knew nothing of my condition. As she laid her hands on me she went right to the place that was affected and said, "What is this? It feels like Jell-O or something. It's very strange and slippery and, oh my, this stuff is not organic." At this she asked, "What's going on here?" As I explained, Tiffany worked on me and said, "the Lord wants you to know He hears your prayers, you silly girl!" At that, I knew exactly what she meant. My prayer was that God would create a barrier so that no more silicone would leak into my body and that's exactly what God did.

It was through my prayers and Tiffany's reinforcing work to create strength in this barrier that 5 months later I finally had surgery. Even though an M.R. I. scan showed there was "no rupture," the doctor believed me and operated. He said afterward that 90% of the silicone had leaked out of the sack yet had somehow been trapped in the breast area, so he'd gotten it all out. Even though the M.R.I. scan showed everything intact, he was very glad he had operated on me. And indeed everything had stayed in place - miraculously God had created a barrier which held for over 5 months. Now I am all organic, blessed, and continuing to heal beautifully with post treatment from God through Tiffany Snow.

* (*Side note:* when I first saw Susan, the toxins in her body from the rupture where creating depression, illness, and skin and facial rashes. Since silicone had also moved into her arm pit area and down her side, sleeping at night had become very uncomfortable. During the healing, I visualized her whole; the Spirit gathering the silicone back into place until it could easily be disposed. Meanwhile, Susan stayed in prayerful agreement throughout the following months, continuing to see God protect and heal her. Also, her determination to listen to Spirit and persuade her doctor when the M.R.I. showed a false reading is commendable - God truly is the Great Physician!)

Can Only Christians Pray for Healing?

No. But, in my experience, it certainly helps. We as humans are made in the likeness of God and are *all born* with an amount of ability to heal. And through the years I have noticed that there are many people who have stimulated this small amount of natural ability into a larger amount - many of these have spent years focusing love through their hands in one matter or another; whether as a musician, artist, florist, animal handler, surgeon, massage therapist, etc. They have widened the natural channels we were all created with. *Natural* healing is Love. Divine healing is *Supernatural* Love, complete with a vast amount of miracles and immediate healings. *There is a difference in the results.* I have only seen immediate healings and "falling down in the Spirit" in the Christian churches, with Christ-centered prayer. But, keep in mind that God is Love, (1 Jn. 4:8) and prayer is Love, so *any* prayer that is prayed in Love will have God's Power in it, *no matter what the spiritual view!*

The Spectrum of Healing

There is a wide spectrum of what might happen in a healing. At the very least, there will be a sense of peace, stress relief, less pain if there is any, and better sleep at night. At the other end of the spectrum - cancer cells, heart disease and chronic pain disappears, brain tumors shrink and eyes see! One never knows *where* in this spectrum a healing will fall. Personally, I have immediate, spontaneous healings in about 10-12% of cases, which is considered very high. I have learned to never place limits on what might occur - including *miracles* - and I feel this percentage will grow over time, as *my* conduit of faith widens, and as *others* open to the fact of Divine Healing, including the results from scientific research!

Will the Healings Be Immediate or Gradual?

Both can happen. Do not limit what may occur. Also, be persistent! *Orare est laborare, laborare est orare* – "to pray is to work, to work is to pray" (ancient motto of the Benedictine order). In most cases, healings will happen over a period of time,

12

sometimes beginning with a single prayer, and more often with a course of several over a period of days or weeks. Over all, it seems that healing is like Divine radiation therapy - the longer the sickness is held in the force-field of God's love, the more it shrinks, until it finally disappears! And, just because improvement seems to be slow at one time, does not mean it will be that way the next. And as I said before, always be open for immediate healings to occur. Remember one of my favorite sayings? Be Realistic...*Expect Miracles*!

Immediate Healing - 93 Year Old Woman Escapes Surgery
(As received by letter from V.H)

The gift of touch and the touch of healing is truly a gift from God that a person can be anointed in. I wrote this letter to show that God still uses people to do healing work, just like in the days of Jesus, through the Holy Spirit. Then it was a sign of God's Love and Power working for his people, and I believe He still uses it today because I saw it in my life!

This is what happened when God moved one of His Gifts into our lives in a mighty way, and the woman who brought the gift, who I can truly call my dear friend.

Reverend Doctor Tiffany Snow and I met in a special and unique way while she was still in Tennessee, and she has been a blessing and teacher to my family since she moved here to California this last summer.

My mother is 93 years old and she has a keen sense of discernment for people. When she first met Rev. Snow she immediately took a liking to her. Because of this bond, she looked forward to each session with her. With each session, healing in and through mom's body was occurring. Both eyes were clearing, one eye had nearly been blind, and her ability to walk greatly improved. The power of prayer and God's mercy and grace stretched our belief in healing hands by touch.

In September of this year, my mom was diagnosed with a spot (4 cm) on her right lung, and abnormal pap cells. Suspecting cancer, the doctor, Dr. G. M.D., FAAFP., was recommending a biopsy and possible surgery. At mom's age this was an impossible vision to foresee and one my family and I questioned.

The night before my mom was scheduled for a cat scan, Dr. Snow came to visit. Upon greeting my mom with a hug she informed me that my cousin and I had to be powerful prayer warriors this evening.

As Dr. Snow gently laid her hands upon my mom's head and on different places of

13

her body, and started her healing prayers, God used her in a powerful way. The presence of the Holy Spirit not only filled the room my mom was in - He filled the entire house with His Glory! The power of prayer was awesome as we also had several prayer groups across San Diego County uniting with us for healing of mom's body.

There is no other explanation, but we knew that whatever occurred after this evening it would be God's will, and I was okay with His decision.

Mom's visit on Thursday morning at the imaging center in Riverside was intense, not knowing, but believing a miracle had occurred on that previous Tuesday night. The doctor entered with mom's chart and test results saying "Ladies...someone's been praying." My cousin and I replied, "Yes, we have." The doctor said "No! I mean let me read the test results...!"

The only word I remember is "benign" and the praise began as the tears flowed. The doctor informed us that "only a residue" was left in the area where the spot had existed and they would treat her with medication for the cervical area. No surgery was needed!

This stretched my faith in healing - when we allow God to use us and with Dr. Snow as a healer anointed by God, because of her Love and respect for God and her desire to be obedient and a vessel empty and ready to be filled. This miracle has touched the lives of so many people who know my mother - friends, relatives, doctors and nurses. I am hoping it will inspire you to Praise God! And to know that His hand is never too short to reach us, we are never too old to be helped. And that He is able and wanting to show us Love in every way - if we are just open to it, He can Heal us.

* (Side note: the grandkids weren't too happy about Grandma seeing again, since now she was getting after them about picking things off the floor! And the daughter did have to put her foot down when Mom wanted to drive the family car! This wonderful woman lived almost two years longer, with the "spot" never returning.)

"Laying-On-Of-Hands"

"He said to them...and these signs will accompany those who believe...they will place their hands on sick people and they will get well." (Mk 16:18)

I work in three clinics, and am able to schedule appointments to see people at specified times for Divine Healing treatments. Clinics allow a comfortable setting, muted lighting, and soft background music to aid in relaxation. I have a massage table available, and a chair, and it is easier to have the person on the table, although healings will occur in whatever position the person is in. The table allows me to freely move my hands from one place to another, starting from the head down. This affords me the ability to use my hands to be a conduit of prayer to specific parts of the body. I don't "push" anything into the person, the place that needs healing seems to "call out" and the Connection is made between them and God. It helps humans to have a visible "touch-stone" to the Invisible, and a person can see by the historical facts of using prophets, healers, etc, that this is not unusual. Similar to a smiling child going with Dad to his job, *I get to be there when The Big Guy goes to work!*

Once, I had a physicist on the table, who felt he knew how this Connection works. He said, "Everything in nature wants to remain whole; even at a cellular level - if one cell doesn't have what it needs, it takes from its neighbor so that it itself can be complete. Somehow, I think in what you do, you create the ability for this to happen, for the cells to take what they need to be whole."

It seems to me that the Holy Spirit bathes all the individual cells with a "cosmic energy soup," stimulating recuperation time and promoting "cell memory" of how the original cell structure was made. There certainly are a lot of changes that happen. Who can know exactly how the process occurs? I'm just glad, as are thousands of other people...that it does!

"For I know the plans I have for you," declares the Lord, "plans to prosper you and not to harm you, plans to give you hope and a future." (Jer. 29:11)

Respectfully laying your hands on a person gives additional insight to the one facilitated for healing, and adds validation to the one receiving healing that what is happening is genuine. Sometimes, the person may not tell why they came for healing, or may only tell the major reason. So, as your hands heat up over the places that need healing, verbally verify those places with the person, this will help them be more receptive and allow even stronger healing to occur. Please remember, unless you are a medical doctor, *you cannot diagnose.* But, you may ask if they are aware of any problem here or there; then it is up to them to see an M.D. if they desire. Always encourage clients to continue to see their regular medical doctors, and to continue taking all current medications unless their *doctors* tell them not to. Do encourage more tests, because there are changes that are occurring that the doctors may not be expecting or looking for. By doing these tests, the doctors, nurses, client, family and everyone around will be able to see the positive results documented, and this will help them believe in the God of all healing.

At times, there may be a "Catch 22" because the problems can disappear *at* the healing or *soon after!* This is what we want, so be happy for it, instead of always needing the ego to be stroked by medical diagnosis to validate what you "see." As you grow as a blessed child facilitated for healing, you will need less and less "proof" of the problems you see disappear under your hands. You will have seen enough validation, and enough chins drop and eyes light up, to know that you are involved in a very special work!

Hot Hands and Vibration

Heat is a by-product of work being done, and I may stay in one place for three minutes, or 20, depending on the need. My hands will cool down when the spot is done, and it is time to move on to another. In my case, I also have "God-sonar" or what is often called "medical intuitiveness," which lets me "see" even deeper into what is going on. And often, a vibration will occur over a more difficult injury, or over a place that seems to be a good access point to another that needs healing. When a vibration occurs - which means I'm "really plugged in to the 220," I know that the deepest healing is occurring, and I keep my hands there until all the vibration is gone. It comes in waves, or oscillations, and I stay there until the vibration slows down and stops, the heat also leaves, and the place cools down. If I have a place that does not want to cool down, I may leave it to see what else is going on in other places of the body, and then return to it later. By using heat, The Big Guy can also let a person know where to go, and when to move on, without medical intuitiveness being necessary at all.

Gradual Healing - God is Stronger than Chemo and Cancer

When I first met "Charlotte," her sister "Karen" had brought her to me for pain relief. She had received a mastectomy and reconstruction by surgery that cut one muscle off her back and wrapped it around to the front to be reattached. She could not raise her arm without considerable pain. She had lost a lot of weight and had no appetite. She wore a wrap around her head, having lost her hair due to the chemotherapy. Both she and her sister were both Godly women who frequented church.

After the first healing treatment, Charlotte felt so relieved from pain that she started flapping her elbow up and down like a bird, announcing, "I'm hungry, let's all go out to eat!" Whereby I sat astounded as she proceeded to down a hearty southern meal!

As time went by, we were together for several healings and wonderful spiritual discussions. But, when the day would come for the chemotherapy again, she would have another bad reaction. One day after a chemo treatment, Karen called 911 and me. Since we lived in the country, the ambulance could sometimes take quite a while to get to where it was going - but I *happened* to be (Divine Coincidence!) driving in town

16

right by her road when she called. Charlotte had been throwing up all morning. I made a quick detour and found her lying on the bed unresponsive.

Charlotte seemed like she was in a coma. Her eyes were sunken with darkness, she felt cold to the touch, and it seemed her heart and blood was barely moving. I placed my hands on her head for a few seconds; then her solar plexus; then her feet. Her body felt barely responsive to the groaning of the Spirit; her body had already shut down so much. Again I placed my hands on her head, stomach and feet. I call this the "shock therapy" treatment. I kept in prayer and repeated all three positions again and again, feeling her energy grow stronger and stronger…eventually cycling wildly and hotly through her body!

When the ambulance got there thirteen minutes later, Charlotte was sitting up on the bed waving them off, saying, "Go away, I feel better now. Really! Go away!" Both her sister and I implored her to go to the hospital anyway, I reminded her that God uses doctors and medicine as his tools also - we had to force her to go! Against her wishes, they took her out on a stretcher, Charlotte complaining all the way!

Later, I found out why she had felt so much better - her body had responded well to the healing. The hospital wouldn't even admit her or keep her overnight because her blood cell count wasn't low enough! All this after she had been at the brink of death!

Due to the continued adverse reactions, Charlotte was *not able to continue her chemotherapy treatments*; one more time she tried it, and once more she almost died. She was not given much of a future by the medical doctors. But, it is now well over a year later, and her faith in God and his desire to heal continue to prove all of the doctors wrong! God is Good!

When You are Down to Nothing, God is Up to Something!

Hello My Angel Friend Tiffany
(As received by letter from "Charlotte")

As you well know, I was as low as one could go; just short of dying. The chemo nearly took my life twice and the last time; I was barely alive. We have to go all the way down in order to go all the way up. PTL! One has to have been there to know what a wonderful feeling it is. You and I know this feeling. Out of everything bad, there comes good. Look at YOU; using your personal life here on earth as an example to lead others. What a blessing it has been to have had the pleasure to know you and have those precious Godly hands of yours touch me. I will always remember

17

the times when you made me feel so much better. May God Bless You Abundantly Always!!! I know he will.

It was one of my life's greatest joys to listen to you talk and have you touch my sick cancer-stricken body, with those lovely healing hands that God gave to you. I know you continuously praise God for striking you down so that you can be His servant. Most people are angry at first and some never heed to God's way for us to live life. I'm so grateful that I can truly say that I never became angry with God for my getting cancer. I asked him for acceptance and the endurance for the things that I could not change. I know that God heard and granted my prayer for this. There has been such a multiplicity of peace within me. PTL!

Now, I feel good...just like before I was sick. I have opened up the salon again and am cutting hair for all my friends. My hair is growing back and is a beautiful silvery salt and pepper. Everyone whom I meet cannot believe that I look so good now. It is not me...IT IS A GIFT FROM GOD!!! PTL!!!

I am writing my poetry again and have even started a website which keeps me in touch with those who have supported me, and as a way to support others. I feel so Blessed! I am so thankful that our paths crossed. I know that God meant for this to be. When you are down to nothing, God is up to Something!"

What Does A Hands-On-Healing Feel Like?

A hands-on-healing treatment feels like a wonderful glowing radiance that flows through and around you, similar to warm honey flowing from the top of your head down through your legs to your feet. The clients will be asked to slip off their shoes, and be invited to lie down on the table, face up. I suggest leaving jewelry at home, and to take off any metal objects (belt buckles, bracelets, etc) since it can disrupt the Energy around that area, making it harder for me to sense what is going on there (gold seems to be the exception, it conducts Energy very well - its just a distraction to the medical intuitiveness). I place a bolster under the knees, to help relieve strain on the lower back. *There is no disrobing of any kind.*

Before I begin, I explain a bit about the process, including the hot hands and possible vibrations. I answer any questions, and give the option for the client to state why they came. If they elect not to (as is sometimes the case in emotional healing), no worries! The healing will occur just the same, whether I know about it or not. The Holy Spirit is like aspirin; it goes to where it's needed! Also, The Big Guy will probably let me see anyway, especially if it is something he needs me to address; for example, an issue or blockage on some level that will aid in healing so full wholeness can occur.

18

As I begin, I place my hands on top of the head and begin with an out-loud prayer, and then go into silent prayer; inviting the client to also make silent connection. "For where two or three come together in my name, there am I with them." (Mt. 18:20) This treats the whole person: physically, emotionally and spiritually. It also makes them part of their own healing, instead of just something "being done" to them. In this way, the person is acknowledging an *acceptance of responsibility* in their healing process. For example: if the person wants to be healed of lung cancer, the acceptance of responsibility would also be to actively throw his cigarettes away and stop smoking. If a drug addict or alcoholic wants to be cleansed of toxins, the acceptance of responsibility would naturally dictate that he does not use these substances anymore nor associate with those who encourage him to do so.

In this participation in their own healing, and with their own connection with Source, it also makes for less possibilities of "fanatical enthusiasm." This is where an immediate healing occurs and the clients then feel that you're better than sliced bread, and want to follow you home! Now, through silent active participation in prayer, they will see that you are connecting with Source just the same as they are, and this acknowledgement helps them understand the Power comes from Spirit touching spirit, and not from you, personally.

Does the Process of Healing Continue After I Leave?

Yes, after the healing is initially finished, the Spirit's energy is still in the body for several days, *continuing the process of healing.* It is similar to unplugging a fan out of the wall; just like fan blades which continue to spin, taking them a while to slow down and stop, it takes a while for the Holy Spirit to dissipate. I always encourage drinking a lot of water through this time - there is much cleansing and changing at a cellular level, and the body needs to flush it out. Also, I suggest for this duration to avoid alcohol and deep-fried or heavily oiled foods. It seems to slow the Spirit down in the body. People often feel very peaceful and relaxed, as all the Wonderful Energy of God touching them leaves a lovely residual effect! If they are dizzy, I have them walk around a bit before driving home. They usually report sleeping very well that night, and awakening refreshed, lighter, and feeling better in many ways.

Sometimes clients will immediately fall asleep on the table - another way for Holy Spirit to move without restriction beyond the "I wonder if this is working" phase. Sometimes it happens so fast that I know it's the same thing I see when healing in the churches, an action of "falling by the Spirit" or "slain in the Spirit," where The Big Guy knocks people out so he can heal them quickly and without interference, by-

19

passing the analytical brain. At other times, the sleep appears to be just a progressive slumber that occurs from being in a comfortable setting; a natural sleep. Either way, the circuits being bypassed allows for the best possible healing to occur.

How Does the One Doing the Healing Feel?

The one facilitated for the healing will also feel the Glow - for me it starts at the top of my head, a feeling of effervescent warmth and sparkle, then slowly descends down through the rest of my body. It's always accompanied by a feeling of peace and bliss – it's that feeling of Communion that I live for! I find that if even a couple of days go by and I haven't yet been utilized for a healing, that I'll become anxious. I need my "fix!" Working for the Supreme One is the best addiction in the world! The healings make me feel peaceful, calm, and as warm as stepping out of a hot Jacuzzi. I also receive a healing too, every time, and feel totally embraced by love. Who wouldn't want that 24 hours a day, seven days a week!

Another of the many "perks" of working so closely with the Almighty is a *feeling of being connected to all living things* - I seem to know where every bird and squirrel is in the trees, where every bunny is under the bushes! Colors themselves seem to be brighter, and hearing and smelling more intense. A sense of *well-being* and *peace beyond words* descends upon me, and at night, *truly blissful sleep* comes from knowing that I am fulfilling the true purpose for my life, in service to others. And I know it makes The Big Guy smile!

As you choose to work as a vessel being yielded, you are choosing to work hand-in-hand with the Very Persona of God. You may even notice that during a treatment your own breathing is altered to become slow and thin, almost as if your own life-force were yielding to leave room for the Spirit of God within. What a feeling! You will see his guiding hand as people and situations are brought into your life in such a way that could *never* be possible before. "Divine Coincidences" abound, as you grow used to "blessed uncertainty," having confidence that God knows the destination of your path, has put your foot firmly upon it, and all you have to do is plunge straight ahead. Run after him! He will work out the details! Such a sense of freedom could never be imagined, until you see it in your own life. Everyday is an adventure as we keep our feet on the ground, our eyes lifted to heaven, and our arms outstretched to mankind!

Doctors and Medicine versus Divine Healing

First, there is no "versus!" Yet, this thought is often vehemently disagreed with, on either side. People who see things as only black or white hit a note within most people's consciousness that aches to the core, for better or for worse. Why can't we just agree to disagree? Why does it have to be either/or? Perhaps there are things that you need to see from the other point of view. Let's take a lesson from history on this. On the *medical side,* there was a time when even the concept of "invisible germs" was considered lunacy. In 1847 Dr. Ignaz Semmelweiss said that washing hands would prevent the spread of disease from cadavers to the new mothers in their hospital, thus preventing the shocking amount of their "unexplained" deaths. He was laughed at and heavily opposed. The world of medicine at that time had no way of proving his theory. Throughout history, we find many "discoveries" have been made *after* the results have been noted. Today, we are living at a time when all sorts of studies have proven and continue to prove that prayer works. So, for a doctor to scoff at the power of prayer now, puts him in *direct conflict with the scientific facts!* He is simply misinformed, or *un*informed.

On the flip side, there are those religions and individuals who feel prayer alone should heal everything and no thought should *ever* be given to using conventional medicine, or alternative medicines; often with deadly consequence. Yet, that thought goes against much of the scriptural ideologies of the Loving God they claim to follow. An example: did not God himself give us the plants to make our bodies healthy? Yes! Now, 85% of the medicines we have on the market are synthetic versions of what we first *found in the field.* God has made us intelligent, and able to use our brains to discover many medicines and new technologies. How many of these technologies and medications (i.e. penicillin) have been *inspired* Holy gifts? Exclusivity with choosing to look at only *one* of the ways to heal, may show we have within us another place that needs mending; the *ego.*

"All things are from God. The antibiotics, for instance, are a source of power implanted in nature for man's use, just as electricity is a source of power implanted in nature for man's use...To insist upon getting well by our own efforts in such a case might be a gesture of faith, but is equally likely to be a gesture of *spiritual pride.* "- *The Healing Light* by Agnes Sanford (Random House, 1972)

Do you remember the story of the man stranded in his house during a flood? As the water level rose, a neighbor came by on a raft and offered to take the man to shore. The man disagreed, replying, "God will save me!" As the story progresses, the man was given other opportunities to save himself, including a boat and a helicopter, as he progressed to the roof of his now-flooded house. He refused all forms of rescue, stating "God will save me!" The man drowns. Next, we see him before the gates of heaven, very angry and demanding to speak to God. "Why didn't you save me," the man demanded, shaking his fist into the air, "you didn't do *anything!*" "Well," God quietly replied, "I did send you a raft, a boat and a helicopter..."

Hospital Immediate Healing - from Pneumonia, Acute Pancreatitis
(As received by letter from Mrs. G., RN)

On Easter Sunday, my daughter was hospitalized at Alvarado Hospital, San Diego, in the surgical intensive care unit with acute pancreatitis leading to pneumonia, followed by a second pneumonia from aspiration. She was on morphine for pain, a respirator, TPN, N/G tube (to keep the stomach empty to prevent further vomiting), and much more. Her doctors had prepared us for the worst, saying her condition was serious and could be fatal. If she recovered, she was expected to be in the hospital for at least another week to 10 days followed by weeks of recovery at home.

I had asked Tiffany Snow to do a Reiki treatment (an alternative therapy recognized by the AMA) on my daughter but was told by hospital staff I needed to get a doctor's order. The doctor had heard of Reiki and graciously agreed. On the third day in ICU, Tiffany did the Reiki treatment with hands-on-healing and healing prayer. The nurses showed respect and worked around her schedule to avoid any interruption. Tiffany asked me to stay and pray.

In the middle of the treatment, which took less than an hour, my daughter felt hot, and asked for a fan. The treatment was paused, as my daughter ate two bowls of broth and some Jell-O, which she was able to keep down (her first day on liquids). After another 10 minutes of treatment, Tiffany said a final silent prayer, and gave us both words of encouragement, "To watch for big changes about to occur," and left.

That evening, my daughter was tolerating liquids so well, that they took her N/G tube out (2 days earlier than expected).

The following day she was transferred out of ICU and discharged home on Sunday after being in the hospital only 8 days (4 days after the treatment).

The doctors were astounded with her speedy recovery and attributed it to her youth. I was told that other patients with the same problem are hospitalized much longer as pancreatitis takes a long time to heal.

I felt it was a miracle that my daughter not only survived, but recovered so quickly.

Three days after hospital discharge, she went back to school part-time.

I am extremely grateful for the powerful healing that was given my daughter, the many prayers from family and friends, and the excellent care she received at the hospital. It was a perfect example of Alternative and Western medicine coming

22

together. I will never know exactly how much of the miraculous healing and speedy recovery was from Tiffany and the prayers, my daughter's young age (18), or exceptional hospital care, but I have no doubt that the healing that came through Tiffany (and as she says, "from the Big Guy"- from God) was powerful and made a difference.

*(Side Note: Just from the double pneumonia alone, the staff said the daughter should have been in the hospital for 3 weeks before being released. This mother is a registered nurse, and kept a strict and trained eye on every nuance of change. She had a lot to look at! Just a few days after being released from the hospital from the brink of death, this daughter touched by God enjoyed her senior prom.)

Prayer is Absolutely Necessary

The true elegance of Divine Healing is being able to let go of the results. The flesh is not the main concern - that is only a temple for our spirit to live in. Through time, we learn that the truly important thing is our spiritual journey. We learn by the obstacles in our life that we gain success only when we lean upon Spirit. We know and have the confidence that all of our needs are being met, *in God's own way and in his perfect time.*

"Trust in the Lord with all your heart and lean not on your own understanding; in all your ways acknowledge him, and he will make your paths straight." (Pro. 3:5,6)

Not all people are going to be healed physically. Perhaps an emotional or spiritual healing is going to occur first, or even in place of, a physical one. We just don't know. *We* don't use the Holy Spirit - it is *he* who uses *us!* Realizing that *we* cannot heal everyone, that *we* can't always do what *we* want to do, shows us that *we are only instruments,* a tool. We have no control over what God does. And, in saying that, please note that it is not your "fault" if results do not seem openly noticeable. It is not our job to defend God; he can do that for himself! Remember that *physical* healing is only one of several parts of healing. Perhaps the healing that has occurred is within the other places that needed it.

Your Job is to Get Out of the Way!

Your job is to be a yielded vessel, and not "clog up the channel" by any preconceived notions on how or when the healing should occur. This "non-clogged" attitude extends to having no prejudices about race, gender, social standing, religious affiliation, etc. Just keep out of the way and let the Real Healer come through! Get rid of the ego. You are just a physical representation, a "touch stone" to aid others to "see" what is

23

invisible, and to relax into it. Just a humble vessel of clay, a fleshly body, just a lover of God wanting to share the love, and see his kids be touched by his Healing Hand. Let it flow like a river, a river of life.

You Can Manifest into Reality the Invisible

To increase your ability to help others, yourself, and really see *extraordinary* things manifest in your life, try living 24 hours a day in an Undertone of Prayer. This lets you absorb the Love of God like a battery stores up energy, and then you can use it freely to help others. This will help in other matters of your life too. It is similar to the battery being able to use its energy to do a multitude of tasks, such as start a car, make a radio play, or a flashlight shine. At this stage, you are truly living the life of a *mystic* ("one who has experience of union or direct communion with ultimate reality").

This allows you to not only heal at a moment's notice but also to live a phenomenal, Supernaturally guided, blessed life! Do you find any scriptures where the *prayerful* Jesus or the *prayerful* apostles stopped to pray *right before a healing?* No! Become a conduit of light at a moment's notice, living with one ear to Divine and one to this world. But keep in mind, the Big Guy is *big* on Free Will. You have to ask for this, he won't force you into something you don't want, with all of the immediate responsibilities that go with it. How do we ask? How else…by prayer!

I have been aware for quite some time that changes occur even when I just enter a room, without my conscious effort of prayer or healing at all. And I have seen entire floors of hospitals be affected by God's Spirit as he utilizes me to heal one person in one room. God knows my Free Will is to *always* be facilitated for his Spirit, and he uses me accordingly. The letter below emphasizes this point; the moment I entered the room the healing began, Spirit seeing a need and fulfilling it:

Immediate and Long-Term Improvements with Brain EEG Recordings
(As received by letter from Dr. Greg Cantu)

"A subject utilized EEG Neurofeedback for fifteen days straight, except for one day, to establish a baseline for attempting to document improvement after hands on healing from Tiffany Snow. The objective was to enhance Beta waves (15-18 Hz) at A2-C3-T4, and inhibit Theta waves (4-7 Hz) at A2-T3-T4 while reducing excessive Alpha waves (8-10 Hz) that were not being filtered from the raw EEG, only observed visually.

The most obvious result from Tiffany being present before the laying on of hands had begun, was a decrease in the regular production of excessive Alpha waves.

24

There was thirty minutes of Tiffany's hands on the subjects head while EEG recordings were being taken, but the plots were hard to read due to interference from Tiffany's hands touching the electrodes. There were some more recording done, hands off, with Tiffany still in the room and some done after she left because she needed to eat. It had been about almost nine hours since Tiffany had last eaten. The recordings appeared worse compared to when Tiffany was in the room but improved compared to the baseline readings.

The following day the subject was recorded again. The results revealed that the pattern had clearly improved but did not look as good as with Tiffany in the room. Both frequencies had improved compared to the baseline readings. The recordings showed both consistently higher Beta and lower Theta production. Excessive Alpha production had also improved visually.

In conclusion: positive changes in the brain waves of one subject was observed with Tiffany in the room, even before the official thirty minutes hands on healing had begun. The EEG recordings appeared worse when Tiffany removed her hands, but still looked better compared to some baseline readings of days before. The following day the subject was recorded again, and the pattern had clearly improved compared to the baseline. The recordings showed that the subject was now consistently producing more healthy Beta waves and less of the problematic Theta waves. Excessive Alpha production was also improved. More energy and better concentration in the subject would be expected from this kind of outcome. This preliminary study was done under the direction of Dr. Greg Cantu utilizing the Neuropathways all digital real time EEG neurofeedback instrument."

The Mother Said, "This Is the Boy I Remember!"

Seven-year-old "Jason" lay on the table fidgeting a bit - his mother "Lily" was sitting in a chair nearby. I didn't know why they had come, but that they had come from far away by referral. Under the muted lights and with soft music I put my hands on his head, and moved them into the "third" position. Through the eyes of prayer, the Lord revealed a tumor nestled deep at the base of his brain - directly between his ears, and straight down.

I asked Jason to imagine floating in a big swimming pool, and enjoy the warmth and freedom of the "warm water." I knew he was feeling the Power coming through to him, and I did not want him to be afraid. The center of my hands felt like laser beams were attached to them, and a strong pulsation was occurring - I knew we were doing good work. After half an hour, I sent Jason out to wait with his family, and spoke to his mother, asking why she had brought him here. She said he had bad headaches, stomachaches, unusual twitching, and nosebleeds. He would not participate with the activities of the other kids very much, and would often wake up in the middle of the night crying. Feeling that something was very wrong, Lily had taken him to a doctor, "he didn't think anything of it, just growing pains." But Lily knew something was wrong with her boy.

I told Lily "God brought you in here for a reason, either for me to encourage you to get an MRI, or for the problem to be fixed, or both - maybe it is fixed even now. But, you need to know of the possibility of what was found. I am not telling you for sure, this is just what it feels like to me. You know I am not a medical doctor. I just feel strongly that you need to get this checked." Since they had come to see me from far away, and were staying with relatives in the area, I knew it would probably be a little while before they could see their regular doctor again, but felt it was important for me to tell her this.

Two days passed, and I was working on Jason again. He thought he was coming to see me because of his stomachaches. In talking to the mother, I found out that Jason had gotten very sick after the first treatment, even vomiting that evening. He had also been sleepy all day long. I knew that sometimes these were indications of a very strong healing. Often I have seen that when the Holy Spirit stimulates rapid cell regeneration and cleansing, and toxins are released, big changes are occur, and the body needs plenty of rest to recuperate. Drinking a lot of fresh water helps, and if the belly is nauseated, steamed vegetables (alkaline based - not acidic like fruits) also help. Jason had told his mother that during the treatment, "I had a bee buzzing around in my head." He also said, "I like her, but her hands are so hot!"

This time Jason's head felt different under my hands - the vibration was different, and the heat was not like a laser. I grew very excited, but did not say a word. I felt there was still a bit of work needing to be done, and I would let the Lord tell Lily what was going on.

Two more days went by, and I came out into the waiting room to greet Jason and his mother. Her face was glowing! I didn't ask why, but I knew within five minutes of touching Jason that all sign of the tumor was gone. The joy inside overwhelmed me, and I excitedly ushered Lily out of the room. "I don't feel anything wrong!" I said. "I knew it!" Lily answered. She went on to relate that yesterday Jason was playing baseball, and running the bases, and not getting tired! There were no nosebleeds, no stomachaches, and no headaches! She then said the words that touched my heart so deeply, and which I will never forget - "this is the little boy I remember!" we both cried

26

and held each other, so grateful to God for putting us together and bringing his grace into our lives.

The next day, Lily's husband flew in and I saw him for a healing treatment. With each hand placement where I would find something on him, he would smile and validate it. During the husband's treatment, Lily told me of something extraordinary that had happened with Jason the night before. They had been in a store, and Jason and his brother were up ahead of Lily in the aisle. All of a sudden, a "black thing flew out of his ear - it shot straight out sideways and disappeared." Lily couldn't believe her eyes! Jason didn't seem to know that anything had occurred. She wanted to know why this had happened, and what it was.

I didn't know why either, it was a mystery to me. So, I prayerfully listened for the Words to be said, with one ear toward heaven and one toward earth, and told Lily that she had been shown this as a validation that the problem was gone, and not to worry about it anymore! She was thrilled. So many blessings for this family! As I saw the father carefully gathering up several business cards off the counter, I called to him and offered several brochures too, so that the work could be explained to others. He came back down the aisle and took them from my hand.

"Thank you," he said with tears in his eyes, "for my boy."

"Thank Him," I said, pointing up. "He is the one who heals, I am nothing."

"Well, just the same, he used you to do it," he nodded and left.

How Do I Feel the Love Necessary for Healing Complete Strangers?

There will be a time in your life, if you choose to spiritually progress, that this *will not* be a problem, and you will genuinely feel deep love for *every* person you meet, always seeing the Divine Spark within and the great possibilities ahead for them. Even the most hardened of criminals will feel like your own son! In the meantime, you might try this: remember a deeply moving incident in your life that made you feel great joy and love, and use that memory as the catalyst, then spread that love to others. Here are some examples:

Do you remember the first time you held your newborn baby in your arms, all fresh, tiny and new? How did it make you feel? Perhaps a loving memory was when your husband brought you a surprise that was not affordable, yet gladly given, just to make you smile! Perhaps it was when your daughter first announced there would soon be a grandchild to love! Find anything that gives you the sensation of absolute, deep, loving

27

commitment, and imagine this person in front of you as being part of that experience, and then place your hands upon him in prayer. Soon, finding love in your heart for strangers will come as easy as breathing, and you will see love all around you, and the universe will respond to you in a way that it never has before.

Be a personification of Love!

"This is my command: Love each other." (Jn. 15:17)

Goethe said, "I can be a tool of torture or an instrument of inspiration, I can humiliate or humor, hurt or heal. In all situations, it is my response that decides whether a crisis is escalated or de-escalated, and a person is humanized or de-humanized. If we treat people as they are, we make them worse. If we treat people as they ought to be, we help them become what they are capable of becoming." How true!

Why Does God Need A Mediator for Healing?

He doesn't. We know *he can go direct* by Divine Prayer, without any "middle man," and he *often* does - we see that when we are by ourselves in our room, our car, or outside. Just him and us, without a mediator. In the same way, he doesn't need a mass of flesh and bones to yield himself to him as His Hands to work on others. So why does he use "healers?" Simply because of this - he is a good, loving father who wants all of his kids to *work together, love each other and to learn to get along!* It's the same as when he decided that male and female should come together to create a child. He actively wants us to *interact together* for the common good and to help and encourage one another. He doesn't *need* to use us at all, but he does, because he just wants to, it's for the Highest Good of humankind, and a visible touch-stone to faith.

I Don't Feel Worthy Enough to Pray

Moses was a murderer and a stutterer, yet God forgave him, refined him, and used him to free the Israelites from Egypt. He did this through many miracles and manifestations of power, including numerous plagues and parting the Red Sea. King David was an adulterer and murderer, yet he was forgiven and anointed by God to be a great King, ancestor of Jesus, and the writer of one of the most popular books of the Old Testament. *Psalms* has inspired poets and writers throughout time.

"But God chose the foolish things of the world to shame the wise; God chose the weak things of the world to shame the strong. He chose the lowly things of this world and the despised things - and the things that are not - to nullify the things that are, so that no one may boast before him." (1 Cor. 1:27)

28

He always amazes me! So remember this when you think, "I am not good enough to pray." It's not about *us* being good - we can't *earn* any of this – it's about *him* being good. Very Good!

Medical Intuitiveness as "Words of Knowledge"

Sometimes I start a healing treatment at the clinic without even knowing what is wrong with the person. And I have found some places my hands get hot are actually injuries or broken bones that go back forty years or more. This is the main reason for a full body hands-on-healing, so the person feels the place of injury being acknowledged. Holy Spirit does not need this method to activate a healing - my hands may be touching one spot only, as on the forehead, hand or heart. The Spirit will work if I am only holding onto a toe or a finger - such as in a hospital bed with very little skin exposed. He will even act with the hands being held over *or just towards the body,* without the person being physically touched at all! And, as we will discuss at length later, long-distance healing can occur across the room, the state, or the country! Don't tie the hands of Divine! His hand is not short!

Medical intuitiveness is not a necessary for healing to occur. Just as with the hands feeling hot against the body where there is a physical injury, or an emotional one, "God Sonar" just gives more details to the *convince the brain what the mind already knows.* Sometimes the vision in my mind is so clear when I'm working, that I can readily see through the skin, down past the muscle and tendons, through to the inside of bones, and down to the wood in the table underneath them! Often I will draw diagrams of what I see on my charts, especially if it is a tumor, cancer, or an artery blockage, just for my own information, to compare the changes that have happened if and when I see the client another time.

Heat & Vibration of the Hands

Heat is a by-product of working being done, whether it is warm, hot or lack of, all is a sign of what the body will accept. Different things *feel* different under a sensitive hand. There are different vibrational qualities attached to different problems. Through time, I have been able to "assign" colors to different vibrations that I feel; in this way it makes the diseases and ailments easier to remember. At first I didn't know anything at all - I would pick up a certain vibration, and find out afterward what it was when the person would say "I have diabetes," or "I have high hepatitis C." Then I would keep that vibration in memory and assign it an easy color pattern. When I felt that same vibration again in someone else, I would softly venture the question. In this way I learned. I am still learning, and come across new things all the time.

29

I have also found that there are some types of drugs and medications that make the vibrations in the body difficult for me to "see" through. Two of them are cocaine and morphine-based medications. I am *not* saying that *healing* can't be done through them - who am I to limit God? I am just saying that the vibrational level is *so extremely high* that I cannot feel the Spirit moving under my hands, or the "intuitive knowing" that he sometimes allows.

Some things are now very easy for me to detect, cancer being one of them. It seems that the vibration of cancer is so all-invasive that even just touching a person's hand is all that is needed to know that the disease is somewhere in the body. I assign it an "orange" color. Aids is an "orange-brown." The list goes on, with several color combinations coming from fine-tuning the knowledge given, and training the brain to respond with a color when a certain vibration is sensed. But, I also make mistakes and misinterpret vibrations, especially with new problems that I'm not familiar with yet. I use the medical intuition openly when the person I am working on knows beforehand about the disease or ailment. Giving the additional information can lead them to a greater belief in the One who sees what is hidden, and lead to better treatment of the problem. *I refuse to use it as a "parlor trick" to impress.* This would be *unjust use* of the power of the Most Just, whom I *really* do not want to offend! I don't want to be out of a job!

"For you created my innermost being; you knit me together in my mother's womb. I praise you because I am fearfully and wonderfully made; your works are wonderful, I know that full well. My frame was not hidden from you when I was made in the secret place. When I was woven together in the depths of the earth, your eyes saw my unformed body. All the days ordained for me were written in your book before one of them came to be." (Ps.139:13-16)

Do Not Diagnose Unless You Are a Medical Doctor

Not being a medical doctor, I do not diagnose. But, I do encourage people to get things checked out when I find something "wrong." Keep in mind, God uses doctors, machinery and medications to facilitate healings too!

Some things will feel different under my hands from just the difference between hot and cold. Often, a tumor will feel like a cold spot - almost like a lump of scar tissue, with edges that fade out into the warm surrounding area. A broken bone will feel like a definite cold line, with sharp contrast to the surrounding bone. A fracture is much more subtle to feel - a soft cold line, with minimal contrast; often I will miss a fracture unless there has been additional trauma to the surrounding tissue.

The first time I "looked" at the brain, I thought I was going to faint! An entire city under a cap of bone! The pulsating of blood and electrical currents jumping synapse gaps of nerve cells, passing back, forth, and through, the brain folds look like so many translucent earthworms under glass! What a complex and marvelous machine the brain is, capable of so many things! I also found it relatively easy to identify the places where a stroke had damaged the soft tissues, those places being a different, darker "color" than the surrounding area.

Besides the physical indications, *emotions* are also easy to perceive here, and placing the hands on the head can reveal many buried traumas, stresses and fears. This "head" position is also a good position to aid the one who is crossing over in death. But, as always, please remember that prayer, like Divine aspirin, *goes to where it is needed.* We, as mortals, need not be too concerned about hand-placement. It seems that the major issues that need to be healed first, will be the "priority places," and will be the hottest and perhaps receive vibration, while everywhere else receives on a "secondary" basis. Thus, the entire body gets what it needs.

The Colors of Healing

Don't be surprised if this "assigning a color to a malady" facilitates your having immediate diagnosis of an ailment, even by just shaking a hand. It is much easier to allow God to "pop" a color in your brain to let you know what is going on, when you have been training your brain to recognize and coordinate the two. But, as always, keep in mind that unless you are a licensed medical doctor, you cannot legally tell the client anything. You cannot diagnose. It must be viewed as God giving this information for you only, to sharpen your intention to heal and the progress being made under his care. Sometimes I can "see" problems change *right before my eyes!* This is a boost for my faith too!

If you see "red flags" and need to tell the client about what is going on (nearly-clogged artery, extreme blood pressure, cancer, etc), you must tell them: "I feel a lot of heat here; and heat is a by-product of work being done, so the Spirit is definitely working on something here. If you don't know what this might be, I suggest you go to a medical doctor and find out." This should be enough to encourage them. Then continue with the treatment. Who knows if what you saw is not being cured right now? Call the client in a week and ask if they've gone in for a diagnosis. This call will encourage them to do so because of your level of concern. Or you may even state, "in all good conscious I cannot continue to do treatments unless you see a medical doctor first." Of course, this again can be a "catch 22" as God will often take care of the immediate problem, and leave nothing to be diagnosed! When this happens, you must not let the ego get in the way, but just be happy that the problem has been corrected.

More on "Words of Knowledge" and Wisdom

Supernatural Knowledge is specific insight or understanding of a situation that would *not be known* by natural means. This includes medical intuitiveness, and even prophecy. Supernatural Wisdom is how to deal with a situation that would not be known by natural means. In the scriptures, they are called Spiritual Gifts. (2 Cor. 12:8) This incorporates visions or words that may be given that will need to be passed on, whether the one facilitated for healing knows the meaning of them or not. You will know these things are not of your own, if you dare to hold them back! They will rise up in you like a hurricane ready to explode, and no matter what, you need to let them out.

"And they were all filled with the Holy Spirit and spoke the word of God boldly." (Acts 4:31)

"Help Me to Hear God"

This is a wonderful request that I receive all the time. Often, we find ourselves intensely looking for direction and receive so much variety of information from various sources, that we don't know how to process it. We may not know what is of God, ourselves, or others. This is again where intercession works - having another to step in with us and help sift out the wheat of truth from the husks of confusion. A Divine Healing treatment is an opportune time to be a "cell phone" or maybe "satellite receiver" for God, and he often uses the occasion to give a message in behalf of the one asking. Often, it just validates what the client already knows deep in their soul, but brings it out in the open, up to the surface, to be resolved or acknowledged. Here are some examples:

(1). "Bebe" is a woman in her fifties, whom I had seen several months before. At that time there had been hormone imbalances with all the accompanying problems, and she had not had her period in eight months. The *day after* the healing, she received back her period, and in the four months since, received her period every 28 days like clockwork. She was feeling so much better! As she stood there in the clinic thanking me, I teased with her, "Yes, you are thanking us now, but if you get pregnant, you'll think again!" We laughed, and she got up on the table to begin. She was here this time for emotional healing; she described an undertone of despair, uselessness, and lack of energy which had recently been pervading her life. She hadn't a clue as to why.

I finished my prayer and placed my hands gently upon her head, beginning the silent *amour* to Father. In my mind's eye, a vision appeared. I saw a man; it felt like a father-figure, although not a relative; and he and his wife were both old. They were alive, but

32

sickly. I felt the high emotion of love and tension between Bebe and the man, and unfinished business needing to be attended to. I gave the physical description of the man, his wife, and all the other information to Bebe. At first, Bebe was quiet...then her eyes grew big. "Oh my God!" she said, "You are describing some very good friends of mine - and the man is like a father to me! I was just on the phone with them yesterday, and I have wanted to go up and see them so much. They have both been sick for a while now, but now the man has gotten worse – but he'd said not to visit, and not to worry. So I don't know what to do. I really would like to see them again, and help out if I can."

"Well, this is the main problem of why you're feeling the way you do," I replied, "this vision has been brought up so we can talk about it, and for you to choose the way to resolve it." We talked for a while, and as I continued in an undertone of prayer, the words she needed to hear flowed off my tongue like a cooling salve on an injury. And the word I was hearing from my own mouth was a salve to my ears too, spirit once again touching Spirit, and me getting to be there for it!

(2). Sometimes, accessing Spirit is like dialing up on a phone line, and getting a party line! The information you receive *may not* even be for the situation or person at hand. For example, I was doing my morning home visits, which I try to do for people who are not able to come to the clinics. About five minutes into my first healing of the day, I received an adrenaline rush through my body, and I saw a vision of a woman in a hospital bed, with red lights flashing in the air all around her. It was a previous client of mine, who had had major surgery the year previously for a critical aneurysm. I felt such a calling to see her, that I asked the wife of the client I was still working on to call the hospital where she had been the last year, and ask if she had been admitted again. She called, and my client *had* been admitted.

I went back into prayer to finish the healing I was doing, knowing I would be rescheduling my afternoon. Ten minutes later, I heard the muffled hum of my cell phone go off, and I had a "knowing" that one of her friends was calling me. It *was* one of her friends. I left for the hospital.

One of the interesting points from this experience, one that I would really like to call attention to, is that I had received the "God call" *while being in service to others.* This hadn't been the first time that day that I had been in communion; I spend 2-3 hours every morning in prayer and meditation, and during this time, nothing had been said. I've noticed this before, not just with myself, but with my clients also - they may bring in a friend or family member for healing, and they themselves are the one who receives the healing or the message. It seems that when our hearts are the most open, in surrendered love on someone else's behalf, we truly receive the ample full measure

33

back to us! When we become a true channel of unselfish love, we can receive all his gifts more fully. Truly a demonstration of "Give, and it will be given to you. A good measure, pressed down, shaken together and running over, will be poured into your lap." (Lk. 6:38)

(3). Quite often, when you are in prayer for someone else, Spirit will also talk privately to you. I was at a point in my life where I wanted to have a home. Being very cautious about not wanting to put a strain upon my finances or time for the ministry, I lifted it up for Our Dad to give me an answer. That night, no answer came. The next day, when Spirit volunteered me for a healing after a friend's speaking engagement, the answer came. The moment I laid my hands in prayer, I heard: "Yes, you can have both - a home and a ministry. It's been there for you all the time." When connecting with God for another, God took the occasion to connect with me, because my own high emotions concerning this heart-issue had been blocking me from hearing his word. When I was relaxed and in prayerful concern for another, I was not blocked any longer, and he was able to talk to me, and *then* I was able to hear!

What Does the Future Hold for Me?

Prophecy, or "a prediction of a future event that reveals the will of a deity" (Encarta Encyclopedia) can give valuable insight about where our true destiny lies, in the path of Spirit. It can give us clues to look for along the roadmap of our life. It brings us hope, joy, and a clear focus. When are we the most likely to hear true prophetic words occur? Around a person or group of people in prayer - and healing and other manifestations of Spirit will often happen at the same time. Remember, God is BIG into marketing! When he has an opportunity to be listened to, he'll take it every time! For me, a prophetic word occurs in about 20% of cases, where I get to witness this form of life-changing Connection. Since these are so personal, I will not share examples of them with you here, for privacy reasons. But, it is constantly in my prayers that every person reading this book will one day experience prophecy and healing happen for them!

"Above all, you must understand that no prophecy of Scripture came about by the prophet's own interpretation. For prophecy never had its origin in the will of man, but men spoke from God as they were carried along by the Holy Spirit." (2 Pe. 1:20,21)

Now, we have seen how many physical illnesses have their basis in emotional or spiritual dis-ease, and how prayer can lead to accessing many gifts of healing. The next chapter will go into the mental health/physical relationship more deeply, including how to help break through the blockages of unforgiveness and victimization to receive deep, long-lasting healing.

34

CHAPTER 2

Inner Peace & Emotional Health
Healing the Deeper Wounds; My Near-Death Experience

One of the most shocking things I have noticed in my work has been realizing that *not only the men* have heart disease, but the *women* do too. A lot of it! Women, do you know *heart disease is the number one killer* among us, cancer being a *distant* second? How many people do you know who have heart disease? A friend, a neighbor, a brother, a spouse…yourself? What does heart disease have to do with emotional health? A lot. Studies continue to show that our physical and emotional selves share information with each other. One part of our being *definitely* knows what is happening in another part.

So, who is the one person most prone to have a heart attack? We know the profile - the one who is under high stress and responsibility, nitpickers, always in a hurry, no time to exercise, and is probably overweight or smokes. Statistics also show more disease for single people, and those who work for an employer instead of for themselves. Also prone are those with the "Type A" personality, and those who habitually see the glass as "half-empty" instead of "half-full."

But, I'm not one of those, you say…well…maybe *subconsciously* you are.

●

What do you see above? Ask a group of people, like I often do when holding speaking engagements, and they will all invariably say, "a black dot." Uh huh - *how many of you focus on the black dot* when you see this page? Look how little this dot is! There is so much more white around it than dark, and yet we focus on this speck of dark. Now, isn't it interesting that we are focusing on maybe 1% of what we see, instead of the other 99%? Often, that's what we do in real life too. *Look beyond the black dots in life, you'll live longer!*

Your Mental Reaction is Important to Physical Healing

"Even in the entirely physical illness the sick person's mental reaction is almost as important in evaluating his chance of recovery as is his physical reaction. In such obviously physical conditions as pneumonia, or tuberculosis, or diseases of the heart valves, or even, let us say, a broken leg, there is not only a physical problem but an important attendant emotional problem as well. It is the way a person feels about his illness that determines to a large extent whether or not he is going to get well at all. Certainly it determines how he is going to live with his illness if it does continue; it determines both the length and the nature of his convalescence…This is why every surgeon knows how much more dangerous it is to operate on a frightened patient than on a confident, fearless one. The decisive factor seems to be the presence or absence of the will to live - a will backed by a strong, sometimes even unconscious, courage and faith." *Faith is the Answer* by Norman Vincent Peale, D.D. & Smiley Blanton, M.D. (Fawcett Crest, 1978)

It is quite possible that the emotional/physical relation of healing is also referenced here in the scriptures. "He heals the brokenhearted, binding up their wounds." (Ps. 147: 3)

The Link between Physical, Emotional & Spiritual Health

There are numerous studies available that prove that the physical and emotional health of the body is interlinked. If we are depressed, our immune system goes down and we get sick. Or, conversely, if we are sick, we get depressed. As we have seen, science is releasing more and more studies about the correlation between spirituality and physical health. So, for perfect balance in maintaining our health, we need to take care of ourselves physically, emotionally and spiritually. It's a balance. Even in a precarious world! How do we do that?

A Glass of Water and Dirt

Often, the cure for our inner trauma cannot depend upon our own willpower or intelligence. Over and over again we try, and again and again we fail. We need something Greater than ourselves to help us. We are all like a clear glass of water with a couple of tablespoons of dirt in the bottom. Most of the time, we go through life keeping the top part clear, as more sediment steadily accumulates at the bottom. As the sediment gets deeper and deeper, we tend to move more slowly, get sick more easily, get angry more quickly, and all we can do is wait and "let things settle." Finally, we may get to a "breaking point" in our lives and not even know why! It's because of the years and years of dirt!

How do we get it out? This is a place where Divine healing comes in another one of its glories. Imagine a kitchen water faucet turned on full blast - now take the glass of water and place it under the faucet. What happens? The fresh blast of water agitates all the dirt in the glass, *as it cleans it out and overflows the top!*

That is how a God-directed healing works. Slowly, the muddiness in our lives can clear up, if we keep filling the top with a steady stream of Connection. But, you may find, as the water starts to clear, that there are still pieces of rock and hard sediment that are not gone. These are the things you are *still holding on to,* that have hardened and become so big that it seems there is no hope. There is. You simply need the Power beyond yourself, *along with* the Free Will choice to not hold onto it any longer. *So, how much sediment you release also depends on other factors,* such as your own ability to *forgive.* We will talk more about forgiveness further on. But for now, just know that you can move from being a toxic drink of silt and muck, into a clear, fresh, sparkling glass of cool water!

"If there is physical, mental, or financial darkness, be assured the Presence of God dispels it."- *Consciousness Transformed* by Joel S. Goldsmith

Why Do I Feel Dizzy After a Healing?

Sometimes, in this agitating and cleaning-out process, the physical and emotional bodies may need a couple of days to detoxify, since so many changes are taking place at the same time, and at an incredible rate of speed. At times, this may cause dizziness, or an upset stomach, or other symptoms of detox, which seems to be lessened by eating some steamed vegetables and getting more rest. Think of yourself as having just completed a long-distance run - the body needs time to recuperate, and rest and nutrition helps it do the job. Light-headedness after a healing is a common side effect of the Spirit working in the body. It seems the average human being is not used to so much "current" going through it. It is a pleasing feeling, and is accompanied by a feeling of joy, calm and peacefulness. Drinking some water and walking around takes care of the dizziness - and please be sure to wait before driving home when you feel this way!

Emotional Healing for Black Belt Instructor

The first time I met "Jason," the Spirit let me see that the real reason he taught martial arts, had a black belt, and was a "trained warrior" was because of a previous emotional injury. I could see through the eyes of Spirit a very definite gray triangle superimposed on the back of his head. Physically, he was in good health. I had been asked to speak about Reiki to his Tai Chi group there at the YMCA. As part of my presentation I offered Divine Healing in a little room off to the side. Jason came in and I placed my hands on his head and closed my eyes, listening in the stillness for any information that The Big Guy would have me pass on.

Jason said he had received "energy healing" before, and that I had the strongest "energy" he had ever felt (another difference between spiritual healing and Divine Healing, the Energy of Spirit is Powerful!). I asked him if anyone had ever used prayer with his previous healings, and he said no. I explained that this was the reason for the healing feeling different. I also talked to him about why we must let go and forgive others and ourselves for injuries and pain of the past. I told him why I have faith in a God that Heals. The words I chose were not my own.

My hands were extremely hot on his head, and I felt an emotional release coming on, although he showed no outward emotion. I saw the gray mist dissipate of the superimposed triangle fade into nothing. I knew the pain of the past that he had been carrying for so many years had been absolved, and let go.

Now, I told Jason what I had seen. He then told me about his father. The father had been overly strict, and had been verbally and physically abusive - often the father would hit him. He especially remembered the time he was hit with the end of a water hose on the back of the head, exactly where the gray triangle had been. Jason left the treatment feeling much better; and with a knowledge that he didn't have to fight back anymore. Now, he had a *Bigger Guy in his corner.* Now, Jason seemed encouraged to progress in his spirit journey; and with a new awareness of what the God-Spot was, and the need to fill it with the right things.

"The ultimate weakness of violence is that it is a descending spiral, begetting the very thing it seeks to destroy…Darkness cannot drive out darkness; only light can do that. Hate cannot drive out hate; only love can do that." - Dr. Martin Luther King, Jr.

Then God said, "I Have Always Loved You, Don't Give Up on Me, or Yourself."

"Tony" was skeptical, but he would try anything to get rid of the huge "lead weight" that hurt him in his solar plexus (belly). He told me of how he used to be in a monastery, his heart fully dedicated to God; but had later left that life and became sexually promiscuous. Now, he was a law student, but wanted to be a teacher, and a writer. He felt "stuck" and unable to focus, and was not making progress in anything. Even the bar exam he was qualified to test for now, he had no desire to take. He also confided that he had to fight suicidal tendencies. I went into prayer and laid hands on him, inviting him to also be in an undertone of prayer. Although I could not sense any *physical* reason for the pain, my hands got hot and I could feel healing happening, on a

38

very deep level, *emotional healing.* So could Tony. He became excited about what was occurring, and the skeptic disappeared, replaced by a man eager to schedule another appointment.

At our next visit, Tony shared with me that he had felt a "little hole" open up in the "lead weight" in his belly, and that it had gradually begun expanding since the healing. Now he was feeling much lighter and had much less pain! He also shared that he had *just taken his bar exam!* As we began the prayers and treatment, he started weeping, and crying out in a wonderful emotional release. He tried to cover his face with his hands, as he felt embarrassed. I told him that it was OK, and that it's not usual for men to cry out during a healing, and handed him a box of tissues. This is a common reaction for men, to be ashamed to show their vulnerability - but it is the Lord who is touching them, softening the heart, and healing past scars. There's nothing to be ashamed of with that! We don't need to keep our defenses up around the Wonderful Counselor - after all, he not only sees us in our birthday suit, but even deeper that that - right into our soul. Nothing hides from him! That's one of the reasons he loves us so much - he knows how hard everything is, what a struggle life can be.

As I quieted back into the stillness, and brought my hands back to the top of his head, I received precise, slow and well-defined Old English words in my head. "Oh my goodness Tony!" I said, "I have a message for you, from God himself! This is what he says: 'I have always loved you...don't give up on me...or yourself.'" I shook with chills, like I always do when this Most Wonderful Power comes over me, and sat down. "Wow, Tony. God really loves you. And you were beating yourself up about that, weren't you!" And Tony started crying again, joyfully and without restraint. A few months later when I heard from Tony, he was still happy, completely focused, and pain-free.

But I Have Prayed Many Times, and Nothing Happens

If you have prayed about the problem many times and don't think anything has changed, don't feel hopeless - that is why God allows mediators, and *intercessory* prayer. If you feel God doesn't love you anymore and your candle of faith is burning low, let the faith required come from the one praying in your behalf. And if you are moved to, unburden yourself upon the one helping you, and as before, feel all the emotions there are to feel. You can do this with someone you feel safe with, who has an *active* prayer life. You can also go back to one who is facilitated for Divine Healing, planning to spend at least an hour, so that Spirit can flow naturally, in a private setting. As his kids, we have one another other for a reason. When one is down, the other can lift him up, we are meant to need each other and get along. "He comforts us in all our troubles so that we can comfort others. When others are troubled, we will be able to give them the same comfort God has given us." (2 Cor.1: 4)

We also need to be persistent, and know there is right timing for everything. He does love us. He does hear us. He does communicate with us; perhaps you are just not seeing it clearly at the moment. And, making sure what we are praying for is not about ego or excess, we learn to wait in expectation with love and obedience. Then look for the results: "Devote yourselves to prayer, being watchful and thankful." (Col. 4:2)

"As our prayers, our mental training and our acts of forgiveness fuse into a high consciousness of God's indwelling, we become more and more aware of an outer source of power; a protecting and guiding influence that surrounds our day's work with blessings and guides us into paths of peace." - *The Healing Light* by Agnes Sanford (Random House, 1972)

"No, dear brothers and sisters, I am still not all I should be, but I am focusing all my energies on this one thing: Forgetting the past and looking forward to what lies ahead..." (Php. 3:13)

Lack of Self-Love a Major Barrier to Healing

Judith MacNutt has her Master's Degree as a Psychotherapist, she and her husband Francis are co-founders of CHM (Christian Healing Ministries). In a conference I attended, she spoke of something she found in her clinical work which was most interesting. She found that *if a client did not love*, they were emotionally and spiritually dead, *and soon would be physically dead. It did not matter which healing path they took.*

I have found in the thousands of cases from my own experience, that this is *absolutely true.* If there is one major thing that is a barrier to receiving healing, it is this attitude: *"I don't deserve to heal."* Whether spoken or unspoken, it can easily be seen by a discerning eye. Sometimes, people don't love themselves. They don't feel worthy. They feel healing will happen for the *other guy,* but not for *them.* Self-love is not an ego thing. In fact, it is one of the basic teachings of most religions, including Christianity, "Love your neighbor as yourself." (Mt.22:39) We need to love *ourselves,* and have respect for our uniqueness and individuality, whether or not that conforms to what our personal ideals are or to those of society.

Can you discern for yourself if you have lack of self-love? The scriptures show us that the *heart is the seat of motivation,* it also says *"what ever the heart is full of, this is what the mouth speaks."* (Mt. 12:34) Hmmm. Let's look closely at that and see if we

40

can *remember our last few conversations*: Were they problems about the kids, or how frustrated we are about the bills? Were we complaining about work? "How come so-and-so got her vacation days and I have to wait?" "I have to bring the food for the office party again, no one else has time, and so I was nominated. How could I say no? But I don't have time either!" "I don't get any credit for how hard I work, no one respects me!" Is this what your heart has been speaking of, out-loud?

Often when we are not happy with ourselves, and we need the constant approval of others, our self-worth is in question, and the sediment in our water glass grows that much deeper.

The Tape Recording in Our Heads

We talked about what we are speaking out-loud. Now, what has your heart been speaking of, *inside your head?* We all have a *tape-recording* inside our heads. It picks up all the programming we have received from childhood on, and is commonly mistaken for intuition. Sometimes this tape recording needs to be reprogrammed, if its messages are not healthy. If it's saying things like the following, then it's time to re-record: "I'm not good enough, not thin enough, not young enough, I don't make enough money, my thighs are ugly, my bald head is ugly, NO ONE COULD EVER LOVE ME!" We could *never* measure up to all of these unrealistic outside influences, please everybody, and our internal ego. *And we shouldn't want to!*

"He heals the brokenhearted, binding up their wounds." (Ps. 147:3)

Empower yourself, and become the best you possibly can. *Realize your full potential as a Child of God - you have control over your programming, about what you will accept, or reject.* That is Free Will. That is one of the "made in his image" qualities we were born with. Because these undesirable programmed thoughts have taken a long time to be instilled, they often take some time to be replaced with positive ones. Be patient and consistent. Utilizing all these concepts together will speed the process. *Incorporate all five senses to "re-train your brain."* Doing this trains our brain easier and faster.

Sometimes, God in his infinite mercy and desire to see us happy and whole even while we are struggling here on earth, will use very unique ways to help us re-record the tape in our brains. Sometimes during a healing, or while simply interacting with one another, he will allow visions or words to be said to help mend the broken places that only a Supernatural intervention will allow. Such is the case with "Emily," a woman in her 60s.

41

Emily's Story - a Mother's Love

During a class on healing, I lost all train of thought, stammered, and looked up from the podium. Essence of Spirit was calling, loudly!

"Emily," I said, looking out over the group, "has your mother passed?"

"Yes," she answered, quizzically.

I continued, "There is another woman here with her, like a sister. Did she have a sister who passed?"

"Yes," answered Emily.

"I am hearing 'VV' for a name, is this connected with her?"

"Yes!" Emily answered, "Oh, that is my aunt's daughter, Vivian!"

We put down our books and let Spirit lead where he wished. Holy Spirit was working out a wonderful plan.

"OK, Emily," I continued, listening quietly to the words being placed in my head, and starting to see the vision clearly forming in my mind. "Did your aunt have black hair to her shoulders, and pale skin, and talk very demonstratively?"

"Yes! She had black hair to her shoulders and my mom used to tell me that she would always get her into trouble, because of the things that she did. Amazing!"

"Your mom, Emily, she had blonde-brown hair and it was very short?"

"Yes, she used to call it 'mousy,'" Emily answered.

"Did people say you looked a lot like her?"

"Yes," Emily said.

I continued in Spirit, "Your mom wants you to know that she loves you, and visits you a lot, and watches over you all the time. She has seen everything you have done and is very proud. She just wants you to know that." Emily's eyes grew glossy. Healing was occurring in her spirit, years of wondering and wanting the approval that only a mother could give her child. How long had this emotional healing been needed?

"Oh my gosh, this is so big!" Emily said, "She died when I was just *twelve years old.*"

42

The tears flowed from all of us. Healing tears!

When we don't put limits on God's ability to heal us, and let *him* lead the class, we can witness the best teaching of all, which is that *love never dies*. Our Heavenly Father knows what we need for emotional and spiritual healing too, and makes opportunity for it. A God who cares for us would not keep us from Connecting with our loved ones when appropriate; he would seek to help heal and soothe our wounds. And he does!

And the Father said: It's Time to Let Me Go

Two sisters flew down from Canada for the Christmas season to visit their family. Their mother and sister had already been to see me, and they had experienced such wonderful things, that the sisters wanted to visit also. Could I squeeze them in on their limited time schedule? We made the appointments, and their brother was able to drive them. I invited all three family members into the healing room, and explained what I would be doing, and what they might expect. I gave each of the sisters the opportunity to have their family in the room during the healing, or to have their time in private. They chose to stay together, and after reminding the group to be focused only in the present moment, I led the group intention with an out-loud prayer to the One Who Hears and Heals.

Soon, "Monica" got up on the table. Then we continued on in our own silent prayers, each one in our own way of Connection, petition and praise. As I felt the sparkling heat descend upon my head, and flow down through my body to my hands, back, and feet, I breathed a deep sigh of joy and relaxation, surrendering to Spirit. My hands were on Monica's head, and a vision was forming.

"This pain in your neck is more than physical, although you do have some bone degeneration here ('did I say that out-loud? No, cannot diagnose, cannot diagnose…I need to keep reminding myself!') between your vertebrae, right in this area (as I placed a finger hot on the spot). It looks like it's been that way for a few years, perhaps even six or seven; was this a car accident?" She verified that it was, along with the whiplash trauma I was seeing in her throat and jaw.

Now, I was feeling the canvas stretch out for God to paint on, and was beginning to see the beauty of the Artist's renderings. I started to speak what was in my head, "I see a man - this is your father; I'm certain it is - he wants you to complete your business with him. You still have things to say to him, and he wants you to know he can hear you, even though you don't think so. Just go to him and speak, and he can hear you. You still have to forgive him, and finish your business."

43

"My father is still alive," Monica said.

"His spirit is here." I said, "If his body is still alive, it is functioning on automatic. It is difficult for him to be in it. Does he have Parkinson's, or Alzheimer's disease?" I asked.

"Yes, he does!" Monica said. A gasp came from the couch of relatives.

"He is spelling out letters now, these are some letters in his name, 'A, I, R, N.' Does this make sense to you?" I asked. Another gasp, and the brother sat himself erect on the couch, his eyes wide.

"Yes!" The brother said, "Amazing! He was born in the Middle East, and those are the major letters in his name!"

I continued, "He gave those letters to show you it's really him talking. Monica, you are carrying much emotion, barely under the skin. Much of your pain will disappear when you let go of your father, and forgive. Whether you choose to go to his physical side, or not, whenever you have the prayerful intention of talking to him, that will draw his spirit to you. Then, you need to say *everything* that is in your heart." I moved my hands to her shoulders, still listening with one ear to heaven and another to this world. I continue, "He was very dot-to-dot, very demanding and strict, when he was here (the brother nods his head affirmatively). He wants you to know he is not like that now, all of that he has let go of. You need to let go of it too."

I continued the healing, the entire family in tears of joy and forgiveness, for such a special healing moment having come into their lives. I praised the Son of God for his compassion, seeing Jesus make the dead come to life again, "resurrected" in a very different way, even when the physical body still remains, however unresponsive, on earth!

(For the record - I have also seen this kind of movement of spirit when a person is *comatose.* It might be compared to an "astral travel" type of situation, where the "silver cord" is still attached to the physical body, since the person is not dead. When the cord is severed, the spirit cannot come back into the body, but is greeted by an escorting angel, and family members who have already transitioned to heaven, to help bring the new spirit into the Light of God, thus completing the physical death of the body on earth.)

What's that on Your Wall?

If we don't transform it, we transmit it. That is why the exercise about what our last conversations are about, *are so telling* about how we truly look at life through our own hurt. We must forgive, not only others, but ourselves. We must show love to others, to God, and to ourselves. Here is one way to transform negative feelings from bad experiences, an example mostly taken from a speaking engagement I attended with Colin Tipping, the author of *Radical Forgiveness: Making way for the Miracle*:

"Imagine a wall hanging a friend gives you, they tell you to hang it on your wall because it is growing in value and will be worth a lot one day. You look at it, and all you see is a ugly mix-match of chaotic colors woven here and there with no random pattern, and loose threads and knots. You can't imagine what he is talking about, but you take it home and hang it on your wall. One day you notice some brown paper hanging down off one corner; the backing is torn so you turn it around to mend it. Underneath this torn backing you notice something usual, so curiosity gets the better of you, and you tear the entire backing off. There in front of you is an exquisite woven tapestry! A landscape so beautiful, with all the most inviting colors and fine craftsmanship imaginable! And then you smile to yourself, because now you understand that every piece of colored yarn and every place where the chaotic colors where, and every knot was *exactly where it was supposed to be!* Everything was as it should be, you were just not aware of it! Such it is with your life. You just aren't seeing the bigger picture yet."

So it is with our own chaotic life. We are the weavers of yarn, each working on a different place, at a different time, on a different scenic tapestry, in our spiritual journey toward God.

"And we know that in *all things* God works for the good of those who love him." (Ro. 8:28)

You are not the victim anymore. Now, shift your consciousness toward your memories, and apply this to them. Now, can you see them in a different light? It's by climbing the mountains that we become strong, not by wandering around in the gentle valleys below. Every time we move through an obstacle, it provides an opportunity to learn lessons; even if they seem confrontational. But, we can use these lessons as an encouragement to keep in balance and conscious of our physical and emotional needs. Confrontations also always help us practice Godly love, since it gives us incentive to work toward a more spiritual manner of living.

"Do not repay anyone evil for evil. Be careful to do what is right in the eyes of everybody. If it is possible, as far as it depends on you, live at peace with everyone. Do not take revenge, my friends, but leave room for God's wrath, for it is written: "It is mine to avenge; I will repay," says the Lord. On the contrary: "If your enemy is hungry, feed him; if he is thirsty, give him something to drink. In doing this, you will heap burning coals on his head. Do not be overcome by evil, but overcome evil with good." (Ro.12:17-21)

Affirmations Using the Five Senses

Write down (sense of touch) a list of positive affirmations:

(1). "I am perfect exactly the way I am."
(2). "I am worthy to be loved."
(3). "I deserve to be treated with dignity and respect."
(4). "By grace, I am worthy to receive all that God has to give me."
(5). "I know I am forgiven, and I easily forgive."

Add what other affirmations you like, and make the list as long as you wish, all reflecting *positive* ideals. Now, this is the most difficult and beneficial part - *stand in front of the mirror and say them out loud!* In this way we are also using our *eyes (sense of sight)* and our *ears (sense of hearing)*. This is how we reach the deepest parts of our heart and mind…it is O.K. to have an emotional release, go ahead and cry if you want, let the emotions wash warm though your very soul. We all have felt pain for *such a long time.* Our Father doesn't want us to beat ourselves up anymore - he never did.

By using this method of Five Senses Affirmation, we are touching as many re-education processors as we can. In this example we are using three senses. If you have an addiction that you want to release, see if you can add a physical representation of it, in this way also utilizing taste or smell. It does not matter if you initially *believe* what you are writing down or saying into the mirror. The subconscious brain accepts everything as fact, even when we don't want it to! That is why we have to keep an eye on it, exercise our Free Will, and clean it up on a regular basis.

The reason why the advertising giants rake in the big dollars is because they know this works. My secondary major in college was marketing. The advertisers know that repeating three commercials within a short span of time sinks it deep into the subconscious brain. Have you ever notice a commercial repeated one after another, and thought it was just a glitch? No, it was on purpose. Our conscious mind knows that buying the new X brand of soap won't make us be the talk of the neighborhood because of our children's white shirts. Or, that buying a particular brand of soda will make us beautiful, give us endless energy, and popular at the beach.

46

But our subconscious is another matter. Be careful what you feed the "computer." You may not like the results that spit out the other side. Parents take note! Do you monitor what your kids are feeding their "computers?" Do you approve of what is coming out of their brains? Especially if you are having family problems, you need to address this issue.

Use the Affirmation List everyday - when you first wake up in the morning, and when you retire at night. "Bookend" your day with it. Hang it on the back of the bedroom door, so you don't forget. See and feel yourself as God wants to see you: totally in control of your Free Will, and whole emotionally.

NDEs, a Glimpse of the Bigger Picture

Often in the cases of near-death experiences, a glimpse of the bigger picture (the real front of the tapestry) is shown to those who die and come back. Have you noticed in these cases that the persons come back are incredibly different; the priorities change in their lives, and they become more purposeful and "in the moment" with everything they do? They often go into some kind of service for mankind, discard many of their unnecessary material possessions, and have an inner glow mingled with exuberance that is seen by everyone they meet! They know that all the chaos is nothing, love is what really matters, and giving love is the highest mission. It aligns them in the flowing current of God's waters of life everlasting. So, they can do *nothing else* but "go with the flow!"

The apostle Paul describes an experience which many believe is a NDE, which may have been linked to when he was stoned and left for dead. (Acts 14:19,20) Please note that he is talking about himself when he says, "I know a man in Christ:"

"I know a man in Christ who fourteen years ago was caught up to the third heaven. Whether it was in the body or out of the body I do not know - God knows. And I know that this man - whether in the body or apart from the body I do not know, but God knows - was caught up to paradise. He heard inexpressible things, things that man is not permitted to tell."

In 1999, a glimpse of the bigger picture was shown to me. It changed my life forever, for the better! I am including a large segment of it to prove that *a time of brokenness is often a catalyst for very important things to happen in our lives!* Brokenness gives an opportunity for being rebuilt into something even better than the original. Also, please pay attention to the "life review," and how we are *accountable* for loving one another!

Struck By Lightning! My Near-Death Experience

Not everyone needs to be struck by lightning, or have a miracle happen, to understand God's will for his life. But, that is the method that God used to fix up one of his most broken kids: me.

It was summertime in Tennessee. A time of good green pasture for the horses, ripe tomatoes on the vine, and long drives in the country. Life seemed wonderfully slow for me that gracious summer; as slow as the drone of the honeybees in the apple trees, as slow as the preparations for the upcoming county fair.

For the first time in many years, all four of my children had come together for vacation time, and I knew that it would probably be the last tick of the clock before their lives would get too busy to experience this again. I was making every opportunity to show them a full and adventurous summer. Life had never been so materially good! I was thankful to share the riches of my new life as a new wife. We would swim in the pool, watch movies and ride the go-cart. We would drive the jaguar in the country and go camping and have picnics. We would ride the horses.

I could overlook the growing detachment of my husband and the late night phone calls. I could also ignore the mysterious apathy and disdain my oldest daughter had for me. I could overlook the bill collectors' constant threats and the new expensive toys being brought home that we couldn't afford. I thought I could make it through anything - hadn't I just survived my fourth encounter with possible death? Even the doctors were amazed. The venomous spider bite had tried to shut down my breathing and my heart, but the doctors knew what drugs to pump through me and I had made it through - and this had happened just the previous week!

My husband and I had been married only a year and a half. The marriage counseling would work. He would stop comparing me unfavorably to his "special friend" of seventeen years, telling me about her just two weeks ago; and for me to "just deal with it." He would stop needing her. He would remember he loved only me. I hoped time would blow away the ominous gray clouds gathering in my personal life. I kept telling myself *time would help, and I would adjust again, somehow.*

I hoped that if I closed my eyes and wished hard enough, everything bad would just disappear. Hadn't I gone through this enough times? Why did this keep repeating itself? Why did I continue to make bad choices about the mate in my life? One thing I had learned - that I would feel that I didn't deserve this and that God had abandoned me. Then I would usually try to fix things myself. When I would fail, I would then call upon Him, and he would bail me out, change the situation, and slowly mend all the broken parts. But this time, I felt there was no way my life could be fixed. *I was broken beyond repair.* I felt I had no mission, that my life had no purpose.

I was so tired of starting over. For the first time in my life I felt I had some material advantage, and I did not want that to change - the children enjoyed it so much, and so did I. *I chose not to pray about it* - I felt I would sacrifice my happiness for the material gain of the children and I. I had messed up my life too much, too many times. There was nothing left for me. I decided I would do what my husband said, and just "deal with it." I would resign myself to ignoring the problems around me, and just struggle from day to day, with a fake smile and heavy heart. Love between people seemed only a façade for control. I felt already dead; my heart knew no joy. I was without hope, and felt helplessly broken.

Although I refused to see the storm swirling under my own roof, I couldn't ignore the rain and thunderclouds gathering outside over the valley. Strong winds were blowing up the hill over the pasture. The rain was pelting the garden and sounded like marbles dropping on the metal-roofed sheds. I had to go check on the horses. I had to make sure they were safe. That's when *I ran out of time.* And I would never look at time, and many other things, the same way again.

God, Lightning and Healing Hands

"Stars!" I shouted through the thunder to the appaloosa pacing behind the chain link fence where we kept the farm implements. "Stars! You are always the one getting into trouble! In the middle of a storm trying to find fresh grass!" As I let the chain down off the shed with one hand, I steadied myself against a wooden structure pole with the other. The horse bolted up the pasture, as the finger of God bolted down. Standing in the pouring rain with my arms outstretched, I was killed by a bolt of lightning.

The last thing I remember about the strike itself was doing an uncontrollable electrical dance as my muscles spasmed and contorted this way and that. *I felt no pain.* In that split second, I remembered that electrical shocks often stop the heart; so I pivoted around and pushed my chest against the corner of the truck parked there, thinking to start it again. Before I could even put any weight against it, my eyesight narrowed and I felt my body slowly slide down the bumper onto the wet earth; and all went black…

The next thing I knew, I found myself standing on nothing, way up in the universe, and there were distant colorful planets all around me. I could see misty pinpoints of stars when I raised my right arm, and when I moved my arm back and forth it made

49

the stars look wiggly, like a reflection on water. I felt dizzy. I had a sense of being able to see not only in front of me, but all around me at the same time. Floating just a few feet from me, I saw a man with a spirit body just like mine (no wings), though he was short and had slanted eyes. He spoke to me with a voice that I heard inside my own head, saying: "Don't be afraid, it's ok."

On the other side of me, another spirit person, this one much taller and with chiseled facial features (again no wings), nodded approvingly at me. All the while, we were moving with great speed toward a great ellipsed ball of spinning light; it was brilliantly white in the middle and yellowish on the outside edges. The closer we got to it, the more I felt overwhelming Love; it seemed so warm and comforting, it encompassed my very being...like the security of a favorite grandfather's arms wrapped around a child as he crawls up onto his lap.

We stopped. The bright light was still far from me. I wanted to go on, I felt like a magnet, irresistibly drawn. The desire to "blend" had grown stronger the closer we got. I knew it was the very Presence of God himself.

Why had we stopped? As I stood there confused, yearning toward the Great Almighty beyond my reach, a glowing luminousness appeared in front of me. A Divine Presence was here!

A gentle voice called out from this realm of golden sparkles massed brilliantly in front of me – "What Have You Learned?" he asked, in a nondiscriminatory and non-accusing way. The voice was so soft and tender, yet the presence of Divine Authority was there; I knew that it was the voice of God's own son, the empowered Jesus Christ.

Then - all of a sudden, life events unfolded before my very eyes. Key moments where I showed anger, and where I showed love, appeared like a movie. I could feel the anger and hurt of the other person whenever I had been mean; and I also felt the anger as it rippled on through to others. I had never before faced the horrid deepness of my own sin. Then, where I showed love to people, I felt that too. And how much further that rippled out from person to person, as a warm pulse triggering cause and effect in all things that were wonderful and blessed...I had never before experienced such joy!

Then the presence of Christ said, "The Flesh is the Test of the Spirit...Love Each Other." Words of wisdom imparted to me! I felt overwhelmed with love, and so privileged.

I wanted to stay! I wanted to join myself with God's swirling life force, His Essence,

His Heaven, was just beyond the presence of Jesus! But, I wasn't allowed to go any further. I wanted to go to God! I wanted to feel more Love! "Why can't I be with you now Father? Please, Abba, Please!"

I listened as hard as I could listen, waiting for His Words. Then, just on the outside of my understanding, I faintly heard voices singing the most beautiful melody I had ever heard in my whole life. I felt a "knowing" that these were the blessed voices of those joined with God, and angels, and came from His Swirling Presence.

I knew it was praise for The Father, but I just couldn't make out what the words were saying. I felt so sad…I knew I was supposed to go back to the earth. I knew it would show love for his kids to do so. I also knew *I did have a choice* in this, although I wanted to stay. I also knew I had to make a "better movie." But, there and then, I vowed to be a vessel to do only His Will, if he could use me. I absolutely gave myself to him. His Will, not my own, would govern the rest of my life. If he could use this broken piece of clay from the earth, it was all his. I totally dedicated myself and surrendered all desires. Instantly, I felt a child-like sense of wonderment *as a warm flood of bliss and peace overpowered me, and a warm tingling sensation filled me to my very toes.* What was happening to me?

Again the spirit on my right side talked inside my head, and while I floated there before the Christ Consciousness, the very Presence of Jesus, the spirit told me something that I didn't at all understand: *"Welcome to the world of healers," he said.* This was a shock - I had no idea what that meant. I had never believed in such a thing. At this point the Christ Consciousness sparkled and faded away and the stars and space behind his glowing features were visible once again. Such effervescent beauty and colors twinkled around me, like being in the midst of a sparkling aurora borealis! So many shapes of heavenly bodies transfixed in the cosmos, all unique and necessary, all untold distances away. Yet they felt so close that it seemed I could reach out and pluck them out of the sky, and carry them home cupped in my hands.

Then the slant-eyed spirit went on and *answered* the many questions I was having about this experience. He then pointed out different stars, planets, distant colorful swirling lights of all kinds, *and gave names for all of them.* Then he gave me *answers* to thousands of questions that I never had questions for! Reams of information seemed to be exploding in my brain, like an empty library suddenly being realized! Details flooded my being about many wonderful and sacred things. I wondered: were these things newly learned, or just somehow remembered?

Most of this information I am still trying to integrate and understand. It is almost like

51

trying to learn another language without being given the basic alphabet for it. So, at this point, there are deeper things I have told no one, and keep only to myself. Often, when in prayer to the Father I will ask him to further my understanding on these matters, yet I get the distinct feeling that true understanding will only be revealed on a "need to know" basis. However, for some reason a seed was planted within me. I do know some of this information came through as I was writing this book. There are things in here that I never knew that I knew!

I must remember that everything he does is for the Highest Good, always happens in the Perfect Time for it, and that it is His Will, not ever mine or anyone else's, that matters. His is Perfect Love Personified! I am just a sinful (but forgiven), impatient person! But, for some reason a groundwork has been laid within me. I know that if he wants me to share this information later on, he will tell me, and give me the reasoning ability to articulate and understand it.

The spirit who was speaking to me did not offer his name, and I did not ask. I wanted to be careful to show homage only to the True God and Christ, not to any one else. I then felt myself sinking, as if falling through a bed. *I was being pulled back.*

With that, I woke up, my husband shaking me by the shoulders. Somehow my physical body was now lying on the front seat of the truck, *although I had left it out in the mud.* Since I had gone from the house to the tractor shed, *three hours had passed.* The storm had gone, but left evidence that at least three other strikes had occurred on the pasture, besides the one that had struck me.

"Welcome to the World of Healers"

At the emergency room I was hooked up with wires and given tests to check my heart. A thorough exam revealed that it had not been damaged. But, my eyes and ears were affected very badly, as was my sense of balance. I felt dizzy, but keenly aware of the reality of my experience. The only piece of jewelry I was wearing was a single diamond earring. A brown burn mark encircled the gold stud where it went through my ear. My skin tingled all over and was extremely sensitive to the touch, especially on my arms and in my hands.

The doctors told me that I had been very lucky; the doctor said that often an arm or leg gets blown off during a strike (was he kidding?). People often die (and don't come back – yes, I knew that). They reasoned that because I was holding the chain-link with one hand and the wet wooden pole with the other, the current had passed through me, instead of grounding in my body. I knew they wouldn't believe me if I told them it had been a Divine Strike, that God used this as a wake-up call, and that I had been before the Presence of God (and oh, by the way, Jesus spoke to me)! They would have kept me a lot longer than they did, and probably in a little white jacket, in a locked padded room to boot!

I spent a few days in bed, oscillating between a wild mixture of extreme happiness and unbelievable sadness. The emotions ran deeper than any I had ever felt. I was glad for the experience, but I had wanted to stay there! I kept re-living the event over and over in my mind, every detail emblazoned into my brain. I was determined that even if I forgot my own name, *I would never forget this.* I tried painting what I had seen - oil paints on canvas. The colors, no matter how I mixed them, were not brilliant enough. Nothing could capture what I had seen and felt. I felt sad again. Then once more, happy for the experience. Then confused. What did it all mean?

My First Healing Experience – a Horse!

After a few days, I was back to my chores, including putting salve on Star's skin infection. For six weeks I had smoothed on the medicine the vet had given me, but still the red blisters kept spreading and killing the hair all around his girth. Now I had run out of medicine, so I just rubbed his belly lightly around the outside of the infection because he had grown used to the attention. I noticed that my hands were getting very hot. I thought it must be bacteria from the infection, and when I washed my hands under cold water it went away. I didn't think anything of it.

The next day, I walked up to rub his belly again - reminding myself to get new salve soon - and noticed that all the blisters had turned white and some were falling off. I once more rubbed around the infection, and my hands turned hot once more. The next day when I went out, *all* the blisters had fallen off, and there was evidence of new hair growing back. But, since I had been religiously trained that hands-on-healing died with the apostles (and that near-death-experiences were just created by chemical reactions in the brain), I thought this was mere coincidence.

The next week, I took my cat in to be spayed. The vet said it would take 10 days for the stitches to completely heal. On the first day, she didn't want anything to do with me. But, the second day, she was in my lap as much as possible. She just would not leave me alone - even yowling for me if I left the room! Every time I would rub her and pet her, I found that my hands would heat up again. On the third day, she tried pulling the stitches out with her teeth. On the morning of the fourth day, I decided to look at what was going on, and found that the skin had healed so well that the stitches were puckering her skin up tight. I found myself embarrassed to take her back to the vet - what would he say? So I carefully cut the threads and pulled them out myself, *through skin that bore no surgical scar*. I began to understand what was happening…but, would this work on people?

It Works on People Too! My Purpose Becomes Known

The next day, I said a prayer to God, laid my hands hot on my forehead, and on various parts of my body. Then, I made an appointment with the doctor. A previous mammogram had shown lumps in my breasts. A former doctor had told me I had fibroid cysts in my uterus, which could only be removed through surgery. Also, I had a torn rotator cuff in my shoulder, which had prevented me from sleeping well for the past six months.

I anxiously awaited the test results:
…the mammogram showed the lumps were all gone.
…the diagnostic ultrasound showed clear, the fibroid cysts had disappeared.
…also, I could sleep at night without any pain; my rotator cuff was healed.

God had blessed me with the gift of healing! This is what he had meant!

Hesitantly, I started sharing this new gift with my friends - and that's when I ran into trouble. *I found that I was taking the pain of their ailment onto myself.* If they had a migraine, *I* would get a migraine. If they had stomach pain, *I* would get stomach pain. That scared me - I found myself afraid to use the gift. Maybe I was using it wrong? Why would God give a gift that would cause me harm to use it? I felt I wouldn't last very long in this work. And yet, I knew in my heart that God wouldn't give me something that would be unsafe for me to use. What was I missing?

I thought I might find answers if I watched the healing ministries on TV. For the first time in my life I wondered if they could actually be legitimate. I had never believed in this sort of thing - I had felt it was a fake, showy display to raise money and give people false hope. Now I wanted desperately to talk to one of them. Did *they* feel sick afterward? Had they each been told, "Welcome to the world of healers?" in some way? Was I part of this same group? What did God want me to understand?

I continued on this way for a time, confused by the gift. I thought maybe I would work only on animals; I did not feel their pain. Maybe I could work for a veterinarian, alone in a back room, quietly healing the animals. I didn't know what to do.

So, I prayed for understanding, and what I found was the Lord's words overflowing back at me. On and on the scriptures popped out of the Bible, the pages randomly falling open to pertinent information, my eyes emblazoned on the scriptures he wanted me to see. They popped out *as brightly as if a yellow marker pen highlighted them!* Dozens of scriptures! Here are just a few:

"For I know the plans I have for you," declares the Lord, "plans to prosper you and not to harm you, plans to give you hope and a future." (Jer. 29:11)

"You are the light of the world. A city on a hill cannot be hidden. Neither do people light a lamp and put it under a bowl. Instead they put it on its stand, and it gives light to everyone in the house. In the same way, let your light shine before men, that they may see your good deeds and praise your Father in heaven." (Mt. 5:14)

"...fan into flame the gift of God, which is in you through the laying on of my hands. For God did not give us a spirit of timidity, but a spirit of power, of love and of self-discipline." (2 Tim. 1:6)

Through his Word he kept reminding me that when the Lord gives his people a commission or Divine gift, *he does not do it without a specific purpose.* I knew I had to use the gift however *he* saw fit. I knew that gifts came with responsibilities, and I was prepared for that. I was going to be working for the Greatest Boss in the whole world! So many times I had been absolutely shattered, yet he had still held me gently in the palm of his hands. There had also been many times we had walked together hand-in-hand, and many times I had turned away from him, hid my face in shame, and withdrew my hand from his. Yet, his arm was still outstretched, and he still loved me…I was astonished. Everything I had done and *He Still Loved Me! Unbelievable!*

And now, he gave me a real purpose, a job to do - he wanted me to work daily under his guidance! Work for *Him!* What a wonder Father we have!

He had gone through all this trouble to let me know my life's path. I had been so stubborn and resistant, that only an empirical, first-hand experience would do it. I had a purpose now, and I did not have to suffer in silence or ignore my plight. I could be strong again, *because his strength was in me.* Everything was made anew! I had *died to self at the foot of heaven and upon the earth* - and he had *resurrected me* up again as an adopted daughter, an heir of the kingdom! My father is the richest person in the universe; and now I was his princess. And I have *so many* brothers and sisters, princes and princesses all of us! We have all been bought with a price. And there is a price for us to pay to be with him. We must die to ourselves, and give all glory and worship to him! I was happy to do it.

"Let us then approach the throne of grace with confidence, so that we may receive mercy and find grace to help us in our time of need." (Heb. 4:16)

I was amazed that he was giving me a job where I would be working in direct communion with him everyday. He wasn't tired of me yet! I would also be making friends and helping people from all walks of life, social standing, color and religious background. *He opened me up!* I vowed I would never allow myself to be closed down again.

I asked to blow in his direction as easy as the wind, and that I would go wherever he led me. One of my favorite scriptures came to mind: "The wind blows wherever it pleases. You hear its sound, but you cannot tell where it comes from or where it is going. So it is with everyone born of the Spirit." (John 3:8) I prayed to God to be used by the Holy Spirit fully, to touch as many people as I could, *to bring people to faith.* I had vowed to be a vessel empty, ready for him to fill. I did not care if it hurt. I would not fear. *His Will be done. His Will be done through me. "Here I am, send me!"* (Isa.6:8)
Reiki Healing in the God-Spot

One day, a trusted friend invited me to a Reiki ("ray'key") Open House near my home in Nashville, Tennessee. She said there were people being healed there. I cautiously went with her. I found people praying and laughing, and the laying-on-of hands. Their hands were hot like mine; and the people they were attending had come from the community, mostly the poor and the curious. Twice a month they would gather here in this upper room and invite any who wanted to come. I watched them, and it made me wonder. I felt comforted that there was a large painting of Jesus hanging predominately on the wall. On the desk was information about this Japanese technique, and I thumbed through it. There was a picture of a man, a Christian minister, who had given Japanese hands-on-healing this name of Reiki in the early 1800's, although it had been known for hundreds of years before. I looked at the picture and gasped - I knew this man!

This was the spirit with slant-eyes and rounded belly that was beside me during my near-death experience! The very same man! My Goodness! God works in very, very mysterious ways!

Dr. Usui had been a teacher and minister at the DoShiSha Christian University in Japan, and died many years ago after starting several healing clinics. With this, I knew what my next step was; and I went through the training classes of Traditional Usui Reiki, eventually receiving what is called the Reiki Master Degree. The pain I had been feeling was gone. Now, I felt energized and euphoric after the healings! I was not taking upon myself the other person's pain anymore. I believe the pain was merely a catalyst to keep seeking answers, and lead me to my next step. So, now I was using the "Gifts of the Spirit" offering "Healing Prayer" and "Divine Healing" under the title of

"Reiki Practitioner." But why had God led me up this path, one that I had never heard of before? Why was this strange name added to the calling of my mission?

I have given *much* thought and prayer to this question. And this is what I have been given as the answer. And since he continues to use this vessel for even more powerful works, I know His Blessing has been upon it. I have learned not to judge where his Spirit places my foot, because wherever I am he places an angel to protect and shield me with a flaming sword of Unconditional Love. So, please do not judge too quickly, and give weight to the words of God; including "By their fruits you will recognize them…" (Mt. 7:16-20) At the least, please remember that even Jacob's son Joseph (who had been sold as a slave by his brothers) abided for a while in Egypt; it was for God's Higher Good and helped the most people. Joseph said "…God intended it for good to accomplish what is now being done, the saving of many lives." (Ge. 50:20)

Reiki is now recognized by the American Medical Association as a Complementary Alternative Medicine (CAM). It is used in many hospitals by trained nurses and doctors as a complement to normal health care needs. It has consistent and measurable results. There are more and more studies (including double-blind studies by NIH) and more research is being conducted. This form of hands-on-healing is easily accessible, and more and more accepted by the public. Reiki is also a healing modality that allows me to submit legally appropriate insurance claims for integrative healthcare interventions using ABC codes (this is not available for "Healing Prayer" at this time). This ability to bill insurance makes Hands-On-Healing more available for those who really need it, and legitimate as a recognized tool in healthcare.

I have also received my certificate from the California State Board of Nursing as a "provider." This means I can teach about the Divine Connection of healing (by the name of Reiki) to nurses for their necessary Continuing Education requirements. This helps the medical healers become even better healers - as they actively ask for the power of the Spirit to come directly into their work, by their prayerful intention and loving touch.

This is nothing I earned. It is nothing any person could *ever* earn! Yet, I know that if The Big Guy wanted to, he could make the rocks speak, so I am in good company. I know I have been hard-headed, extremely stubborn and completely sinful. Through difficult lessons and time he made me see my self-pity, false piety, and selfish desires. I also had a false form of love; *I was giving love conditionally, with the aim to receive back.* God's way is pure, Unconditional Love. I was also putting in God's place of worship other things, including spouses, and all of them were failing me miserably. Only he can fill up that yearning inside us, only he can fill the God-Spot he created within. The true acknowledgement of my failings made me see all these things clearly. He had removed the veil, and now I could see. I was free!

Now, my entire life is an adventure and an *aware* spirit journey! I meet people from all over the world, get to be there everyday when incredible things happen, and form friendships that are deep and loving. I praise God continually as I enjoy every day, every moment, and every experience I have! I am always amazed how he brings his kids together. It totally humbles me to be involved in this kind of work.

The point that I want you to remember from my experience is this: you don't have to be struck by lightning to show love, or to have a special connection with God. Love is the key to everything. Remember, the life-review *you* have will be about the love you showed, or didn't show! It's all about love! What will your words and actions reveal about you?

"But I tell you that men will have to give account on the Day of Judgment for every careless word they have spoken. For by your words you will be acquitted, and by your words you will be condemned." (Mt. 12:36,37)

When I was before the Ultimate, I wished only to love and be responsible to him. But what *he* wanted was for me to be responsible and *love everyone else*. So, we prove our *love* by *loving* everybody else!

My brokenness led me to a mending of the very highest kind, and everything in my life has changed, in align with fulfilling that purpose. I feel blissful, every night and every day!

Brokenness, and emotional trauma, can often lead one to a place of "Birthing Spirit." It may be difficult now, just as a woman giving birth has pain, but when the baby is born, what joy there is! So it is with the surrender of ego and Self Will, as you begin to allow the rebuilding to occur. And you don't have to be struck by lightning to do it!

CHAPTER 3

Spiritual Therapy
Self-Care; Conscience; Forgiveness; the Spirit Within

People who are in balance spiritually have certain qualities that shine forth in their personalities like luminous beacons in a foggy night. These people love without judging others, and understand that the Divine Spark is within every person, and they see each person as a child of God. They take responsibility for all they do and are very careful that their words and actions do not cause harm to others or to the earth. If they are not in some kind of career that involves service toward humanity, they often fill their off-hours helping to resolve problems in their neighborhood, environment or schools, or they are on the phone encouraging and supporting their many friends. They have a desire to help others and receive much satisfaction from it. They know who they are inside. They know how to give, and how to receive. *They know love!*

Spiritually balanced persons seem to be able to "roll with the punches" and come out on the other side unscathed. They come from a place of profound faith, and reliance on One greater than themselves. They will never be found guilty of gossiping, backbiting, cheating, blaming, faultfinding, or making any person feel inferior. They truly listen to others, are encouraging, tactful, humorous, humble, personable, compassionate and always willing to offer a listening ear or share a word of wisdom. They see their lives as being blessed and guided, have a sense of deep peacefulness. They look for Divine Coincidences every day of their lives. Truly enjoying life, they see every day as an adventure, and desire to consistently show unconditional love to every person they meet, as if they were meeting God himself. They accept each with tolerance and respect. They understand we walk alongside each other on our mutual journey of obtaining true potential.

It doesn't matter if their physical body is whole or not - their spirit is, and others see it also and bask in the glow. What a wondrous life is theirs; and it's potentially attainable for every human on the planet!

Knowledge Comes Before Wisdom

One of the first things a person must do to become spiritually balanced is to clean out negative and false thought patterns and redirect and relearn new ones. When we err by ignorance, we *still* receive the full impact of consequence - the law of cause and effect. We must let go of our lack of self-esteem, insecurity, fear, and unforgiveness; we must embrace the Spirit of Love in all we do, and in all we are. It is surrender, a trust in what is not seen by human eyes, but embraced by spirit. Our Invisible Father, whispers to spirit that we are not alone, and that he loving cares for us. Every step on the path is progress, and it takes ample time. But, the effort is *well* worth it. Spiritual revelation is an on-going process rather than a completed, segmented event.

Didn't you learn the alphabet before you learned how to spell and read? Didn't you learn numbers, addition and subtraction before you learned algebra? Yes, you did. It was a natural and gradual process. You did the same thing when you were choosing a marriage mate - you dated, did things together, enjoyed each other's company, and did a lot of communicating. *The love grew as you got to know the other person.* So it is with the number one concept in Spiritual Awakening. Look at the three aspects of love in this famous scripture:

"Jesus replied: "Love the Lord your God with all your heart and with all your soul and with all your mind." This is the first and greatest commandment. And the second is like it: "Love your neighbor as yourself." All the Law and the Prophets hang on these two commandments." (Mt. 22:37-39)

So there we've got it. *Love God. Love Ourselves. Love Others.* Simple concepts! But, as we have seen, we need to lay a basic foundation by spending time getting to know who these folks are, including ourselves. We also need to clean out some concepts that may be damaging to you or hampering your spiritual growth.

Why Do I Feel Guilty for Getting Sick?

Sometimes people have the belief that an illness is always a physical reflection of a spiritual imbalance. If they get cancer, they wonder what they did to "deserve" it. *Trees* get cancer, as do animals. Do we blame and criticize trees and animals for their illness? No! We give them love, understanding and support. Yes, some things we bring upon ourselves because of emotional and spiritual imbalances. But, we also need to acknowledge many other factors including, but not limited to: genetics, environmental pollutants, addictions (parental addiction while in the womb), working conditions, childhood nutrition, etc. Now, can you blame yourself for all these things? No! You are bombarded by many factors. Take note that also, sometimes the cells in our body *simply malfunction.* We are a long way from the Garden of Eden and perfect bodies. So, *stop feeding off the guilt platter* and decide from this day forward to use your energy to fix the problems, instead of all the energy it requires for placing blame!

Restoring Your Soul

The health of our spirit greatly influences both our physical and mental health. We've

60

all seen the person who is incapacitated because of chronic illness or injury. Perhaps he is a paraplegic, and that is how his life might stay, without much possibility for change. Yet, we find people with the *same* injury but of *two* different attitudes. One is angry and withdraws, is abusive toward others and self-pitying. They hate their life. The other is happy, outgoing, creative and spends their time doing whatever they can with whatever ability they have, doing something good for people. They love their life! Perhaps all they can do is simply hold a paintbrush in their teeth - with which they have painstakingly learned to produce intricate, beautiful pieces of art. What ever they do, the true joy is from finding meaning in their lives by joyfully offering to others what has made their light shine. Ones afflicted with an illness and live in joy know a wonderful secret: Spiritual Wellness. Spirit goes beyond whatever state the physical body is in. Spiritual wellness also heals emotionally; and the two are linked into wholeness.

If a human life puts itself willingly as a hollow straw in the direction of the flow of God's great river of spiritual power, wouldn't that power have to flow through that life? By the practice of faith a person can completely surrender his cares and worries, and let the love flow. That means you learn to *receive* love, *embrace* it in your life, and then *give* love, completing the progression of *flow*. Not all at once, but presently, like dawn stealing across a darkened world; the quiet strength of God will come into your life, gifting you with vitality and an amazing capacity for love.

"The Lord is my shepherd, I shall not be in want. He makes me lie down in green pastures, he leads me beside quiet water, he restores my soul." (Ps. 23:1-3)

The Uniqueness of You - Finding Out Who You Are

The first thing you need to do is to *know yourself.* Who are you? What do you like to do? What is your favorite color? Why? So many times we forget about our own uniqueness or consider it vanity to know who we really are. What is your favorite way to make eggs - as an omelet, scrambled, over-easy or poached? Have you *tried* a variety of ways to really know, or are you just in a habit and so consider *that* must be your favorite? Often we go along in life not really making the choices that we ourselves want, but to please someone else or just following a habit. Maybe it's something as simple as how we choose our eggs, or maybe it is as complicated as what religion we learned as a child. *How do you know what is right for you?*

Sometimes we need to spend the time to re-evaluate how we do things, and *why.* We wouldn't want to wake up one morning and feel that everything in our whole life has been "not really what we want to do." When that happens it makes us feel resentful and empty. When we try to please everyone, we find it can't be done; and we often lose part

61

of ourselves in the process.

Self-Care and Overextending

Self-care is important. Jesus often went up by himself away from the crowds to be alone. Were all the people healed, all the parables told and every question answered before he left? No, but he did what was needed at the time and then "filled up his cup" again. When people manipulate you (or you are forced by your own need to please) to give more than God wants you to give, think about this. This is an important point, and will aid your emotional and physical health too. So remember - *when people want you to give more than God wants you to give, remember Jesus withdrew to a quiet place!* He would take care of them again, another time, after he recuperated, after he took care of himself.

In following the Lord's example, we will not experience burnout syndrome or resentment from overextending ourselves. We can exercise the God-given choice of Free Will and say "no." It gives us a chance to come back, refreshed, and ready to help in another situation, at our best. And that's better for everybody!

How Do I Relieve Stress?

The dictionary describes stress as "mental, emotional, or physical tension; strain, distress." The world we live in is fast-paced and competitive, and causes stress in our lives. Changing schedules, budget concerns, credit card bills, car repairs, mortgage, relationship problems, children difficulties, endless appointments, etc. - it all requires *a lot* of energy. A *depletion* of energy means a need for *replacing* energy. Again, the law of cause and effect comes into play. Rest, exercise, trips to the beach or to the mountains, a bubble bath, a babysitter and a dinner out, a massage, a drive in the country, a picnic at the park, solitude, a movie - all these things can help relieve stress. But sooner or later, you have to face those things that created the stress. How do you restore a weary heart, build courage, or hope for things to get better? This *only* comes from *filling the spiritual need.* We were created with an empty "God-Spot."

Just like a car can only work well feeding on gasoline, our spirit can only work well feeding on Spirit.

"He gives strength to the weary and increases the power of the weak. Even youths grow tired and weary, and young men stumble and fall; but those who hope in the Lord will renew their strength. They will soar on wings like eagles; they will run and not grow faint." (Is. 40:29-31)

You cannot keep overworking and overstressing yourself without paying the high cost on your body and mind. Look at the symptoms: *For the body* - look at all the medical research that has shown heart attacks, strokes, headaches, insomnia, high blood pressure, extreme fatigue and even cancer are related to stress and burnout syndrome. *For the mind* - emotional exhaustion such as crying easily, a pessimistic attitude, being quick to anger, inability to shake depression, irritability for no reason, taking drugs or alcohol to "get away from it all," criticizing, and bitter about other people's good fortune - these are all symptoms of burnout and stress.

"Cast all your anxiety on him because he cares for you." (1 Pe. 5:6,7)

Most people wait until their "stress balloons" keep growing bigger and bigger, until one day, they "pop!" Then they lose control and go off in all directions - they leave their job, their family, the country, find a lover, etc. Everything breaks down, falls apart, and crumbles – often like dominos leaning against each other, everything tumbles down. There is another alternative! Instead of "breaking," all it takes is *one step at a time,* a progressive letting air out of the stem of the balloon, releasing its pressure *gradually* until it is safely deflated. It can then remain resting there whole and unbroken. Learning to see opportunities in many situations develops character and confidence.

"Consider it pure joy, my brothers, whenever you face trials of many kinds, because you know that the testing of your faith develops perseverance. Perseverance must finish its work so that you may be mature and complete, not lacking anything." (Jas. 1:2-4)

Why Should I Make Time for a Spiritual Life?

Take a step back and look at your life. Are you happy, no matter what life is giving you? If your answer is no, they you must *buy out the time. Buying* means we have to exchange something for it. That is what we normally do for things of *value.* What happens when you buy out time for spiritual growth? You will find peace, understanding, answers for many of life's questions (big and small), endurance, strength, and love. What else occurs when you make time to look for God? You find him!

"You will seek me and find me when you seek me with all your heart. I will be found by you," declares the Lord." (Jer. 29:13,14)

"Examine your priorities and ask the tough questions. Are the things you're investing your time in, things that will last? Will you have anything to show for your hard work and frantic pace when you come to the end of your life? If you're too busy for God, then you're too busy." - *Stress* by Melanie Jongsma (The Bible League, 1992)

63

Make Friends with the Inner Child

What hobbies do you like? When was the last time you did them? What did you do as a child? If people were to buy you a gift, do they know what you like to collect? *Do you?* We were all created different. *We are perfect in our variety!* Accept the differences in yourself and embrace them. Accept the differences in others too, and embrace them!

This knowing of oneself will take some work to do. The mind doesn't want to change its set patterns, even if they are not good ones. It will do anything to protect the old beliefs and find a way to adhere to its comfort zone, even in little things. And our comfort zone doesn't mean those things are necessarily good for us, it may be that we are just used to them, and have adjusted. This is the reason why so many abused women divorce only to re-marry another abuser. The same thing happens with alcoholics. Breaking a pattern is never an easy thing to do. Perhaps we even grew up in this cycle because our parents had an unhealthy habit (even *lack* of discipline, or being *overly strict* is a pattern we learn), and our grandparents before them. But, we need to break the cycle of events, for our own good, and those of our habit-following children.

This is one of the reasons that free coupons and free samples work in advertising. Marketing firms know that once we've developed a pattern, we're more likely to stick to it, without actively looking much further. In the case of business, this applies to which brand of clothes, food, or drink we will purchase. Free samples and coupons help this process. It's time to re-make ourselves! Set aside time everyday, even if it is only fifteen minutes, to ask yourself questions. Pretend you are a celebrity and interview yourself about every imaginable nuance! If you *know yourself* first - what you like and dislike - you will clearly see God's ability to guide and bless you toward your goals, *because you know who you are!* If you don't know what you want, and can't ask for it, so how can God fulfill your desires? Know yourself first!

We Are Like a Leaky Dixie Cup

We are all like leaky paper Dixie cups. Everyday, our energy is being used for various needs, and if we don't keep filling it up with energy from the top, pretty soon the cup goes dry. Not only that, but the container itself ends up crumbling in on us, and pretty soon we become a broken vessel. But, what happens if we have *more than enough* coming through the top? Turgor pressure! Even if the entire bottom were to fall out, we still wouldn't crumble in!

What are you filling your cup with? I call this cup the "God-Spot." It is the hungry spirit within us, created by God to continually reach out to him. It can't be filled up from just anything - more material possessions, more money, becoming famous, these things don't fill this empty space. No matter how much you throw in it, it will still just be an empty hole. Here are just a few suggestions that can help satisfy this hunger. I'm going to outline just a few simple things - I don't want to spend much time detailing these, because I spent a full two chapters detailing a *multitude* of tools we can choose from in my previous book, *Psychic Gifts in the Christian Life – Tools to Connect*. But, I would like to emphasize that you actively *find* those things that are particularly useful for spiritual growth, resonant within your being, and then *use* those things consistently, whether it be from my book or someone else's.

(1). *Create Sacred Space* - a place inside, or outside, where you can go to for relaxation without being disturbed; an inside altar acts as a quick and visual reminder to increase your prayer life and the sanctity of all things. The Water Wheel; True-Spirit Compass; Making a Memory Chest.

(2). *Meditation* - active listening in the stillness, as you open your heart and mind to God. Some favorites: the Glass Elevator, Counting through Thought, the Perfect Mantra; the Twilight God-Spot.

(3). *Visual Imagery* - where you incorporate all five senses to transport you to a favorite memory or place you have been, or would like to be. There you have complete freedom even with the natural elements (i.e. you can fly, etc.) Also, it is a good place to go to hold conversations with those who you need to release in forgiveness and love. Incorporate the Cabin of Family Forgiveness; What Scent is Grandma; What is Left is Right, Right?!

(4). *Communion with Nature* - go for a walk on the beach, a camping trip to the mountains. Be in creation and see the natural flow of change and beauty in all stages of life, and feel the Presence of the Maker's hand. Creating a Spiritual Retreat; Fasting; 5 Minute Life Escapes.

(5). *Communion with Animals* - spend some quality time with Fido and Fluffy, animals are a mobile "sacred space!" Feel the love! One favorite: Activating the Human Purr-box.

(6). *Carry a Sacred Object* - your grandmother's locket, your father's watch, a native coin from your ancient homeland, a cross. This is almost like bringing your altar with you; you are never out of touch with what is important to you. Remember when you were a kid and always got in trouble because you filled your pockets with crazy, special-only-to-you things? Here's your chance to get in touch with your "inner-child" and acknowledge the sacred at the same time.

(7). *Read the Sacred Book* - Dust off your Bible and open it to the book of Psalms. It's a good place to start because many of the Psalms are conversations with God, written by people who were in stress. There is an anointing on the book; even if you read just a paragraph or two a day, you will find your day is more peaceful, and goes easier.

(8). *Affirmations* - if you aren't using them already from the Emotional Healing chapter, it's time to put them into the program for your spiritual therapy too.

Fear Stagnates Growth

Fear is the opposite of love. Love is always a verb, a *moving* thing. Fear stops, freezes, *stagnates.* If you were in the forest and needed a drink, what kind of water would you choose? The still pond with the layer of green moss, silt and floating debris, or the stream running fresh, clear, cascading over the rocks? There are many dangers to drinking from a stagnate pool; it could adversely affect your health. Fear is stagnate water. Love dances and shimmers as it makes its way along. *Love invigorates health!*

"Fear is like a wound within our emotions. You heal a fear much like you heal a cut on your hand. If you ignore a cut on your hand, it will get infected. But it will heal itself if you pay attention to it and give it time. It's the same with a fear. First, recognize its existence - what kind of fear is it? Is it fear of poverty, of loneliness, of rejection? Then use common sense. Don't let the fear get infected. Often we burn 70 percent of our emotional energy on what we fear might happen (90 percent of which won't happen). By devoting our energy to our other emotions, we will heal naturally."- Quote of Za Rinpoche, *What Should I Do With My Life?* by Po Bronson (Random House, 2002)

"Part of our inner fear is that we do not know or trust ourselves, so are afraid to be in situations that give us opportunity to evolve. In order to take control of our lives and accomplish something of lasting value, sooner or later we need to learn to Believe...We simply need to believe in the power that's within us, and use it. When we do that, and stop imitating others and competing against them, things begin to work for us." - *The Tao of Pooh* by Benjamin Hoff (Penguin Books, 1983)

"There is no fear in love. But perfect love drives out fear, because fear has to do with punishment. The one who fears is not made perfect in love." (1 Jn. 4:18)

"When we see God in each other we will be able to live in peace." - Mother Teresa

Pay Attention to the Spiritual Subconscious

The spiritual subconscious is that part of us that tells us what is right and wrong, good and evil, and is part of the breath of life that all mankind has in common. Often it is called the *conscience*. For example, in every culture there is a taboo on murder, adultery, and the most basic things, almost like the 10 Commandments written within our soul. This conscience can also be ignored and defiled; or cleansed and sharpened. It is part of being human:

"Even when Gentiles, who do not have God's written law, instinctively follow what the law says, they show that in their hearts they know right from wrong. They demonstrate that *God's law is written within them*, for their own consciences either accuse them or tell them they are doing what is right." (Ro. 2:14,15) *New Living Translation*

Listen to the Spirit

Within the connection with Divine is the ultimate source of accurate information, and the "language" is learned and interpreted through time. The more we listen, connect to him and look for the meanings, the louder and clearer his words become to us. It fills our hungry spirit, and fills the empty God-Spot we were all created with.

If we are strong enough to get our own *preconceived notions* out of the way, we might even be able to let God-Consciousness come straight through - with all of its purity and power and truth - *without interpretation.* A 'knowing' compared to a 'figuring out,' spirit embracing Spirit. *Oneness!* When we ask for Connection, and for Spirit to have free access in our lives, everything changes. *Bypassing the interpretation of the brain, you can now allow direct access of the unity of Divine Will. No words needed, just an absolute knowing.* Talk about being Connected!

"My prayer for all of them is that they will be *one,* just as you and I are *one,* Father - that just as you are in me and I am in you, so they will be in us, and the world will believe you sent me. I have given them the glory you gave me, so that they may be *one,* as we are - I in them and you in me, *all being perfected into one.* Then the world will know that you sent me and will understand that you love them as much as you love me." (Jn. 17:21-23)

How Do I Know if it's Me Talking, or God?

God gives us a knowing, and a discernment to know his voice over a counterfeit one. Test it out! God would never tell us to hurt ourselves, or others, or to be an extremist. It will not contradict anything that we know about his character of love, his teachings of wisdom (being familiar with his Word lets you know the difference – the personality of God, the history of how he deals with mankind), the undefiled conscience, or the commonsense he created us with. See if what you are hearing resonates in your bones,

67

and makes you feel happy, peaceful, balanced and confident. If it doesn't, it's not True Source.

As for knowing if it is your own intuition, or your own spirit talking, that can also be answered. Ask him to make it clear! This is what I did (remember the freedom we have through Free Will, we have to ask for things first!), and now when the Lord speaks to me, there is a *definite* distinction. He uses my voice, *but* it's more punctuated, has no language contractions, is slower, in colonial English, and has a definite "Old World" flavor to it - I can't mistake it now!

One week, I was sharing this with one of my clients. The next week, she approached me at a grocery store and said, "I tried what you told me to do - to ask for God's voice to be different than my own. This is going to sound crazy, but God has a sense of humor!"

"Yes, he sure does!" I agreed.

She continued, "The voice inside my head now - you know, when he's talking? Now I hear Mickey Mouse!" We started laughing, "It's a good tie-in; Disneyland and Mickey Mouse was the only good time I had growing up. Who would have known!"

Our Father always takes up the slack, and the lack in our lives. It's time to rip apart the perceived partition that keeps us on one side and him on the other.

"Whenever anyone turns to the Lord, the veil is taken away." (2 Cor. 3:16)

Yup – not only is the veil lifted so we can "see" better, but we can "hear" better too! Even if it's the voice of an animated character! God certainly DOES have a sense of humor! He made people, didn't he? That proves it right there!

Wait For Internal Confirmation

These whisperings of God will give an internal confirmation, and a sense of deep peace. I suggest you always wait and give time to what you hear, to make sure you're not sensing your own emotion, excitement, or desire. It is well worth taking a moment every day to spend quiet time, and listen.

"Be still, and know that I am God." (Ps. 46:10)

We have many instances in scripture where he gives information to people about the future (i.e. Noah and the flood, Moses and the Promised Land), and God has a unique and special plan for each of us. But, he won't *force* us to listen to him, or to fulfill our best path, although he will *encourage* us. Often we have to get out of the whirlwind of noise around us and in us, to do this. God speaks in whispers. Find a place internally, and externally, to *listen.*

"A great exercise to practice listening to God is to ask Him if there is anyone He wants you to encourage or bless - then be still and listen. You will be surprised at how quickly He responds. He will fill your heart with godly thoughts and goals. He will name people who will be blessed by your attention to them, and He may tell you specific things to do to encourage them. He has ideas to present to you that you haven't even considered. Listen carefully to Him. Then follow the advice given in John 2:5; "Whatever He says to you, do it." - *How to Hear From God* by Joyce Meyer (Warner Faith, 2003)

Be Open to the Reality of God

"Blessed are the poor in spirit, for theirs is the kingdom of heaven." (Mt. 5:3)

This scripture is basically saying: *Truly happy people are those conscious of their spiritual need.* Happy, that is, because they *know* that they *don't know* everything, because true humility is the first step in being willing to learn. By following our path, we will always continue to learn!

Remember the God-Spot. Nothing else can fill that need but spiritual union with him. It is similar to having an automobile, and trying to put water in the gas tank. Whether it's a state-of-the-art Lexus or an old Chevy, it still needs petrol to operate. Nothing else will do! And just as a car is created with all of its parts on the drawing board for a *specific purpose* and the design sent to the factory, so God created us with a need to have a *"God-Consciousness"* and use it. See it as an "on-board satellite navigation system!" Let it guide you through the maze.

The God-Spot is why we find everywhere, in all parts of the earth, and in all periods of time, people expressing a need to worship; whether it has been the sun, idols of stone or TV personalities. As a person searching for the face of God, it may easily seem like an insurmountable and impossible task. But, yet, a gnawing feeling inside of us keeps driving us - we need to have the validation of God. We need the personal realization in our lives, the manifestation of *"I AM."* Why is that? Why can't people feel complete happiness in just meeting the needs and wants of life? We've seen why. *Because we were made that way!* We were *meant to be empty* without God - the *hungry spirit.*

Illness is an Enemy

"I think it is fair to say that every time Jesus met with evil, spiritual or physical, he treated it as an enemy. Every time a sick person came to him in faith, Jesus healed that person. He did not divide human beings, as we so often do, into a soul to be saved and healed and a body that is to suffer and remain unhealed until the next life and resurrection. We are the ones who talk about "saving souls," but nowhere in the New Testament does it say that Christ came to save souls; he came to save human beings - body and soul." - *Healing* by Francis MacNutt, PhD (Ave Maria Press, 1999)

There is no need to believe that suffering will earn you "brownie points." God wants us to be whole. So also, does your family, friends, and workmates. Subjecting yourself to the thought that keeping an illness somehow saves someone in your family from getting ill, or that you are somehow "earning" God's love because of your suffering, is a faulty concept. Yes, we do find a time in early history when it was taught that the body was a prison that confined our spirit, "hindering" spiritual growth. In that ignorance, the physical body was abused, starved, beaten and looked upon with mistrust and hatred. But, that is *not* what Christ preached. God made the human body. It is a miraculous work, intricate in its every detail, and still has many mysteries that science hasn't yet been able to figure out.

"For you created in my inmost being; you knit me together in my mother's womb. I praise you because I am fearfully and wonderfully made; your works are wonderful, I know that full well." (Ps.139:13,14)

"God has no contempt for what he has made. Further, he has no disdain to serve us in the simplest requirements the nature of our body demands, for the love of the soul he has made in his own likeness." - Juliana of Norwich (c.1342 - c.1413)

Prayer to God

Do you remember in the garden, how he sought out Adam and Eve to speak *face to face* with them? That was his original purpose. He still wants that kind of close connection today. Remember to be in the stillness, so that you can listen for replies. It is two-way communication we have with our friends, mates, and relatives. How long do you think these relationships would last if we did all the talking and never allowed them a word in edge-wise? Think of God as a buddy who "hangs out" over your right shoulder. You are not talking to yourself when you pray. You are communicating with the Power of the Universe, and if you are listening in return, *you will know he's talking back to you.*

Treat the Almighty Father as a dear respected friend. Know that you can talk to him casually, without any fancy words and in any setting. People often feel that they can manipulate God into doing whatever they want him to do, if they find the "magic formula" of words to say, then they drone on and on, all within ear-shot of other people.

Did that work to manipulate your earthly father at home? I doubt it! It doesn't work with your Heavenly Father either! A lot of people use God like a Santa Claus, just begging for things. Don't use all your time trying to convince God into making deals! He knows what you need before you even ask for it. Spend time in praise and common thought and ring him up through "prayer phone." His cell phone is never out of range, never has a low battery, or even a busy signal! Picture that every time you pray, you are making a deposit in your grace bank account. You do not have to even pay a nickel for this cell phone. In fact, you receive the benefit. Become a millionaire!

"People often act as though you can manipulate God into doing what you want him to do. If you believe enough or say the right things or if you have enough faith, then God has to work. But God doesn't change to suit us. In the process of praying and through prayer we change to fit into God's will."- *Miracles Do Happen* by Sister Briege McKenna

"If the only prayer you said in your whole life was "Thank You," that would suffice." - Meister Eckhart (c.1260 - c.1327)

Healing of the Memories

This "unfolding" is the reason why many people experience healing of the memories as long as three weeks after a healing treatment. Different memories may come up that were thought to be long forgotten; such as memories of trauma, physical and emotional abuse, and unforgiveness and destructive thoughts. Often we think that these are things we had *already* gotten rid of, when we had merely suppressed them.

Remember how we are like the glass of water with dirt in the bottom. These hidden, unhealthy emotions are part of what Divine Healing stirs up and brings to the surface, to be given another opportunity for release out of our systems. So, when this unfolding happens, one thing I suggest is that you allow yourself to totally feel all the emotions of the experience, and not to push them back down into suppression. Then, see the memory as simply an experience that you moved through, and that it is over now, and done. You are not the victim anymore. You must forgive the situation, the other people, and yourself. What we receive in forgiveness will be in direct relation to that which we give.

"Forgive us our sins, just as we have forgiven those who have sinned against us." (Mt. 6:12) - New Living Bible

"The secret of life isn't what happens to you, but what you *do* with what happens to you."- Norman Vincent Peale

When these hidden things are brought to light, talking it out with another person can also help, and praying always helps. Remember prayer is tapping into the Supernatural Power, which is mightier than us. Often, we just can't truly release the memory on our own, and this is where calling upon strength mightier than ourselves is necessary.

"The basic idea of inner healing is simply this: that Jesus, who is the same yesterday, today, and forever, can take the memories of our past and *Heal* us from the inner wounds that still remain in our memories - or in our subconscious memory - and affect our present lives…bind the effects of the hurtful incidents of the past…and fill with his love all these places in us that have so long remained empty." - *Healing* by Francis MacNutt, PhD (Ave Maria Press, 1999)

"There is no fear in love. But perfect love drives out fear, because fear has to do with punishment. The one who fears is not made prefect in love. We love because he first loved us. If anyone says, "I love God," yet hates his brother, he is a liar. For anyone who does not love his brother, whom he has seen cannot love God, whom he has not seen." (1 Jn. 4:18 - 20)

Also, please note that we can change the pain and fear of past and future situations through Long-Distance Healing Prayer, since *time and space make no difference to God.* We will go into that more fully in a later chapter.

Forgiveness for Yourself, and Others

Frankly, it doesn't matter what happens to you, it matters *how you deal with it.* It's the *re*action to the action. *Not being able to forgive is pride.* It is a matter of trust to be able to let go, even of the bigger things, and in this way surrender to our next stage of spiritual development where we can *quickly* and *easily* forgive. Surrender is not a one-time occurrence. It is a constant and long-term process that occurs in stages. Scripture says that God will *not listen* to the prayers of those who continue to hold unforgiveness in their heart. It's considered a sin, grave imperfection, to do that. That's how important it is!

"If I had cherished sin in my heart, the Lord would not have listened." (Psalm 66:18)

"Love your enemies, do good to those who hate you, bless those who curse you, pray for those who mistreat you." (Lk. 6:27)

"Forgiveness is a complex act of consciousness that frees the psyche from the need for

72

vengeance or retribution. Energetically and biologically forgiveness heals. Let go of all angry thoughts. Holding anger in your being hurts you." - *Reiki, A Way Of Life* by Patricia Rose Upczak (Synchronicity Publishing, 1999)

I've Really Messed Up My Life!

We are loved! The reason we needed Christ to come and be offered up as a sacrifice for our sins is this: back in the Garden of Eden we had two perfect people make the Free Will choice to rebel against God, even after God had told them where their choice would lead - to unhappiness and death. They cut themselves off from the perfect *Connection* they had with their father. They "unplugged" themselves from the Universal Energy current.

Similar to a hot cup of tea that cools down when it's left sitting unattended on a countertop, the Energetic "heat" of once-perfect mankind now lived a shorter and shorter lifespan until finally after the flood man died after an average of only 70 years of age (this is why in Genesis you see Methuselah living 969 years, Lamech living 777 years, etc). It is similar to a dent being put in a mold - every piece that now came out of it would reflect that same dent. So it is with us, the defective children of our first parents, Adam and Eve.

Depending on where you are spiritually, you might look at it as a bunch of "karma" that mankind could *never undo.* Darkness cannot exist around Light. "Eye for eye" is the perfect law - cause and effect. How would this "curse" be taken off the kids and *each one* be allowed to make Free Will choice for themselves? *The scale needed to be balanced again,* hence, a perfect human who would freely choose to follow God, no matter what temptations were presented to him. That is where the miraculous and perfect life of Jesus came in; he balanced the scale by submission to God, even to his death. So now, each one of us can come into a position of *Grace* before God, which includes forgiveness of sins. This kind of healing is the greatest miracle of all.

Physically, we still bear the dent. We still get sick, grow old, and die. But spiritually, we are now allowed access to the Presence. And because of all that Christ suffered for us (when he could have chosen not to, by *his* choice of Free Will), we are admonished by the Father to "glorify the son." (Jo. 8: 54) This is also the same reason that Jesus told us "no one can come to the Father except through me." He opened the door to our life continuing, whether we acknowledge that fact or not. Knowing why we have a "dent" and that the scales are now balanced and how it occurred, helps us to understand why mankind in general has had a communication problem with Dad for a long time. If my earthy father told me as a child, that I needed to take a shower, I would do it. If God tells me I need to be cleansed from dirtiness, this isn't because I'm worthless; it's because I'm too precious to stay dirty!

"For since death came through a man, the resurrection of the dead comes also through a man. For as in Adam all dies, so in Christ all will be made alive." (1 Co. 15:21)

"The thing you need to do is forgive yourself, but be specific. You don't sin generally, you sin specifically. Go down a list if you have to and write it on a piece of paper and say, "I did this and I did this. I had sex with this one. I hurt that one. I stole from this one. I lied here. I did all these terrible things." Write every one of them down and then say, "God, in the name of Jesus, I nail them to your cross. I bring them to the cross of Jesus." Then take that piece of paper and tear it up and burn it and say, "As far as the East is from the West, that's how far your sins are taken from you." And then say, "Lord, from this moment on, I'm going to live with you, restore unto me the joy of my salvation." That's how you do it. Be brutal on yourself. Don't leave anything out. OK?"
- Quote by Pat Robertson

Think of it as cause and effect - except we aren't being held accountable for what we deserve - we could never undo all the karma. No matter how much life we had.

Finding Your Unique Path & Purpose

What is your purpose in life? Have you ever asked someone else, or even paid someone, to tell you what it is? Did you actually believe it, or did you still have your doubts? Sometimes people go to fortunetellers, or Tarot card readers, or consult a Ouija Board. But often, people still end up feeling that there was something missing to the experience. Often, the fortuneteller is merely giving the person an interpretation of what is being read from the vibration of the person, and not actually anything of deep meaning from his soul.

At other times, it can be even a dangerous thing, because the connection being made by the fortuneteller may actually be a connection to dark energy (fallen angels); though even the teller themselves may not be aware of it. This can do much damage, because you are by Free Will calling upon that which is in direct opposition to what you are striving for; darkness instead of Light. Evil instead of Good, Demons instead of God. You don't want anything following you home; or giving you wrong information. Humans have a bad habit of accepting *anything* supernatural as being from truth, and from God. Remember it is not at all that simple! You can't believe everything you hear – not just because the *interpretation* may be faulty, but because the *information* may be misleading to begin with.

74

God Speaks Through Our Natural Abilities

God speaks through our natural abilities. He created us with certain skills and desires, and each of us is unique in doing these things, and they "come easy" to us. We gain pleasure in doing them. What are you good at? What do you like to do? Pursue your natural talents and find a way to use it to enrich the lives of people around you, then watch for God to bless your efforts. If you spend your life doing the things you hate to do, having a job that you hate to go to, and live in a place that you hate, why are you still there and doing these things?

Years ago a best-selling book called *What Color is Your Parachute,* highlighted the burnout syndrome and suicide rates of the weary worker, and the life-long drudgery of those who would rather be doing something else. Then it basically said, "do what you love to do and the money will come." That's true. The Lord came to give us an abundant life, not one of misery. Trust that all your needs will be met. He gives us a sense of peace and joy when we are fulfilling his plan for us, using the abilities we were each uniquely created with.

Yes, it is a scary step to change our mindset on this. So much responsibility weighs on our shoulders. But, perhaps you can adjust slowly, create a business on the side, and test the waters. Pray about it. If grace is *not present,* there will be a continuing struggle, and you will need to look at your other creative assets. If grace *is present,* doors will open and opportunities will appear!

"Trust His ability in and through you, and don't be afraid to be unique." - *How to Hear From God* by Joyce Meyers (Warner Faith, 2003)

Now this is important - if your passion and Free Will are *not* engaged in what you are doing, you cannot create anything dynamic in your life, because there is nothing to Bless. *Nothing to Bless!*

Remember, truth comes in softly, even if it will change your life. And spiritually, there is no turning back after you have tasted Divine nectar!

"Taste and see that the LORD is good; blessed is the man who takes refuge in him" (Ps. 34:8)

CHAPTER 4

Long-Distance & Remote Healing
Quantum Waves; Space and Time; Ancient & Modern Use

How many times have you been on the phone and a loved one starts complaining about his bad health? Did you want to do something more than just wish him well? How many times have you picked up a newspaper and felt sorry for the family whose house just burned down, for the teenager in the car accident, for the innocent shooting victim?

If you ever wished you could do something to make things better, well guess what - now you can! Through Long-Distance & Remote Healing, now you have the opportunity to help *anyone* at *any time!*

Supported by Science?

"Consider many therapies that are now commonplace, such as the use of aspirin, quinine, colchicines, and penicillin. For a longtime we knew *that* they worked before we knew *how* they worked. Today we are in a similar situation with intercessory prayer: data suggesting its effectiveness have arisen prior to the development of a generally accepted theory. This should alarm no one who has even a meager understanding of how medicine has progressed through the ages. Sometimes scientific facts are accepted but never explained. In the 1600's, when Newton invoked the idea of universal gravity, he was attacked…because he could not explain *why*…"This sort of worry no longer bothers us, but *not* because we have answered it," observes philosopher Eugene Mills of Virginia Commonwealth University. "We've simply gotten used to the idea." So it may turn out with intercessory prayer." - *Healing Beyond the Body* by Larry Dossey, MD (Shambhala, 2001)

There is now *much* research available on prayer, including *distant prayer* - results that show that surgery patients have healed faster, crops grow more abundantly, loved ones die more peaceably and with less fear and need for medication. There are studies that show incredible differences between test groups in double-blind studies, of those being prayed for and those not. I encourage you to go on the internet and research the various colleges and institutions for the summary of their test results – and read, read, read! Since there are just too many to be quoted here, I have chosen to stay within the parameters of my own personal experience. There are many good books on the subject of prayer, and healing, and a few that combine both topics. I especially enjoy Dr. Larry Dossey's large body of work, and Daniel J. Benor, M.D, who is completing a set of volumes on various Healing Research modalities, i.e. *Spiritual Healing: Scientific*

Now it's also possible to read about several of the many experiments our military has used for years regarding "remote viewing." This is the ability to gain information about a distant location without employing any physical senses. The "Stargate" program was a multimillion dollar program that was in effect by the CIA for over 20 years (*Mind-Reach* by Hal Puthoff and Russell Targ, *The Stargate Chronicles* by Joseph McMoneagle).

The viewers went into meditation, and accessed something that was beyond normal means to grasp. How did that happen? Sounds similar to prayer, eh? Does it also sound similar to this passage where Elisha was chastising his servant Gehazi, who had done a bad deed *miles away* from his master? "But Elisha said to him, "Was not my *spirit with you* when the man got down from his chariot to meet you?" (2 Kings 5:26)

Centuries Old Practice

"When Jesus had entered Capernaum, a centurion came to him, asking for help. "Lord," he said, "my servant lies at home paralyzed and in terrible suffering." Jesus said to him, "I will go heal him." The centurion replied, "Lord, I do not deserve to have you come under my roof. But just say the word, and my servant will be healed…Then Jesus said to the centurion, "Go! It will be done just as you believed it would." And his servant was healed that very hour." (Mt. 8:5-13) See also Matthew 15:21-28.

"Well, that can't happen today, and that was Jesus!" you may say. True! And he said that after his death and resurrection, the Holy Spirit would be poured out and even *greater works* would be accomplished by the people through that same Spirit.

"Believe me when I say that I am in the Father and the Father is in me; or at least believe on the evidence of the miracles themselves. I tell you the truth, anyone who has faith in me *will do what I have been doing.* He will do even *greater* things than these, because I am going to the Father. And I will do what ever you ask in my name, so that the Son may bring glory to the Father. You may ask me for anything in my name, and I will do it." (Jn. 14:11-14)(Acts 2:17-33)

That's why we see in the scriptures people being healed with the laying on of hands; prayer; people touching the healer; long-distance healing; healing for someone who interceded for someone else; etc. Even today, healing comes in a variety of styles - but all require a few basic essentials.

Does the Person Receiving Healing Have to Believe in It?

No, we are not limited to healing through first lifting the understanding of the client into the deeper meaning of God's love. The results of the healing itself, the empirical experience, will often get the person wondering about a Greater Force. As they hear us say our beginning prayer, they hear more about who that One is. Some may also wonder if it's right to pray in the power of Jesus' name for one who is not willing to accept Christ. Let's look at this from a simple point of reason, and not argue theology.

In a hospital, would a patient preparing for surgery ask to look over the doctor's tools, and then disdainfully forbid the surgeon to use the ones he personally doesn't care for? If the doctor is prevented from using the implements he knows and has had much success with, the patient would be harming himself by being so judgmental - perhaps to a disastrous outcome.

The same would be true of a mechanic being limited to the tools he needs to work on your car; the plumber's wrenches, etc. Sometimes it's worth a try to be quietly tolerant, and wait for the final outcome to see if proof of competency is there, to see if those tools actually fix the problems presented to it.

For me, I would want to have the job done right, and let the worker do what he thinks best, and not meddle with his tools. If that means utilizing prayer, the Bible as a "how-to" manual, and Christ as the invisible surgeon hands, then so be it. Let the evidence speak for itself, and let the one needing healing be healed. All I need is for the person to be open to the possibility, and let the results speak for themselves as evidence for Spirit, as evidence for God's Love.

Long-Distance Prayer

Anyone can send love and good thoughts and intentions to a loved one a far distance away. The difference with long-distance *prayer* is that the focus is much more intense, since it requests Supernatural Intervention that *activates* the intention to be fulfilled *beyond* what we could "wish" for. Nothing prevents us from prayer, at any time, in any place. It, in itself, is long-distance healing; since the person or situation we are praying about is rarely in the same room with us. Whether it be silently over the expanse of time and space or verbally over the phone, prayer works.

Prayer by Phone

Praying with someone over the phone is a good and simple form of long-distance healing. The person is awake and paying attention, and has the choice to come together in agreement with you. It's a good idea to request that the person being prayed for also says an out-loud prayer of his own afterwards; this strengthens their commitment to fully receive the manifestations of the mutual prayer. Even over the phone, healing in this matter can be instantaneous or gradual, and it's possible you might be gifted with an impression or even prophecy that the Big Guy wants you to share. For those who are called to it, these are the special gifts of Advanced Connection.

"The Lord said to me, "the telephone is a means of communication. People talk to each other on it. I can also use it. You use the phone. People will hear you, but experience me." I don't have to see them, just unite with them before Jesus." - *Miracles Do Happen* by Sister Briege McKenna

You might also picture the person in your head, and talk them through the hand-positions you are doing in your mind's eye. You might say, "Now my hands are on top of your shoulders…your right shoulder is hotter (if you sense heat there)…now my hands are encircling your right wrist." Or, you may have a stand-in, such as a teddy bear, for your hand positions, if the vision in your mind's eye is not so clear. Be sure to have as few distractions as possible in both of your areas, and agree on the energy exchange beforehand for the cost of the call - healings may take an hour or more, and it would be a distraction if you were watching the clock and worrying about cost. I usually have the client call me, at an agreed upon time - also make sure you know the time zone differences in your parts of the world!

Radio Prayers

Healing and miracles can occur over the airwaves through radio, just like they do over the phone. In these cases, *only a few moments* can be taken for a healing, and Spirit moves accordingly!

Have the caller place their own hands on their body where they want to be physically healed. For emotional healing, have the men place their hand over their heart; and the women on their solar plexus (belly); this is where the larger seat of their emotions dwell. Say a short out-loud prayer of blessing, knowing that God knows what is needed, and knows where these people are. You may be surprised to hear Words of Knowledge or Prophecy occur at these times too. When this happens, know that you must speak, boldly, the words in your heart; but at the same time, that the whole world is listening! It is a delicate balance; personal privacy and teaching a group - but if you are in Spirit, what needs to be said and done, will be.

Healing will often happen for everyone around you, too - the host, the engineers, etc. One thing though - Spirit plays havoc on electrical! When under the anointing, it is often hard for me to hold a microphone, or even be near one. You might have to play with different configurations. The same thing happens to my cell phone, and sometimes I need to wait before I can be near a TV or my computer, since bands of white go across the screen when I am still under the anointing of Spirit. I cannot wear a watch at any time. And especially during the two or three hours after a healing, I try to avoid cash registers, gas pumps, and using my credit or debit cards (often I de-magnetize the cards at this time). It is embarrassing to hold up a grocery store line because the register suddenly goes "on the blink!"

I would like to share with you one story about an interview I had on a radio station in San Diego. The host called me up and then sent a letter to me after the fact – and the funny thing is, we didn't even know all this was going on during the interview! Just to fill you in - I had been nervous, so I asked the hosts if we could join in prayer in the back room before we started the 45-minute interview, which calmed me down immeasurably. When I saw the room full of equipment, I again voiced my concerns about the possibility of equipment failure, but was told not to worry. What you are about to read, occurred from the Presence of God and his Holy Angels, the same as though I were doing a healing - Spirit heals people, but kills machines! A small backup tape was still archiving, so the interview still was able to be recorded, and is available to this day.

"The Worldwide Leader in Internet Talk" Goes Silent
(a letter as received from Cheryl L. Sutley, Executive Director/Host of Total Wellness Radio)

"Having heard of Dr. Tiffany Snow through Dr. Scott Robinson, whose reputation and recommendation I held with great respect, I immediately knew that I was to work with her, or have her work with me. I met Tiffany at her office for a healing treatment at the end of February and was immediately touched by her presence of peacefulness and calm. She took my hands and looked into my eyes and said, "Hello Sister Healer, why aren't you doing your work?" What Tiffany did not know was that I had been a body therapist and healer and had shut down that part of my life while going through some life challenges and needing to do my own healing. She spent over an hour talking with me and then another hour doing her healing work on my body. I can testify that when I walked into her office, I was literally a "mess," feeling despondent, frightened, overwhelmed and full of anxiety. When Tiffany finished her "work" on me, I felt calm and completely at peace…

A few weeks after I met Tiffany, I invited her to be a guest on my Internet Radio Program. At this time, Tiffany warned me that she had an unusual affect upon electrical equipment - that if the equipment was in need of repair or old or ready to break-down, the electrical impulses around her from her guardian angels would "push this equipment over the edge" and break down. Believing this to be true, having had some experience myself along these lines, I went to our studio people (the owner, the program director, the head of engineering for the entire station and the electrical engineer) repeating what Tiffany had told me. The consensus was that the equipment was all fairly new (less than 2 years old) and that they had no concerns. They invited me to have Tiffany as my guest.

On the morning of Tiffany's guest appearance, everything quite normal and smooth, we started to broadcast at 9:00 a.m. PST from our studio in San Diego, California. Within a few minutes, I could see that the engineer who was running the equipment from inside our broadcast room was acting "antsy." Several minutes later, the program director came into the room and walked around us, as we were broadcasting the show, and looked very intensely at the computer screen, the equipment and the board. She and the engineer were whispering back and forth, she looked at us strangely and left. Since we were in the middle of our program, we continued to interact and follow our program scripting and were trying to keep things as smooth as possible, which we did. In the meantime, we noticed that the computer screen had gone blank, the engineer was frantically pushing levers and keys around, and music from our "intro's" and "outro's" started to play during our talk time. *We were broadcasting live,* so all we could do was make reference to the "weird things" going on, laugh and continue with our program. Several more times the program director came in, repeated her efforts to solve some sort of undisclosed problem, and left. This continued throughout the rest of the program hour.

At the end of this program, Tiffany, my partner, David Sherrell, and I walked out the studio door and were met by several people who wanted to know if we knew what was going on. Lee Mirabal, the program director, called me into her office and told me that they were experiencing the most unusual problems. That in all her 40 years of broadcast experience from San Diego to NBC in New York and all across the country in dozens of radio station, she had never encountered these "strange and unexplained break-downs." She said that not only did the computer screen in the broadcast studio go blank, but the computer system that controls all the music and advertisements went down. The engineering department experienced complete loss of their programming for the rest of the day. All the programming, advertisement, intro's, outro's, music, etc., that had been set up on the computer for *all* that day's entire programming, was completely lost.

She also could not find any of the graphics, pictures, icons or web pictures for the entire station on her computer or any other computer in the station. So, she called the web development company (at another location, 50 miles away) to reconstruct from their storage, and they could not find any of these graphics in their holding or storage files at their location. In addition, the telephones wouldn't work properly and all the lights on the telephone systems were out. This continued for several hours after we left the studio.

Needless to say, the technical people at the station were upset and asked to reconsider having Tiffany back on as a guest. I felt very uncomfortable, but completely sympathetic, so went to the radio station owner and apologized. Chris Murch, the owner, looked at me directly and said, "I am in complete belief with the work that Tiffany Snow is doing and I want you to know that she is welcome to come back at any time. We will do whatever we can to not have this happen again, but she is very welcome. We admire Tiffany and her work with the utmost regard and respect." – *end of letter.*

*(Note: As of a year later, they have not been brave enough to invite me back – I had suggested perhaps a phone interview would be better. Or would it? What an adventure I'm living! I never know what's going to happen, or where! This review is still available online, and can be heard through a link at my website (www.TiffanySnow.com) or through Total Wellness Radio (www.wsRadio.com), search for my name or by date, 3-11-03. Have fun!

Advanced Remote Healing

Remote intercessory prayer can also include medical intuitiveness, words of knowledge, and miracles. "Now about spiritual gifts, brothers, I do not want you to be ignorant…there are different kinds of gifts, but the same Spirit…now to each one the manifestation of the Spirit is given for the common good. To one there is given…the message of wisdom, to another the message of knowledge…*to another gifts of healing…to another miraculous powers*…to another prophecy…all these are the work of one and the same Spirit, and he gives them to each one, just as he determines." (1 Cor. 12:1-11)

Notice that there is a difference in the healing gifts stated here. *"To another gifts of healing…to another miraculous powers."* Although not expressly stating that this passage is talking about miracle healings, we do know time after time miracles *did* occur, even in the Old Testament. It may also be that other Supernatural gifts are being noted by, *"to another miraculous powers."* There are people with advanced spiritual abilities that have been gifted and trained by Spirit to be a totally open conduit, available at any time. As we will see, there is proof that there were actual ceremonies or

83

rituals that occurred to pass down, or open up, these gifts to mankind.

Although it is God that makes the final determination about where, when, how and to whom he allows the "tapping into" of these precious gifts, we are *all* encouraged to "eagerly desire the greater gifts." (1 Cor. 12:31)

Is *your heart* being called? Could you be a fulltime channel of Redemptive Love into the world, tapping the ever-flowing stream of forgiveness, healing and bliss of Oneness to mankind?

On this path, you will reach a much deeper level of prayer-power. Keep in mind, with the added *responsibilities* also come a vast amount of new *blessings!* Ask the Big Guy! We need more healers in the world! And there are so many gifts that he gives besides the ones for healing. "Supernatural Signs and Wonders" have made my life a daily adventure; I've been facilitated by Spirit to help find missing children; help the FBI; give information on archeological digs, etc. And I have made *long-lasting friendships* with a variety of people from all over the world! What an excellent job I have – I'm one of the few people I know who wake up in the morning thrilled to go to work! I've got the Best Boss in the world, and the job "perks" are spectacular. Who could ask for more? *Come work with us in being a Light of God's Love to the world!*

Next we will learn about advanced remote healing - a long-distance healing that connects so strongly with the person involved that the healer will have hot hands and inside information (medical intuitiveness) that is not possible by any natural means, even at thousands of miles away!

Remote Healing & Medical Intuitiveness – How to Do It

Distance and time make no difference in healing - the One who heals already knows who the person is, where he is and what he needs. So, it is up to the healer to make it comfortable for all involved. I am given simple information about the person: name, age, state (and affliction if they wish to tell it). I receive this from the person themselves - if it is on behalf of another person, I tell them that I cannot share any information with them that I may receive - since the information is personal and would be a breach of confidentiality to the one being healed. I also tell them that I will know on a core-level if the person will receive healing or not - my hands *will not* get hot. All healing is given and received on a basis of Free Will, if the person's spirit will not receive it, the Spirit of God acknowledges this, and does not force the issue.

I arrange the healing at night so that the person is sleeping peacefully in his bed. I am aware of time differences if the client is across country or the world. I lie down and start my prayers, with a medium-sized teddy bear as a stand-in for the person being healed, and my secretary (usually my daughter) in a chair alongside, ready to write any information that the Lord might give me.

Placing my hands upon the teddy's head, eyes, neck, shoulders, etc., I move from the top down to the feet, then roll the bear over and start again. All the while, I am in prayer. Prayer is Key - nothing will happen without aligning myself with the Almighty Power that heals, and allowing Spirit to overflow. God's love is the Healer, I am merely standing in the gap, as we are encouraged to do so for each other. My hands grow hot or start a pulsing vibration where the problem is, and I tell my secretary where all these places being healed are, and any other information gathered, as the healing progresses.

Often, besides the physical, I will receive information about emotional healing that needs to be addressed, sometimes with accompanying pictures of the traumatic scenes unfolding in my head. Sometimes it's previous childhood issues, or an unfolding relationship pain; it can be a varied host of previously buried problems that need surfacing to heal, there are many possible issues. Often when we bury these traumatic things deep inside they fester - and they often cause physical problems as a by-product (science is proving this more and more). The more details the Big Guy gives me, the better able I am to help bridge the analytical brain/spiritual mind gap in the morning when I converse with the client by phone, perhaps helping them to open up a little bit more.

Send Healing into the Past & the Future

In quantum physics it is said that quantum waves can go *both* forward and backward in time. God is beyond time and space, and is in control of it all. Why not send healing into the future? Perhaps for a dentist appointment, a business meeting, a job interview or an appointment with your tax auditor! You can also send it into the past, to help heal old hurts. Try to think of the problem clearly, and pinpoint the year or date as closely as you can. If you have a picture of yourself from that period of time, this will help you mentally focus better. Send prayers to traumatic experiences of past emotional and physical abuses; including neglect, violence, and addiction. Be persistent! See the event as an experience you are simply moving through, release the anger, and be a *victim no more.*

Healing Sent to Future Dentist Appointment

I had an appointment to get out my old silver fillings and have them replaced with new porcelain ones. I knew what day it would be on, and approximately what hour. Having spent years of my childhood in braces and also having had bad reactions with Novocain before, I sent healing prayer to the date. Since I had not been at this office previously, I had nothing to visualize on except my new smile, and I asked the Lord to keep me physically and mentally healthy. The day came, and as I sat down in the chair and the dental assistant prepared the swab and needle for the Novocain, I asked if I could have five minutes alone first, "just some quiet time to relax," I explained. With a strange look on her face, she briefly left the room, whereby I felt a wave of warmth, and a knowing that there would be no problem! I gave a prayer of thanks, glad that my jaw wouldn't feel like it would be hanging to the floor for seven hours.

When the assistant came back in, I told her I wouldn't need any Novocain, and to proceed with the drilling! Of course, this prompted an outcry of disbelief, and the dentist was called in, to whom I verified that if I felt any pain, I would surely let them know. Four molars, including two on top, were soon successfully drilled, scraped, and replaced with new fillings. One of the back teeth was cracked, and I received a crown on that one. The dentist would often stop as he was drilling, grinding and shaping, and ask in amazement if I was feeling any pain, to which I would shake my head, "No!" with a sparkle in my eyes.

I felt the deep pressure of the drill, and the whirling sound was disconcerting, as were the flakes flying around from the process. But I felt little discomfort, and never the need for Novocain! It was the first time the office had ever had a patient like me - which meant all the assistants had to come in to see and hear the story from the dentist. When I had a chance to tell why I didn't need it, it was with a clear voice and no effects from the procedure, that I shared the secret of Long-Distance Prayer. Then *their jaws* dropped to the floor! All I could do was flash my new smile, just as I had visualized it to be weeks earlier.

Healing Sent to Back Injury on Boat

I received a call from a woman at port in Canada, asking for a healing for her husband who had injured his back and was having difficulty getting around. Taking care of a sailboat and moving into and out of ports is a very strenuous and dangerous job, especially for an older couple. Now, they had to stay at the harbor until he got better - the injury had occurred weeks before and had gotten progressively worse, until they were wondering if they had to cut their vacation time short and get off the water. I arranged a time, and that night did the healing. The connection was good, and I could feel my hands get hot over various old injuries, and the vibration occurring over the worse ones. I could smell the person's body odor, which is unique to everyone, and continued in prayer for about half an hour, then the heat left and I knew we were done. I concluded with a prayer of thankfulness for the healing that had occurred. It was

86

about 11:30 p.m.

The next morning I called and spoke to the man, who excitedly told me that his back pain was totally gone. Not even any residual pain was left! But, in addition to this, he had a story he wanted to tell me.

"Have you ever seen the Disney movie, 'Honey I Shrunk the Kids?'" he asked.

"Yes," I replied.

"Well, I never remember my dreams, so I don't think this is a dream - and it must of happened between 11:00 -11:30, right when you were working on me - because I woke up at 11:30 and looked at the clock. In the dream, I felt like I was under a microscope, because I saw this *huge eye* above me, looking straight down on me! It was the most interesting thing! I didn't feel afraid, even though it seemed like an eerie thing. And today my back is healed! Thank you."

Healing Sent to Unknown Affliction

"Denise," an employee I was working with, suddenly became very sick and had to go home early. She was vomiting and dizzy. She had had problems like this many times before and the doctors had given her medicine but not a reason for her distress. That night at 3:00 a.m. I suddenly awakened out of bed with her on my mind. I said a prayer for her to be relieved, and went back to sleep. The next day, Denise was back at work again. I asked how she felt, and she said she felt very good.

I asked if it had happened during the night, and she said, "Yes, when I got up in the night I felt better."

"By chance, do you know what time it was when you got up?" I asked.

"Yes, I remember looking at the clock. Why do you ask?" She said, with a quizzical look on her face. "It was about 3 a.m."

During the next year that I knew her, she had not had any recurring problems with this undiagnosed illness.

Another Healing Sent to Unknown Affliction.

"Kathy" met me at a function and asked if I could help her father who lives in another state, whom I had never met. His health had been deteriorating, and the doctors were starting to do tests now to find out what was wrong. Could I help? I went over the issues of disclosure and the spectrum of healing that could be expected if the client allowed a healing to occur. I explained all healing was by prayerful Connection with The Big Guy, and that he knows where everyone is and what they need. She agreed, and we set up an appointment for an evening a few days later. She chose not to tell her father about it, since she felt he would not readily agree to it. I told her I would know on a cellular/spiritual level if this healing would be allowed by Free Will or not.

The day after the healing, I called up Kathy - and she reported that they had the test results back from the previous week. Before she could tell me what they were, I felt the Lord prompting me to speak clearly to her…so I interrupted her.

"Does it include blockages in the heart?" I asked.

"Yes!" she said, "how did you know?"

"Well, the Big Guy often tells me what he's working on," I replied. "I also saw him in uniform, and…does he smoke? Because his lungs have injury…"

"No…he doesn't smoke. But…he *was* a firefighter, he's retired now."

"Ok, that's where the uniform and the lung problem come in." I replied.

I went on to relate a few other problems, and where there are emotionally blocked places in his body that are causing health problems. "I have something else for you, something I don't get very often, a Word for him from The Big Guy himself! You have to tell him about the healing, Kathy, and you have to tell him these words!"

"He says, *"Tell him I love him, and I'm doing this because I care for you."*

The next week, Kathy came to see me. She said the doctors were throwing a fit, thinking the original diagnosis was wrong, and were doing a multitude of new tests.

"Why?" I asked.

"Because the blockages are gone! And Dad feels so much better!"

"Did you tell him what I told you?" I asked.

"Yes, I did," Kathy said, "I thought he would start in on me, or laugh me off the phone, but the most amazing thing happened. He said, *"…I believe that."*

Making and Using a Book of Prayers for Long-Distance Healing

For covering a large amount of people and situations, making a *Book of Prayers* is a good idea. This is a simple but powerful idea to help heal a large amount of people in a short period of time. Find a simple book of plain paper to write people's names in. So many times we find ourselves trying to recite the names of everyone who needs help, and we feel guilty if we forget even one! *Your intention of love makes a difference.* Prayer moves heaven and earth!

Also, in church, it is often disheartening to hear the detailed announcements of people's health problems when a request for prayers is being made on their behalf. God knows both what they, and we, need. No personal information needs to be disclosed. Truly, this is the time that we can have faith in Romans 8:26, "...the Spirit helps us in our weakness. We do not know what we ought to pray for, but the Spirit himself intercedes for us with groans that words cannot express."

At night before going to bed, think of anyone who has been brought to your attention who needs help. Perhaps it is someone at church, at work, or even on TV or in the newspaper. Write his name down in the book, each one on his own uncluttered line. Be sure to write your own name in the book too.

Hold the book between your hands, in a prayer position, and approach God. "And the prayer offered in faith will make the sick person well; the Lord will raise him up. If he has sinned, he will be forgiven." (Jas. 5:15) Pray for the nations, the government officials, for the oceans and for the earth itself. Let God know how much you care to see "His Will done on earth as it is in heaven." (Mt. 6:9-13) This is a wonderful way to let go of all your cares and worries, having faith that everything will work out the way it should. Know that what you are doing *really, really, really* matters!

Long-Distance prayer is *not* a difficult thing. And it allows you to show your true spiritual balance by actively working with your desires to bring blessing and love upon the planet. You'll never be stuck with just "wishful thinking" again!

CHAPTER 5

Deliverance & Exorcism
Ancestral Healing; Angels; Repetitive Cycles; Hexes, Curses & Spells

"I knew by experience that the invisible spiritual world was every bit as real as this material one." - *Putting On the Mind of Christ* by Jim Marion

"Six out of 10 Americans (59 percent) said they believe Satan is a symbol of evil, and not a literal being. In a seeming contradiction, however, 54 percent said they believe a person can be controlled by spiritual forces, such as demons. More than a third believes it is possible to communicate with the dead. This is based on telephone surveys of 630 adults in the 48 continental states in August 2002. The sampling margin of error is 4 percent."- by pollster George Barna.

"The apostles performed many miraculous signs and wonders among the people... As a result, people brought the sick into the streets and laid them on beds and mats so that at least Peter's shadow might fall on some of them as he passed by. Crowds gathered also from the towns around Jerusalem, bringing their sick and those *tormented by evil spirits,* and all of them were healed." (Acts 5:12-15)

So, if there is such a thing as protecting and healing angels, and devils that can torment, manipulate, and destroy, don't we need to know about them? *This chapter is one of the major differences between spiritual healing and Divine Healing.* This kind of knowledge and healing ability goes much further into the deeper things of Spirit than simple hands-on-healing could ever go.

This kind of healing goes into the very essence - how our spirit can be attacked by other spirits, and what we can do to defend ourselves.

I realize that *much* of what is about to be discussed in this chapter may seem "out-of-this-world" to those who have never witnessed or benefited from deliverance or breakage from spells or curses. All I can ask is to *just keep your mind open to the possibility.* There *is* a need for this kind of healing, because there *is* this kind of "disease" in the world. And, this kind of healing has very specific tools to do it. So, let's start with a little study on what these different spirits are, where they come from, and what they can and cannot do to the human body and mind. Knowledge dispels fear!

True Angel Sons of God

As humans, everything we see has a beginning and an end. There is a spring and a fall, a sunrise and a sunset. Even the giant redwood trees live to be longer than us, but they too have a beginning and an end. Not so in the Spirit Realm. Everything is much *larger* than you could ever imagine! Not everything is as it seems...

I am talking about the world of angels, the battle of good and evil, and the Great War that ripped apart the heavens. The creation of angels occurred before the world was. There is much to be understood, but only a little is necessary to know at this time, for acts of healing; the warrior needs to know who his enemy is, to be successful.

Although many people aren't sure about the *devil* being a real being, we do find that most people believe in the reality of *angels*. A surprising number of hands go up when I ask a group if they have seen, or felt, an angel around them (about ½ - ¾ of the crowd). Books abound now on the subject of angels, and calendars flood the market of cherub-faced dolls with wings. Let me present to you more information on this, since there is much more to angels than this quaint store-manufactured picture. It is important to know what angels are and where they came from, because the one we call the *devil* was actually created as an *angel* himself. There are good angels, and bad angels, and both are powerful. For now, let's focus on the good angels, the True Sons of God.

Angels are some of the most beloved creatures the universe has ever known! Both the Greek words *ag'ge-los* and Hebrew *mal-akh'* actually mean "messenger" or "spirit messenger" and occur in the scriptures nearly 400 times. Angels were individually created by the will of the Most High; *they are not people who were once alive.* They were created before mankind ever came on the scene. Angels have many privileges, which have included giving messages that contributed toward writing the Bible. You see them in ancient times all over the place - announcing Jesus' birth; bringing him food after a prolonged fast; pronouncing his resurrection and ascension into heaven; etc.

Angels communicate with each other, they talk various languages, and they think for themselves - although the two opposing sides of *True* and *Fallen* Sons do not converse with each other. It's almost like a constant civil war between north and south, with the issue of mankind caught in between. The human controversy sparked a war between brothers - the battle lines are drawn between angels and demons, between God and the Devil.

The angels can travel at tremendous speed, past anything we could compare to on earth.

They are superhuman in power, and have more intelligence than we do. But, there are also some things the angels don't know or understand, and they have an active interest in seeing how God works things out with us. Peter once stated: "Even angels long to look into these things." (1 Pe. 1:12) Angels also rejoice at the repentance of a sinner, and they watch the "theatrical spectacle" that we produce as we go about our lives, making our own Free Will choices, for good or for bad. (1 Co. 4:9) This is truly *Reality TV;* can you imagine some of the possible titles? "The Political Comedy Hour - Red Light in the White House," "The Hating Game - How Long will this Couple Stay Married?" and "Religion Today - Why are Humans Playing God?" They don't get to turn the channel when there is too much violence. But, they are allowed some Divine Intervention. "Human TV" - heaven thought of it first!

The Duties of Angels

Angels also have particular duties, responsibilities and rank. There is the foremost angel, Michael the Archangel. There are seraphs (they have six wings), and there are cherubs. Then, there is a very large group of angels whose primary responsibility is to act as message communicators between God and man, besides protecting (yes, we *do* have guardian angels) and reinforcing Love's will and His proclamations. (Mt. 18:10)

At the "founding of the earth" we see the "the morning stars sang together and all the angels shouted for joy." (Job 38:7) How many angels are there? The scriptures record what Daniel saw: "thousands upon thousands attended him, ten thousand times ten thousand stood before him." (Da. 7:10) And those are just the angels to attend and praise God! In the garden of Gethsemane, Jesus could have cried out to his father for *12 legions* of angels to protect him, if he had wanted to. Just *one* "legion" corresponded to the largest unit of the Roman army, consisting of 3,000 - 6,000 soldiers. One angel is known to have killed 185,000 people *all on his own.* (2 Ki. 19:35, Is. 37:36) Powerful stuff!

Angels have names and personalities too. Only two angel names are given in the Bible, Michael and Gabriel; since angels were dispatched by God, in *His Name*, not in their own. There are several references about people in the scriptures asking angels for their names, or wanting to worship them; but they were told by the angels, "Be careful! Do not do it! I am a fellow servant with you and with your brothers who hold to the testimony of Jesus. Worship God!" (Rev. 19:10) Angels are sexless; they don't marry or procreate. But, they are generally referred to in the scriptures as males, although in most paintings they are represented as females. Their wings are not actually feathers. They are likened more precisely to radiant beams of shimmering light. They were created with *their own* Free Will, or moral agency, just the same as mankind. God didn't want mindless robots operating around him. He wanted angels there because they *chose* to be, out of love for him. He feels the same way about humankind; and we were made "a little lower than the angels." (Heb. 2:7)

How to See Angels

Angels are difficult to see because their frequency is so very high. They have to really slow it down to allow us to see them. Sensing an angelic presence is like feeling a very high vibrational quality. There is wonderful warmth. You also feel genuinely motivated toward what you are supposed to be doing, the way that you should go, or what you should say. There is a peacefulness of mind, and nervousness leaves. There is also an "I know this" feeling, a familiarity that our core responds to.

Most of the time, *faithful angels* are invisible, but they *are* allowed to appear and manifest to humans at times. Sometimes they are a mist, bright light, and look like shimmering heat waves or as vibrational qualities of energy. Rarely are they allowed to manifest in forms of matter, in human form. Remember what Einstein said? *Matter is just slowed down energy.* Believe me, they can do it, *if it's For the Highest Good*, and *if that's what it takes to get the job done*, then they will! But, most of the time we will not *see* anything with our eyes - we will just have a *knowing sense* that we are not alone. And, it is *not* a sense of dear ole grandmother sitting beside you. No! *It is so much more!*

When you sense these feelings, try to lift your own vibrational level up as far as you can - go into prayer and meditation, and breathe very deeply, even physical activity and aerobics help. Do a healing on yourself or someone else, thereby bringing Holy Spirit further into play. Now, cross your eyes slightly (as if you were looking at a "magic eye" puzzle of the 1980's) and be open, open, open without fear, asking to see God's messenger. The angel also has to *choose* to let you see him, and to slow down his energy to make it possible. Remember that True Sons do not want glory for themselves, so will only appear if it is in the best interest for the job they have been sent for. Be prepared to see angels in a much different way than Hollywood portrays! They can be so very huge – I've seen an angel almost 40 feet tall, standing head and shoulders over a house that had just been spiritually purified (exorcised). They can also be very small, less than three feet high!

The angels of God didn't just "go away" after Jesus left the earth. They are still very active today. "Are not all angels ministering spirits sent to serve those who will inherit salvation?" (Heb. 1:14) We are still inheriting salvation today. We have a promise from God that we are continuing to be protected. "If you make the Most High your dwelling -

then no harm will befall you…for he will command his angels concerning you to *guard you* in all your ways." (Ps. 91) So, this leaves the question: What do we need to be guarded from?

The Angels that Fell

Because of Free Will and ability to make one's own choices, there were angels in Noah's day that came down to earth and materialized male bodies for themselves.

"The sons of God saw that the daughters of men were beautiful, and they married any of them they chose…the Nephilim were on the earth in those days, when the sons of God went to the daughters of men and had children by them." (Ge. 6:2-4)

These angels who had left their responsibilities for forbidden lust were then called "fallen angels," "evil spirits," or *"demons."* They were not allowed to come back into their original job positions, the responsibilities they were created for. They were now on the same side of the fence as the angel Satan, who had previously rebelled against God, and hence were now under his dominion, rulership or kingdom (the kingdom of Satan as opposed to the Kingdom of God).

The human/angel hybrid offspring of these willful Fallen Sons were called "Nephilim." One of the main reasons the flood occurred was to wipe out their hybrid physical bodies. They were a powerful race of giants, *half man and half angel,* bent on manipulation and destruction. They also had supernatural powers, and used them without restraint. The memory of these superhuman giants must have lingered in the minds of the eight surviving members of Noah's family in the ark. Did the Nephilim ignite the Greek mythologies of ancient times? I think it is quite possible.

Later, a war would take place in heaven with Michael the Archangel in the victorious lead, and *more* angels would be tossed to earth, we are told "a third of the stars of heaven," which is literally thousands upon thousands. Formerly, the fallen angels could come and go out of heaven, (Job. 2:2) but after this war they were not allowed to come back for any reason. Now, they are held in the vicinity of the earth, for a short period of time. (Rev. 4:12,12)

Fallen Angels and the "Puppeting" of Government

Satan himself had once been an angelic son of God, but because of misuse of Free Will, he chose to rebel, and thus *made himself* "the devil" ("slanderer," "rebeller"). None of these *fallen angels* are allowed by God to materialize in physical form, ever again. But, they still *manipulate behind the scenes.* That is why they look for human bodies to inhabit to be their "eyes and hands." Like an invading enemy who sends out an agent to infiltrate the ranks to cause confusion, Satan sends out the fallen angels to confuse and destroy humankind. From the beginning he has been jealous of God's love for us, and wants to come between us and the Father. He is an egotistical, sadistic dictator who knows he is on the losing side, and has the mind-set of an angry child - if he can't have the power over creation, neither should God, *so he wants to destroy what he can't have.*

This is why the world is in such turmoil, and why we see those in political and religious power abusing the people - these head figures are attacked more, because they can influence more people. That's the reason why scripture encourages us to pray for the governmental rulers and those in charge.

It's possible that you may see these fallen angels with your eyes, like true angels; except they appear as a dark mist, shadowy transparent form, or angels of light with dark, hollow eyes. They cannot fully materialize – they will only be ghost-like, and not human. Remember, *you do not need to fear any of them!* Good always conquers evil, and God and his faithful angels protect us. The name of Jesus and acceptance of what his life and death stands for, gives mere mortals of flesh the authority over these fallen angels here on earth to *bind* them; they are powerless before our rebuke, because God the Father backs it up. We have a charge of true angels at our disposal, and we are on the winning team. You can't ask for any better than that!

The Invisible War of Angels: the Human Controversy

Besides the emotional, physical and spiritual problems that we face, we can now behind the scenes to the other reasons why we undergo trauma in our life. The fallen angel Satan has brought problems to mankind all the way from Genesis to Revelation, kingdom against Kingdom. This is why we were taught to pray, as in the Lord's Prayer, "Thy Kingdom come, thy will be done on earth as it is in heaven...but deliver us from the evil one." (Mt 6:9-13) Here in these following key verses, we see a *great drama unfolding* that involves each and every one of us in our daily lives, in this invisible war on the issue of God's *right to rule*:

(1). "Did God really say, 'You must not eat from any tree in the garden'?" The woman said to the serpent, "We may eat fruit from the trees in the garden, but God did say, 'You must not eat fruit from the tree that is in the middle of the garden, and you must not touch it, or you will die.'" "You will not surely die," the serpent said to the woman. "For God knows that when you eat of it your eyes will be opened, and you will be like God, knowing good and evil." (Ge. 3:1-5)

(2). "On another day the angels came to present themselves before the Lord, and Satan also came with them to present himself before him. And the Lord said to Satan, "Where have you come from?" Satan answered the Lord, "From roaming through the earth and going back and forth in it." Then the Lord said to Satan, "Have you considered my servant Job? There is no one on earth like him; he is blameless and upright, a man who fears God and shuns evil. And he still maintains his integrity..." "Skin for skin!" Satan replied. "A man will give all he has for his own life..." (Job 2:1-10)

(3). "And there was war in heaven. Michael and his angels fought against the dragon, and the dragon and his angels fought back. But he was not strong enough, and they lost their place in heaven. The great dragon was hurled down - that ancient serpent called the devil, or Satan, who leads the whole world astray. He was hurled to the earth, and his angels with him...Therefore rejoice, you heavens and you who reside in them! But woe to the earth and the sea, because the devil has gone down to you! He is filled with fury, because he knows his time is short." (Rev. 12:7-9, 12)

Lets take these events one by one:

(1). The Fall of Mankind. The question: *"Man can choose for himself what is good and what is bad, and do it successfully without God."* Why didn't God choose to destroy Adam and Eve after they rebelled, and start all over again with different children? Because God had not created humans as mindless robots, these humans were perfect creations who made a God-given *Free Will choice.* Now, *a question was also raised before the angel sons of God* that needed to be answered, no matter what the final outcome was for Adam and Eve. This is where the beautifully created angel of God rebelled and became known as Satan, and the fall of mankind began, coinciding with the beginning of the War of The Right to Rule and the first rebellion on earth, and in heaven.

This question would take thousands of years and many generations of mankind "doing his own thing" to answer. Now, the evidence speaks for itself. We are peering into a celestial courtroom, where the attorney is compiling the mound of evidence. The final conclusion will stand forever, cannot be brought up as a challenge again, and will never be changed through out all time, in any part of the galaxy. This question will be solved on planet earth.

(2). The Question of Integrity. *"Mankind only loves God for what man can get out of God,"* and, *"When tested as to his flesh, mankind will turn away from God."* This is similar to what Jesus stated at my NDE when I was commissioned for healing - "The Flesh is the Test of the Spirit." But, as always, Satan has contorted it, saying that

97

mankind will always turn from God in time of bodily peril. Most of the time, we see just the opposite occur. We also see that at one time, Satan and his demons still had access to the Presence of God. We also see that God knew beforehand whom Satan was tormenting, and that *God is proud of us when we show integrity.* We also see God *allowing* the test to be performed, as undeniable proof that *those who really love God don't do it for selfish gain.* Again, some deeper things about why healing may not always take place right away. (Job. 2)

(3). Satan Permitted to Tempt the World. "Through time and pressure, mankind will see that God doesn't exist, or if he does, he doesn't care enough about the world to be personally involved. Evil Rules. Salvation is a lie." Here we see that a mighty war took place between Michael the Archangel and Satan, and Satan and his demons lost their place in heaven and were banished to the earth. On earth, they have escalated the world's problems, especially in maneuvering the governments of mankind, in response to Issue # One.

Knowing that the time of being allowed to do so is short, the marketing and advertising program of brainwashing people against the belief that God *exists,* let alone loves and cares about people, is fully underway. This lie is one of the reasons that God allows Supernatural events (such as healing), and "Signs and Wonders" to occur - it is a supreme marketing program of his own making, and also acts as a direct lifeline to his people, and underlines why we must persevere in prayer. *Even though God permits the devil to do his work in this world for a short period of time, God is still in control!*

Divine Healing where No Other Healing can Touch - Deliverance Prayer

Now that you know what is happening in the invisible sphere, it is time to honestly ask yourself if you have knowingly or unknowingly become contaminated by any of Satan's agents of confusion. *It does not mean that you are a bad person if you have.* In many cases, it is like having dog poo on your shoe, and you are simply dragging it along with you. Though the initial point of contamination was far behind you, unwittingly you carry it along to your house, your workplace, and into your children's bedrooms.

When you feel that evil is attached to you in some way and you are constantly thinking evil thoughts, are confused, or want to harm yourself or others, and can't seem to shake it, you may need a prayer of deliverance. If you have compulsions that drive you to distraction, suicidal tendencies, desire to inflict damage on objects and animals, sexual addictions, dark thoughts that "come out of nowhere," and you bristle or anger for no apparent reason (especially around spiritual people), you may need a prayer of deliverance. If your family seems to have "bad luck" following it (even through generations), or you have mysterious physical pain or undiagnosed disease that may even baffle the doctors, you may need a prayer of deliverance.

When these things occur and you do not feel in control of your actions, qualified clergy can pray over you and ask God to "bind" the evil affliction and command the entity to depart. You can also take the authority yourself, and I have included step-by-step instructions. It does not take "schooled" knowledge on your behalf, the "heart" intention of freely and fully submitting to God's Will is all that is needed for God to free you from this burden. Most people actually feel "lighter" afterward, as if a great weight was lifted from off their shoulders. If deliverance is needed, nothing else will suffice. If this is not the cause, there are no adverse consequences (if it is always handled with tender love) from acting on the possibility anyway. *This is a main reason why Divine Healing can heal where no other kind of healing can touch.* Even some long-term physical sicknesses are related to the need for deliverance.

Always Pray for Inner Healing First

Sometimes, instead of deliverance, it is *emotional* healing that is needed and the process of changing the tape-recording in our heads, and healing the traumatic history of rejection in our hearts. The signs of deep depression and unworthiness could need *either* deliverance or emotional healing. But, it is a good idea to *always* pray for this *inner healing* before moving into a prayer for deliverance, unless Spirit instructs you otherwise. I have noticed that there are several occasions where the deliverance prayer needs to be said *before* healing of any type can be done. Sometimes, the person will surprise themselves by the uncontrollable bodily shaking, or instant anger that comes up against the healer when the prayers first begin. It is simply the dark spirit inside wanting to keep his ground. Also, if location and time permits, a person might want to see a doctor first, and make sure there is no hormone or chemical imbalance, or perhaps a multiple personality disorder. We must not jump to hasty conclusions, and we must ask for Divine discernment in these matters. The deliverance ministry is a delicate one.

If You Need a Counselor

Sometimes a professional counselor is also recommended and needed, one who has deep faith besides academic training, to allow inner healing expose the deep hurts and the "infection" to be dug out and cleaned up. Being able to refer the person to someone who can further help and do follow-up work is very important, and especially if there is multiple personality disorder (MPD), we want to have the person help integrate the different facets of themselves back together, and not try to Oust them as spirits. This could cause more insecurity in the person's life and perhaps even splinter them further.

Once again, prayer and spiritual discernment is needed, and doctor information. This splintering effect seems to be a blessing that occurs as people are exposed to trauma so difficult that the only way they can survive it is with an "alter" identity. So, as you can see, the person may need inner healing first, even over a period of time, along with counseling, to help mend the broken pieces back. We would not want to break those pieces off, or even try.

In the area of simple bad inclinations and basic lack of self-control, sometimes all we need is a trusted friend, respected teacher or clergy member to help us see deeper into things that we may not notice by ourselves. And, this might be in the form of professional counseling too. Find someone trained to be unbiased and able to offer all facets of available choices. A listening ear and wise counsel might come from your friend, but be sure to test all things you are told by your God-Given conscious and intuition. Make sure the people you trust are in Divine Communion with God - *and not working from their own ego.* You need their words to be God's words, *not their own opinions.* Don't let other people run your life or make all the choices for you - remember that a wise counselor merely gives you many possibilities and the known "cause and effects" for each one. You must make the ultimate decisions, since *only you* will be taking the full responsibilities for them. Choose wisely! And remember, there are unseen problems that typical counseling may not fix - if deliverance is warranted, deliverance needs to be done.

"Timely advice is as lovely as golden apples in a silver basket. Valid criticism is as treasured by the one who heeds it as jewelry made from finest gold." (Pr. 25:11,12) - *New Living Bible*

What is the Difference between Deliverance & Exorcism?

It is rare that a person is actually *possessed* (thus requiring a solemn *exorcism, by qualified clergy*). Possession is *absolute* demonic control of the person. More often it is an evil attachment/affliction that is occurring *(simple deliverance).* It is demonic *oppression,* where the good and normal nature of the person is attacked. This is very common. Most people have just attracted evil to themselves from past bad decisions (sin), so it has an actual right to be there, a contract as it were, and it just won't let go.

Free Will acts like a protective armor around us - through *lapses of Free Will,* such as drunkenness or drug abuse, we may have received "holes" in our armor, places of weakness where we have been attacked. If your Free Will was usurped by another through rape or other abuse, you may have holes. If you have willfully played games (such as using the Ouija board) that opened a door to inviting in evil, you may have holes. By breaking the contracts and cleaning out the holes, and then filling them up again with solid, strong material, your armor can be restored to gleaming perfection and you will live healthy and well, physically, emotionally, and spiritually. You may even be wearing armor that is full of holes that were passed down to you by your relatives. Isn't it time to repair the armor?

"Put on the full armor of God so that you can take your stand against the devil's schemes. For our struggle is not against flesh and blood, but against the rulers, against the authorities, against the power of this dark world and against the spiritual forces of evil in the heavenly realms. Therefore put on the full armor of God, so that when the day of evil comes, you may be able to stand your ground, and after you have done everything, to stand. Stand firm then, with the belt of truth buckled around your waist, with the breastplate of righteousness in place, and with your feet fitted with the readiness that comes from the gospel of peace. In addition to all this, take up the shield of faith, with which you can extinguish all the flaming arrows of the evil one. Take the helmet of salvation and the sword of the Spirit, which is the word of God. And pray in the Spirit on all occasion with all kinds of prayers and requests." (Eph. 6:10-18)

It doesn't matter how long ago it was, spirits can *attack* and *attach* themselves and they don't just "go away." In fact, rarely do we see only one; they seem to "nest" and call in their buddies when they find a home. Similar to being injured and getting the wound infected, demons often use these damaged places in our armor to dig in and become a sore full of "puss." With time we may develop a thin scab over it and think it is over with, but meanwhile the infection is actually ravaging and eating away at our flesh. This may happen, for example, if we didn't have a father's love.

Our wound of rejection then becomes a rip in our spiritual defenses, and in no time we may pick up the very real spiritual infections of "the spirit of worthlessness," "the spirit of resentment," or even "the spirit of hatred of men." Spirits are usually given the names of the emotions they emphasize. Since they don't have physical bodies, they don't usually have names like George, Ethan, and the like. However, often the more defiant angels want to have their personal name known for ego reasons, and these names can also come up during deliverance prayers, especially in occasions of SRA, or Satanic Ritual Abuse. It's time to rid your body, your holy temple, of any bad tenants!

"Submit yourselves, then, to God. Resist the devil, and he will flee from you." (Jas. 4:7)

"I Feel so Much Better Now, so Much Lighter!"

"Monica" had just come off of the table, it had been a good healing; with much information given, and much confirmation received. The Energy touched Monica's heart and body. Next, it was her husband's turn, who admitted a difficulty with anger; and he quickly lay down and we immediately went into prayer. Both the husband and wife were trained Reiki 2 practitioners, and I invited Monica to join with me, and she placed her hands on "Jeff's" feet. Jeff's body started twitching, first a little, then a lot. Soon he was literally spasming and bouncing off the table. "I'm just sensitive to the Energy," he said. But there were also other things afoot - I knew we had to do a deliverance prayer, and do it immediately.

It is always so interesting to me how people are brought across my path – I see so many Divine Coincidences, everyday and everywhere I look! Monica and Jeff's story is one of those. They had been watching a TV show, and a well-known author was discussing his new book. Interested in perhaps purchasing one, they went online to a large internet bookstore and read the reviews on his book. One of the reviewers basically said, as Monica and Jeff tell it, that his book was good, but "the book by Tiffany Snow is better..." so they went to the listing about my book, and read the reviews. One of the reviews happened to be written by a priest. This priest was the *very same one* that had performed their wedding many years ago! And when they went on my personal website, they discovered that the priest's office is one of the places I work out of, only a few blocks from where they live! It was definitely a series of interventions that had brought them here on this wonderful day.

As I started the prayers, I explained that we were now going to go beyond what Reiki could teach them, into something they may never had heard of before, the prayer of deliverance. There will be more detail later in this chapter about the "how-to" of this kind of prayer. But, this story will give you a sample:

"Jeff," I began, "do you ever feel like there is a voice in your head that doesn't feel like your own? One that says bad things about you or other people, or even a feeling of dark depression and unworthiness, one that is constant and persistent? Does this feeling seem to follow you around no matter what, whether things are good or bad in your life, and you seem to receive little or no joy from the good things?"

"Yes, that is exactly how I feel," Jeff replied.

"Do you want to get rid of this darkness, and find the light and love in your life again?" I asked.

"Yes, I do!" Jeff responded.

"Then repeat after me...'I, Jeff, by the power of God - our Alpha and Omega;

102

Jehovah; Yahweh; our One Almighty Father - and by the authority of the shed blood of Jesus his son, and by *my* Free Will, hereby *bind* all spirits of darkness attached to me, and break any and all of their contracts with me. This includes any generational hexes, curses, or spells. I null and void them. They have no power over me. I send all these spirits to God to deal with as HE Sees Fit...the spirit of Anger, the spirit of Resentment, the spirit of Addiction...'" (Jeff repeated the words after me, with his body jumping around on the table until the *binding* part was said).

Now I said, "Jeff, I want you to say the names of any other spirits that pop up in your mind..."

Softly speaking, Jeff said: "...the spirit of *** Famous by the Sword." He repeated louder, "The SPIRIT OF *** FAMOUS BY THE SWORD! I bind you and cast you out to God. *Leave me alone!"*

And immediately, my hands grew hot, and I could feel the change in Jeff's body, as healing Energy was allowed to flow in and around him, the enemy having been removed. A lightness and peace descended, and Jeff began to cry.

"Look at this, I'm crying!" Jeff said. His wife was amazed. "What just happened here?"

"A beautiful thing!" I answered. "That demon that you named, by its own *personal* name, has probably been with your family since at least the medieval times; the most powerful demons have a powerful ego, and want to make their name known. You were given its name, many of these are difficult to oust unless you have identified them. God told you what it was, and by his Spirit, you got rid of it! You have saved your future family from this fellow's evil too."

"It just came to me, just popped in out of the blue - in researching my family, our name even came from it," Jeff answered. "I feel so much better now, so much lighter!"

"Well, let's continue in prayer, Jeff," I said, "I need you to repeat after me once more...'I now ask and accept from the Lord all love, light, and blessing, to fill up all the empty places and lonely spaces, and continue to protect me with the might of your true holy angels...through the blood of the lamb, we thank you, Amen.'"

Afterward, I noted to Monica and Jeff, "It was interesting that the demons were not allowing you to receive a physical healing - my hands didn't get hot until after that main one left. I guess that highlights how they can affect our physical health too. Once that big one was gone, like a taproot of a tree, all of his other buddies left with him - the less powerful ones, whether we named them or not! Then, I could feel the Holy Spirit flow through you like a waterfall, all the way down to your feet! Go home Jeff! Have your wife drive, drink lots of water, rest, and spend the remainder of the day in praise to God!"

We then talked about the need to begin and continue a spiritual training program, and offered them one of the Bibles that "Corner Stone Christian Fellowship of Jesus our Lord" graciously gives me to freely pass out. It's important to keep the "armor shiny" after deliverance, because these precious ones are a prime target to be attacked again, by other evil spirits "in the loop." (Mt. 12:43-45)

Later, when I got home, I went on the internet and looked up the particular name, to see if there was any known history connected with it. And although I won't give you the personal named used, I will tell you that there is a demon called "King of Swords" who is also related to Tarot cards (another "portal" that Satan uses to mislead people), and many demons in reference to "Famous by the Sword." In the days before modern implements of war, these weapons of destruction would logically be the desired names reflecting fear and terror.

There are games and activities which make a contract with us by our Free Will of accessing them - many times the demons use seemingly harmless things; only to our destruction, such as the Tarot cards. They know no one will drink poison when it's simply mixed with water - the bitter taste would make us spit it out - instead, it's mixed into a sweet liquid, thereby masking the contamination from the people drinking of it, who only see the sweet taste and are unaware of the deadly aftermath until it's too late.

Follow-up is Important

A couple of weeks later, Monica and Jeff came for a follow-up visit. The anger had subsided, but it was still strong enough to cause Jeff concern. In prayer, I saw he was still "clean," and had not been "attached" to again. So what was causing the anger? Simple - learned behavior. Just as a child will imitate the destructive behavior a father might demonstrate, so we also develop habits of doing the things we see. Jeff was living behind those eyes, witnessing everything that manifested through his own words and his body actions. Jeff probably thought that all those years it was truly *him* in control, when actually it was him *out of control,* and in the control of *someone else.* Now, taking the child/father illustration a step further, we see that even when the father is not living with the child anymore, the child will act out the conduct he remembers seeing. So it is with learning to re-train ourselves and allowing our Free Will to *align in the balance of Love without fear.*

Another interesting note in this story came from sharing the information I found on the internet about the history of this particular demon, going back so many centuries. I asked if there were any consistent problems in Jeff's ancestral family line, remembering as far back as he can.

"Yes," Jeff said. "My father died at 52; my grandfather at 53. My brother and I are worried that the same thing will happen to us."

It's possible that this demon had been cutting this family down by early death for *hundreds of years*. Not unusual, this is a common trait of families plagued by dark forces. Suicide, self-destruction in one form or another, and scores of "unlucky" events will continue to follow until the Blood of the Lamb is claimed over the fallen dragon. (Rev. 20:1-3) It's a spiritual war we wage, and the stakes are high. The happiness, protection, long-life, financial security, love and joy of ourselves and our families are at stake. Now that you can see a bit beyond the material veil of this world, into the workings of the other, you have a better understanding than most. Use this power to cut any chains that bind, and act as a guardian for your family; in this time frame, and for the future to come. As in this case, now Jeff had become a blessing for his entire lineage!

Discernment of Spirits

One of the Gifts of the Spirit listed in 1 Cor. 12 is the "discernment of spirits." As you saw, we typically call demonic spirits by the behavior they display. We don't want to give any power to them by referring to them by personal names, even if we are told them, unless we are ousting them. Of course, there are occult books that name many of them, just for the reason of ego, power and personal identity. The demons desire to have themselves deified; becoming a deity or god-like. But, all we need to do is recognize what their major attribute is, and call them by that.

Some people may be more gifted in discernment of spirits than others, and a team of two or three on a deliverance is wonderful, because one can be sitting with the one being delivered, as a friend and companion, while the other two are praying and discerning, and "ousting." Anymore than three people does *not* seem to be a good idea, since it may cause undue stress on the person being delivered. Also, personal discernment from the one being delivered needs to be a contributing factor too.

Ignored in Modern Churches

Deliverance, exorcism, sanctification and purification is now often ignored in the churches, or kept as a sacred secret, known only to a privileged few. *But all Christians must know how to fight against the devil and clean up our bodies, homes and sacred spaces.* It was this way in the beginning. The authority and power of the Holy Spirit helps us resist and deflect the attacks of evil and those spirits who choose to rebel. We have Supreme Authority to bind and loose. Jesus said, "I tell you the truth, whatever you bind on earth will be bound in heaven, and whatever you loose on earth will be loosed in heaven." (Mt. 16:19, 18:18)

Jesus taught his disciples about expelling demons right alongside teaching them about healing the sick and proclaiming the Kingdom of God. "Heal the sick...drive out demons." (Mat. 10:5-8*)* (Lk. 8:26-39) Calling upon the authority for which the name of the Son stands, as the anointed representative of God, gives capability to expel any demons that might stubbornly resist the order to leave. With this authority, we can call for a legion of angels to assist us and reinforce what we say; we can even call a *dozen* legions! (Mr. 5:13) (Mt. 26:53)

Fight Like a Soldier

Just as a soldier on a battlefield must be both well trained and properly equipped, so must we in our fight against evil forces. This means knowing the enemy's tactics and staying alert and ready. Satan has many tactics, and attempts to destroy our faith by fear, temptation, powerlessness, discouragement, lies, unworthiness, etc. All are items of darkness and despair. The Bible teaches that the best weapons for this warfare are the Word of God and prayer. We have authority as Christians to battle, and to win! The mighty angelic forces are at our disposal, the Holy Spirit is active, and everything is at the ready as our powerful invisible team enforces the law of God. If the person involved freely wants to be rid of the thing, *it will be rid.* Good is greater than evil, and will *always* win. Isn't it great to be on the winning team, knowing the outcome even before the war starts!

It reminds me of the story of Elisha the prophet and his servant. They were surrounded by enemy Aramean soldiers, bent on destruction of the prophet, because God had been telling Elisha every one of the enemy's attack against Israel even before it occurred! Elisha was equipped with the Divine "Word of Knowledge," and of "Prophecy." So, *an entire army was sent against this one man.* Elisha's servant was fearful and disheartened, so as he looked at all the horses and chariots encamped around their city that last night, poised to kill and destroy in the morning, he asked Elisha, "Oh, my lord, what shall we do?" The prophet answered, "Don't be afraid. *Those that are with us are more than those who are with them.*" And Elisha prayed, "O Lord, open his eyes so he may see." Then the Lord opened the servant's eyes, and he looked and saw the hills *full of horses and chariots of fire* all around Elisha..." (2 Kings 6:15-17) Chariots of fire, angelic forces surrounding and protecting - in ancient times horses were the symbol of mightiness in war. We have those forces on our side today. We have myriads of angels, and our force is twice as large as that of the enemy - 2/3 of the angelic realm stayed as True Sons, and only 1/3 rebelled - and the Almighty Vindicator Himself fights on our side! (Rev. 4:12,12)

Self-Deliverance, Step-by-Step

In easier cases, *self-deliverance* can be effective. In the privacy of your room, turn off any possible distractions, and decide to acknowledge the strength and power you have as a child of God. Use authoritative, strong prayers, and use the authority of Jesus' name and what it stands for. A prayer for deliverance is different than other kinds of prayers. Other prayers are directed toward God. The deliverance prayers are *direct commands* of Jesus Christ's spiritual authority toward the demons. It is similar to a parent ordering a child to obey. God is in control! A Minister's Guidebook may also be helpful (make sure that it has a part on deliverance), as is a ready list of scriptures aimed specifically at ousting demons, and highlighting the ransom sacrifice. You may want to purchase a prayer book or guidebook from a Christian supply house – and I have included an entire chapter of prayers and scriptures here in the last chapters of this book, to also help.

Since "God" is simply a title, I always address him on a more personal note at such times, by the Hebrew name given in the Bible of "YAHWEH." This is sometimes translated into English as "JEHOVAH." The original letters of YHWH (the tetragrammaton) were filled in with vowels as the person spoke, so the "a" and "e" inserted in modern times may not be accurate, though most scholars believe they are. In the scriptures today, every place you read "LORD" in all capital letters, this name of God, YHWH is meant (in the scriptures nearly three thousand times). "Lord" in lower case letters, signifies the Holy Son of God, the Christ. There are also many names for Christ (Khristos - Greek) in the Bible, Messiah (Mashi'ach – Hebrew) being a couple of them. I believe knowing the deeper things about God allows us to show our deeper love for him, that we want to know more about him, and it shows that we are coming to him not just asking for things, but because we want a relationship with him. After all, the first item of importance in the Lord's Prayer is this…"Let your *name* be sanctified…" (Mt.6:9)

Below, you will find a basic outline for deliverance. First, *pray* about it, and ask for the *names* to be given you of the spirits you want to oust (the energy or attitudes they express seem to give you additional power over them, and sometimes lets you know *how* you were attacked to begin with), and thank God in prayer for the power of Jesus name and the ransom sacrifice. Ask for protection to be upon you and everyone in your household, including the animals. Also ask for protection on all your possessions, property and home, so that no destruction occurs to them as the evil spirit departs:

(1). (Sample - Command to the Demons) "I (give your own name), by Free Will and by the Name and Authority of Jesus Christ, Bind the Spirit of (unworthiness, fear, lust, mockery, etc), Command it to Depart, and Send it to Yahweh to deal with as He sees fit, Never More to Return!"

(2). (Sample - Prayer to God of Thanks) "Thank you Lord, that you free us and deliver us from the evil one, please fill up any and all empty places with your Love, Light, and Happiness, so that never a spirit of Satan may enter them again. Thank you for Blessing us, thank you for Loving Us, Glory to God in the Highest! In Jesus' name, Amen."

To the unseen spirits on both sides, this shows your Free Will motive, the authority you do it under, and "binding" it stops the spirit from causing a major scene as a scare tactic. Name it, command it to depart, and tell it where to go (sending it to God always feels best to me, for he knows the best thing to do with it) and include in your demand that you don't want it anymore. The prayer of thanks to God afterwards includes filling up those now empty spaces with wonderful things. A void always has to be filled.

For me, it was a surprise when I followed self-deliverance for myself, and each time before I even completed the deliverance prayer, *I felt a lump suddenly move up into my throat and out* - a sign that, indeed, I had been playing host to an unwanted spirit! I had been living a clean life for years now, but still had "poo" dragging around with me. I suggest to everyone, to come before God for deliverance prayer, because we get "dirty" in so many ways. Why not let the Big Guy shower you off with some fresh water? After the cleansing, I felt compelled to rejoice in Divine for the rest of the day. He only has imperfect people to work with, and he does that patiently, even though we may still smell like what we stepped in. Deliverance makes an opportune time to continue advancing in your spiritual life, and feel the balance that you've been striving for.

Deliverance for Others

Jesus spent much time expelling demons, and taught his disciples how to do the same, right alongside the healings of the physical body. Both were a way to help the people and manifest God's love. Although there are many variables to the following ceremony, I have found that total reliance on God and absolute faith in his power is the *main intention* behind the protocol. It does not take an ordained minister or priest to see the will of God in these matters (except perhaps in matters of Satanic Ritual Abuse, where the office of ordination seems to be necessary). *It simply takes a faithful and prayerful child of God in Connection with the Holy Spirit.* (Rev. 12:10-12)

In all cases, make sure that you are the one in charge of what time and location the deliverance will take place. And, if you choose, a simple deliverance can be done at a healing service; or, you may want to find a side room for privacy. Try to have a place where you will not be disturbed by phones, noise, pets or unwanted people entering the area. It's nice to have two or more ministering to the afflicted one; do not be tempted to do it by yourself ("…where two or three are gathered in my name"). Never go alone, always have at least one other on your team, preferably two. This also helps prevent any false legal or impropriety claims, and having team members help with spiritual discernment, trading off in prayer when it's going on a long time, and one person to sit as a friend to the one being freed.

How to Do It – Deliverance from Evil
(A).

Just a reminder - this is just an *example* of how it can be done. There are no hard and fast rules, except about using the authority of Jesus' name as a direct command to oust the evil spirit. Everything else is flexible, as you can see in Jeff's deliverance. Be in prayer about it, ask God. Jesus spoke to demons and commanded them to come out just "with a word." He didn't use a lot of paraphernalia; but if it helps us to get the job done, it is OK to do so. (Matthew 8:16) (Mark 1:25; 9:25)

Create a Sacred Space: Before the person comes in, if possible, try to consecrate the room to God. Smudge with sage or burn incense. Anoint your hands and forehead with oil (frankincense is suggested, blessed olive oil is OK). Anoint the doorjambs and windows. Be sensitive to anything that is unclean spiritually in the room. If you have Blessed Water (Holy Water), spritz it around the room. If possible, have the sacraments available, so that the Holy Communion of wine and bread may take place. Have a plastic-lined trash bag, because for some reason, vomiting occurs in some cases. More often than not, a choking or coughing happens, when the spirit is expelled. This is noted around the world, in every country where deliverance occurs, so does not appear as a psycho-semantic American reaction of "what is expected." Also, I have found it a good idea to try to find a place that has no electrical appliances in it - often they will be "fried" or not function properly afterward. This can be a by-product of the True Sons too – angelic power is a mighty thing. Sometimes, equipment will turn on during deliverance, which is a distraction. There is a lot of Energy in the room during healings, and especially during deliverances.

Prepare the Team: Pray as a team for guidance, the success of the deliverance, and pray for angelic *protection* of yourselves and your families not with you (spirits have friends too - and you want to nullify any commands they have against causing you problems). You may want to view deliverance as helping a person get out of the mafia - and all the implications and responsibilities that brings to them, you, and all the families involved. Deliverance and exorcism is sometimes entered into with fasting, along with the prayer. Only spiritually balanced prayer warriors should enter into the work, and always only for the results of saving a lamb out of the wolf's mouth, not for any other reason. Be aware that any hidden faults you have, the demons just might bring out in front of everybody (they have supernatural information too, they've been watching you all your life) as a tool to embarrass or catch a prayer warrior off-guard. They can do this by using the person's own vocal cords, in the person's own words or with a growling, "other-worldly" voice.

Prayer for Inner Healing: Have the person come in. It is best that he is sitting in a chair, and place next to him the one who will be his friend. Spend some time talking with the person, sitting in chairs in front of him, making him feel more at ease, and then praying for inner and emotional healing. Try to ascertain certain things from the person's past to help find out where the problems have come from. There is always a reason for it. Are there sinful acts that we need to be forgiven for, such as perpetrating injury or abuse upon someone? Are there times of lapses of Free Will where we have lost control of our actions (or been forced)? Are there bad choices we have made and we are reaping the spiritual consequences, (including Ouija Board, Tarot card and occult involvement)? Are there emotional rips and suppressed wounds of rejection that are festering and have created a place for entry, where forgiveness of others is difficult?

If the person has committed his life to Jesus Christ, excellent, if not, now is the time. (Jesus is the *only* tool in the mechanic's box to get your "car" back on the road. If you want the freedom and all the good end results, you have to use the right tool to get the job done). Use the Sinner's Prayer. Now ask if the person by Free Will repents and renounces any ties to the occult, and to any activities that are connected with his need for deliverance. Stress the need to burn or discard (not give away) any occult items or items that tie him to a past sin. If possible, anoint the forehead of the afflicted person. Whenever possible, do all deliverance by looking deep into the eyes of the one being helped. *Keep their focus.* Begin by quoting some scriptures out loud; and a partner in the background audibly and constantly reading scriptures can be a real help:

Say: **"The power of the blood of Christ surround and protect every living person in this room."**

Say: **"Thank you Lord, that when the righteous cry out, you hear them and deliver them from all their trouble."** (Ps. 34:17)

Say: **"Thank you Lord, that when the 72 disciples returned back to you they said with joy, "Lord, even the demons submit to us in your name."** (Lk. 10:17-24)

Say: **"We thank you Lord that you have given us the keys of the kingdom of heaven, and that whatever we bind on earth will be bound in heaven, and whatever we loose on earth will be loosed in heaven."** (Mt. 19, 20)

(B).

Ask: **"What Do You Want the Lord to Do for You, (name)?"** They will answer, *"to be delivered from evil,"* or *"to be made clean."* If the person can't say it, have the friend intercede for the person and say the words, *and have the person nod in agreement.* This shows Free Will choice.

With laying on of hands (usually on the head, from standing behind the chair) ***say a prayer, out loud for all to hear.*** Ask if the afflicted soul is ready to **repent** and turn around from his sin, with a renewed **commitment to follow the Christ**, and **be washed** in the redeeming blood of his sacrifice. (If the afflicted one is truly possessed, there may be fits of anger or vomiting at this point, thus the reason to stand *behind* the chair).

Say: **"We come in the Blessed name of Jesus Christ and by the authority of his shed blood, we come in the power of the Holy Spirit, and with the Unsurpassed Holy love of our Father God the Almighty, to grant** (person's name) **the freedom of <u>Free Will without constraint, and to answer us verbally without any restriction."</u>** (Sometimes the demons will actually swell up the person's tongue, or make it nearly impossible to answer, thus the reason for this directive).

Say: **"Do you** (person's name) **choose to have back the control of your own Free Will from whomever and whatever place of sin it may be in bondage now?"** (wait for answer)

Say: **"Do you** (person's name) **repent and renounce any occult activities you have been involved in, and freely give your allegiance only to the son of God, Jesus Christ?"** (wait for answer)

Say: **"Do you** (person's name) **freely choose God's Will as your own will, for his word and Holy Spirit to guide you through all occurrences in this life and**

111

beyond?" (wait for answer)

If the afflicted one has answered by himself, in the affirmative, probably a simple deliverance is all that is called for. Come around in front of the person and have him stand up. Sprinkle with Holy Water. Have him sit back down again with hands in prayer position. Continue.

(C).

Ask the person if he can tell you the names of the spirits. If he can't, use the discernment and former information to identify them. If they can't be identified, general statements such as "spirits of evil," or "spirits of darkness," may suffice. Have the person take more personal responsibility for his choices by calling upon God himself for the deliverance. If he stumbles on words, such as not being able to say "Jesus," keep encouraging him. If the prayer is not able to be completed, eventually step in and say it in his behalf.

Say: **"In the name of Jesus Christ, and by the power of the Blood and the Holy Spirit, and the authority given the rank of our adoption as Children of God committed to Almighty God, we command you, spirit of...** (pride, unforgiveness, sexual perversion, drug addiction, greed, etc) **to leave** (person's name) **and, without manifesting yourself in any way, and without entering into or otherwise bringing harm to anyone or anything else in this room, property or building, we send you straight to the light of the Lord God Jehovah to be dealt with as He Sees Fit."**

(If the afflicted one cannot proceed, <u>you must intercede for the person's Free Will and state</u>: **"We intercede for (person's name) in the name of Jesus Christ and by the power of the Holy Spirit and the love of God Jehovah, to grant freedom from oppression by binding and casting out the evil spirits tormenting and controlling (person)."** Then continue with recitation of above.

Do not allow cursing or throwing of objects - many times the possessed soul may be forced to rebel and try to create fear in your heart (fear is the opposite of love - creates lack of faith in God). Sometimes the person's chair may levitate, the sense of an invisible hand may slide up your arm, and a far-away voice spewing threats may be heard. These are all scare-tactics of these invisible, unruly children. Often, as stated, a coughing will occur when the spirit releases. There is always more than one, as they seem to "nest" around a stronger one. You may want to focus on the smaller ones first, to help "loosen" the bigger attachment. Stand strong and be prepared to see God fight for you and the afflicted one! God's angels, and Michael the Archangel himself, know what you are doing, and will *not* lose the battle. Nothing solidifies faith as fast as

112

observing the Lord fight for one of his own lost sheep - the invisible war of the spirit realm where the Good Guy always wins; our True King of the Mighty Sword, the originator of *"tough love!"* Just stand firm in prayer, and one by one continue to cast out each demon, through Spirit.

(D).

Communion: Pray over the wine and the bread, stating that they represent the blood and body of the Christ, offered up in our behalf. **Include the "Lord's Prayer."** Conclude with each person attending saying consecutively:

**"In Jesus name / deliver us from evil /
and in communion with you/ we start anew/
in body, mind and spirit."**

The last person to repeat this is the *formerly afflicted one*, ending with "Amen."

End with prayer: say a personal prayer out loud to God, ask the attending helper(s) with you to say one also. Or you may use a traditional prayer, such as the Catholic end of mass prayer: "St. Michael the Archangel, defend us in battle, be our protection against the wiles and wickedness of the devil. We humbly beseech thee, O God, to restrain him…" **Be full of thanks and gratitude. Sing a song of praise,** or the Halleluiah song.

Rejoice that another sheep is brought back to the fold, out of the mouths of wolves, then welcome him with Unconditional and Never-Ending Love, just as your Father has welcomed and loved you!

With Ministry Team, End with Cleansing Prayer: Jesus said, "These signs shall follow the believer. In my name they shall cast out devils." (Mk 16:17) Finish with a prayer of cleansing, of thanksgiving and gratitude for Divine working in front of your eyes, and being in the front lines of the battle between Good and evil. Pray also for continued protection of your families, pets and possessions, and safety driving home. Also, be sure to pray continued protection for the person Almighty brought you to help. Follow-up should be tentatively scheduled at this time, a "de-briefing" time where you can encourage and strengthen each other with any concerns, questions, or suggestions you may have. It is likely that the team will feel blessed but tired, and really no in-depth issues need to be discussed at this time. Time to rest and rejuvenate, and feel blessed!

Following Up

Be discerning about the possibility for needing more than just one time for deliverance.

Depending on how heavily the person was involved in different things, you may need to oust a few demons at a time, and mend the spiritual and emotional gaps left behind *before* you progress. The person may not know who they are anymore, without the spirits telling them what to do, and running their lives for them. The person definitely needs follow-up through this time - and the stability of love and support that comes from a mature spiritual couple or person of the same sex. They need a covering of going to worship together, and time in the Holy Book. I always offer a free Bible after deliverances and healings, and a Bible study is especially *necessary* to offer after deliverance. Sometimes the persons are forced into dizziness or bodily pain and can't stay long at Christian meetings, or can't read the scriptures because it gives them migraines, and prayer is in continual distraction by "other voices" or wild thoughts running through their heads. This is all demonic attack. It will get better.

They need a friend to rely on. If you can't provide for follow-up, you are doing each person an injustice, and putting them in danger. "When an evil spirit leaves a person, it goes into the desert, seeking rest but finding none. Then it says, 'I will return to the person I came from.' So it returns and finds its former home empty, swept, and clean. Then the spirit finds seven other spirits more evil than itself, and they all enter the person and live there. And so that person is worse off than before." (Mt. 12:43- 45) - *NLT*

Dawn's Deliverance

Dawn was a woman in her early 50's with a background of Satanic Ritual Abuse. I didn't know this when she came to me at one of the clinics for healing. She had terrible pain in her lower back, with many other medical problems, and she was in constant pain. The problems with her health were preventing her from working all but the smallest of part-time jobs, and she was desperate. She was also a heavy smoker, including medicinal marijuana. As I started in prayer and placed my hands upon her forehead, the Word of Knowledge came rushing in. "Do you mind if I say a prayer for cleansing? Sometimes we get attacked by unseen spirit forces and they attach to us." I waited for a response. She started snoring!

In this case, I knew that she was a spiritual person, and I remembered that when we had talked previously, she had referenced how the Lord saved her life. I said the deliverance prayer silently, and the name of a spirit came to mind. Her body shuddered on the table, and was still. I commanded the next spirit, and the same thing happened. The third time, I had no spirit name, but commanded the spirit of evil to depart, all of these with the power of Christ authority.

114

Instantly, *my left eye went blind* and a feeling similar to a *drill entering my left ear* shook me with pain. I continued in prayer, citing scriptures from memory and *refusing to fear!* I commanded the sprit to stop, and bound it. Depart. Go to God. In Jesus' name. Now! After about two minutes of this, it did. I continued with the physical healing, my client still sleeping through it all. When the healing was completed, I woke her up and told her what happened.

She asked if *I* was OK, and told me that the pain in her back was *gone!* Dawn then explained she had been involved in witchcraft for a number of years ("for the power in it - I thought it was mine, but it wasn't"), she had gotten to the point of human sacrifices, but couldn't bring herself to do it (the demons know the power of blood – often witches know the authority of the Blood sacrifice more than Christians do). By this Free Will choice, she then had several people "Coincidently" placed into her life that exorcised the demons, including a stranger brought to her while in Jerusalem. This man knew immediately that Dawn needed deliverance and "ousted" the strongest one, one that she had been *dedicated and bonded* with through Satanic Ritual Abuse (SRA).

Dawn related the deliverance as a beautiful experience, the most holy time of her life, the freedom to get rid of such a thing, and such a feeling of joy! The man in Jerusalem (a minister) had the authority of Spirit to do what those in her home church couldn't or wouldn't do. So God sent her someone who could, a man who came up to her while she was on a church retreat/vacation in the Holy Land, in the very same garden of Gethsemane that Jesus had been arrested and betrayed in! Truly, His chains were Dawn's release, in modern times as well as some 2,000 years before. Her eyes glistened with light as she retold her story, and her spirit glowed from the refreshing of the Divine Healing and Spiritual cleansing she had just received. She continued her story:

When Dawn came back to the states, she had continued in worship and fellowship in a local Christian congregation for several years. But, she had a "falling out" with one of the pastors, and now *three years* had lapsed since she had gone back to church - any church. Her "temple" had gotten "infested" again - the demons wanted her back. And they were going to make life worse for her than even before, if they could. She needed to seek fellowship, and to do it immediately. She needed the body of the congregation around her, to support her in prayer, praise and fellowship.

I invited her to my church. I invited her to go to *any church* that would support her, where she could talk freely about her needs and experiences without tongues waging. Where she could have a support system of love and encouragement, and friends to call on when things seemed out-of-hand. A place where she would have free access to clean wisdom and spiritual teachings, to protect her from falling back into the situation of addiction, fear, and despair. Those who have been in the pits of "hell" in this life, are traumatized in many ways that we may not understand. They have seen and experienced such brutality; and similar to a former mafia member threatened with death if they talk or leave the "family," they are hesitant to open up. A strong congregation is needed for support. We made arrangements to meet again in a few days, and she would come to church. She was excited about the prospect, and felt it was Divine Intervention, which indeed, it was to become.

Since she had been the last person of the day, I drove to my church where there was a small group meeting. I briefly related that I had been attacked (the ear and eye thing), and asked for healing prayer. My body of flesh was still trembling, and the hair on my arms was actually standing on end. But, *my heart and mind was not fearful at all* - and I asked that the prayers reflect my desire that "my *physical* reactions were not to be seen as a sign of *spiritual* weakness," for truly it was not! And I wanted any on-looking demons to know it! I felt robust and energetic inside my heart, from the Holy Spirit working *so strongly with me!* Only the flesh is weak, but through Christ, *spirit is strong!* (2 Cor. 12:10)

Divine Coincidence gives another Opportunity for Love

That next week Dawn came to church. Imagine my surprise, when we find that of *all* the churches in *all* the neighborhoods in *all* the towns, that the *same pastor* in my church was the one she *previously* had the problem with! The church had moved to a different location, in a different town, and The Big Guy had brought them together to settle unfinished business! After the initial shock wore off of where she was, Dawn took the incentive to go up and speak with the pastor; they agreed that any previous problems were "water under the bridge," and he said he was glad to see her. Divine Coincidence, Divine Intervention! While there, I introduced her to two different people she could call and who would support her, including the wife of another pastor. I also gave Dawn the name of a priest who also has experience with the kind of problems she had been involved in.

There was much more work to do, and even during the meeting she was experiencing demon attacks – that morning she had awakened in pain again, and it had progressed to the point of not knowing if she could even drive to the meeting – a typical attack of the buddy system of fallen angels. Now, Dawn found it impossible to stay until the end of the meeting, she was getting dizzy, couldn't focus, and was having sharp attacks of pain, and flashes of anger come up for no reason. The meeting usually concluded with a lovely group healing, and the opportunity for deliverance. This in itself would be a

116

major reason for the dark forces to do everything in their power to make her leave before then. Both she and I considered it a blessing that she had come; she knew she would have to fight for this – she had been gone too long, and she was weak. Now she had some phone numbers, had met some people, and the healing could begin between her and the pastor of the church. She was not alone, and the Ancient of Days wanted her to know that!

Within the next few days, I received several desperate phone calls. I asked if she had called any of the people I introduced her to – no, she hadn't. And, she didn't know if she could come back to church. She said she still harbored resentment, and couldn't get over it. I asked her to write everything down in a letter, and communicate with the Pastor that way, if she couldn't in person. I emphasized that it was especially important for her to have a support system. I reminded her of the coincidence of being brought into the exact place where she could complete unfinished business. Forgiveness and making things right with one another allows deep healing to begin and God requests this from us before coming to him.

"Therefore, if you are offering your gifts at the altar and there remember that your brother has something against you, leave your gift there in front of the altar. First go and be reconciled to your brother, then come and offer your gift." (Mt. 5:23,24)

Again I encouraged her to find a church - it didn't have to be mine - her falling away was why she had become demonized again. *Just find one!* Get in the middle of the flock – the wounded and weak animals that stray away from the herd get picked off by wild animals.

She missed two more healing appointments, because the pain had returned and she couldn't drive. She wanted me to come to her house and do a sanctification ceremony - but I was heading out of the country in the next few days and could not. I asked her to write down the details of her story, of how she had gotten out of SRA, and had been delivered the first time. That night she tried using a tape recorder, but it stopped working. She took up pen and paper, and ended up in the hospital emergency room. Satan does not want to be exposed.

The next day, Dawn was back home, and Satan was continuing to use fear with her. Her voice shaking with fear, she described the electrical sockets sparking on the walls, the stove burners turning on by themselves, none of her clocks working, and objects flying around the living room. "Dawn, did you call any of the numbers I gave you, and the Catholic priest who is familiar with SRA? Please call! I can't be there right now! But you don't have to do this alone!" Dawn said no, she hadn't called. She was afraid to.

Again, I encouraged her to do so, and to fellowship, go to any church. I told her to forget about writing the story. We will get together for lunch when I return, and I'll write it down. She agreed that would be best, and strongly desired to do it, "even though there will be consequences for me, I want to do it. I want to help you, and let others know about all this, and not to *ever* get involved in it."

She was being brave in some ways, but *not* in others. I was going to be gone for three weeks, and she needed to be strong enough to reach out; I was not her only life-line. Dawn was living the truth of this scripture: "So it (the demon or its buddy) returns and finds its former home empty, swept, and clean. Then the spirit finds seven other spirits more evil than itself, and they all enter the person and live there. And so that person is worse off than before." (Mt. 12:43- 45 *NLT*)

Dawn says Hello – I'm Healthy, Happy, and Strong

When I returned the next month, I found out she had only worked at her job a few more days. I tried calling her, and there was no answer. I mailed her a Christmas card, and it was returned. I thought she must have moved, or maybe went to live with a relative. None of the friend's numbers had been called, including the priest; I asked all of them.

One month later, I'm driving down the road, and the rank odor of strong cigarette smoke fills the car. I rolled the window down, and it didn't seem to be coming from outside. The next day, the same thing happens again, at home in front of my computer. I know someone wants to communicate with me, in Essence, but don't know who. In God's own time, if it was His Will, I would know. The next day I took as a writing day for this book, and turned my cell phone to "silent." I was taking time to add additional stories to various chapters of the book. I had written for several hours now, and needed to get up and take a break, drink some water, and stretch. In the book, I was right in the middle of this story - Dawn's story - and found myself wondering how it would end for her. Where was she? I got my glass of water and glanced at the phone, meanwhile a "new message" had recorded while I was working. It was Patty, the secretary at the Encinitas clinic, calling to let me know that Dawn had been *found dead* in her apartment. It had happened at least three days ago – and no one knew the reason for her death.

I sat back down at my computer, and read what I had just written, Dawn's story. I went into prayer and the Lord let me feel Dawn's presence; her spirit in the room.

"Smoke? I remember you in many other ways than that!" I said out loud.

"I know," she answered. "I'm still learning. It's the easiest thing I can do right now.

118

Can you see me? I'm healthy, happy and strong! Look!"

"No, I can't yet, but I can hear you well. I'm happy for you. I miss it up there. I can feel the brightness all around you. You're really safe and 'enlightened' now!" I teased.

"I thought you could see dead people really clear, why can't you see me?" she asked.

"Well, it has to do with you too; you need to learn how to plug in better on your side. Play with the Energy more. You're brand new, you're doing great! Have you been "Up There" (heaven – before The Big Guy) yet?" I questioned.

"No, I'm waiting for the funeral. Can you see my buff escort? I have a body guard! Nothing to be afraid of here - I'm not alone anymore, or scared. I can see all the demons too, and I'm not scared of them. They can't do anything. *God loves me!* I'm shining, happy, and I'm not poor anymore. I gotta go now," Dawn said, fading out with: "Nice name you chose for me, I knew someone with that name once…(she was referring to the alias I was using for her)"!

I replied, "I *know* he loves you! Isn't it *great!* I'm so excited for you! Check in on me, OK? And when I need to help someone out who has gone through some of your stuff, ask and see if you can hang out and help, OK? And I'll use your real name - your story will help others - you won't be forgotten!" I listen for an answer…nothing. I'm not sure if she heard me, but I think she did.

Another point of interest about this story is the very noticeable Divine Coincidences that continued on even past Dawn's death. Even though there is sadness when we lose someone, there is so much joy too, on their side! This was very noticeable with Dawn. Full and complete healing had happened for her, and it may not have been in the way we expected it would, but now she was past any problems at all. I'm sure that she would like me to emphasize this story by underlining this warning - *do not delve into the occult, it is full of pain.* The power is not your own. *Stay away. Do not even experiment.*

A special note to parents: Watch your children! It often starts early in youth, by curiosity, peer pressure or "friendly" adult indoctrination. That's how it started with Dawn - the father of a girlfriend from school. When they would get together for sleepovers, the girls would get indoctrinated by both parents. Most of Dawn's friends had already died. It is difficult to get out - many churches don't even know how to help anymore. Pray, be aware of what's going on in your kid's lives, and stay in the Truth.

Dawn also taught me that there is an equal and opposite ritual for everything done in the Christian church. *Equal* in that it may be called "communion," but *opposite* in that the host and wine is fecal matter and animal or human blood. The "table" may be the back of a naked and abused woman. Sex depravity, drugs and trances abound. Parents, watch for unusual behavior in your kids. There are meetings that they may be attending, *even without their own knowing.* Ringing a phone a certain number of times, or at a certain time, might actually be a subconscious, hypnotic suggestion they've been entranced with, to come to a ritual meeting. So they sneak out, and when they get back home, they won't remember a thing.

And yes, go to church - and fellowship with one another. *It could save your life.* Thank you, Dawn, the story is told. And nothing could keep you from the Power of God's love, as you can see by your "buff escort" angel! Many Blessings to you, my dear friend.- *Dedicated with Love to Dawn L. Alabach.*

Repetitive Cycles

"You have made your way around this hill country long enough." (De. 2:3) This comes from a place in the scriptures where the Israelites had been wandering in the wilderness for 40 years, as a way for them to learn to develop spiritually and rely on God. They would go around and around, seeing the same rock outcroppings, the same valleys and hills, and still they hadn't been allowed to go into the land "flowing with milk and honey." They weren't ready yet. Then, one day it came! The repetitive cycle was broken. Now progress happened very quickly, and soon they entered and settled in the "Promised Land" and became a mighty nation for hundreds of years. Sometimes *we* get stuck in repetitive cycles too, and wonder why we are being presented with the same problems over and over again, in only a slightly different manner. It's because we haven't learned what we need to from it yet - we keep making the *wrong turn* that *will not* break the cycle.

Please remember that feeling angry and vengeful does not always mean that you absolutely have an outside influence attached to you. It could be that you just haven't learned the emotional and spiritual gifts you need to shift your own attitude. Often repetitive cycles are about just that - producing a shift in attitude. Here is a traditional Native American story, which emphasizes that.

"A grandfather was talking to his grandson about how he felt. He said, "I feel as if I have two wolves fighting in my heart. One wolf is the vengeful, angry, violent one. The other wolf is the loving, compassionate one." The grandson asked him, "Which wolf will win the fight in your heart?" The grandfather answered, "The one I feed."

If you are seeing repetitive cycles in your life, search your heart, and feed the loving, compassionate choice, the one that benefits *others* as well as yourself. The choice that leaves selfishness and ego out of the way, and allows you to become the true potential that you already are. Choose differently, through spiritual eyes. You will be surprised how quickly freedom will come, and how quickly progress will then be made. The repetitive cycle will be broken. You may see patterns that have surfaced throughout your life for many years, and even why you chose the way you did, and the outcomes of those decisions.

This is what happened for me - for example, I kept choosing the wrong mates in my life. Why? Because I had a false form of love - I was loving conditionally, with the aim to receive back; and also, I was putting in God's place of worship my spouses, and all of them were failing me miserably. A man of flesh cannot fill the God-Spot. Through the cycle of events, I saw that I was stubborn and self-pitying, had false piety, and selfish desires. All these things being brought over and over to my attention again led me to see and *do something about it.* If we don't do something about it, here we go again!

Generational Healing, Spells, Hexes and Curses

We in the United States have seen some prominent political families that seem to be under a curse, and we've seen it affect several generations. Is there such a thing as hexes, spells, incantations, and curses? Yes. Is there such a thing needed as generational (ancestral) healing? Yes, there is!

"Today, most people believe prayer results in something positive or that it is neutral and does nothing at all. Almost never do we consider the possibility that prayer can be harmful...Prayer has become a luxury, something we can drag out of our arsenal if the going gets rough. If we took seriously prayer's negative side, we would not be so sanguine, and we would respect the power of prayer much more than we do now. Knowing that (negative) prayer could harm us, we would be on our toes. Prayer would become real in every living moment, not an optional frill that can conveniently be ignored...Anyone who is intolerant and narrow can be a source of harm to others." - *Prayer is Good Medicine* by Larry Dossey, M.D. (Harper San Francisco, 1996)

Just as we know blessings are of love and good intentions, we also find the contrary to be so. In fact, for every good ritual or in God's Kingdom, we find there is *a fake ritual in imitation of it* in Satan's Kingdom too, to defame it; just like we have seen in Satanic Ritual Abuse. And just like we have prayer partners and prayer-chains in our world for blessing and healing, Satan has people who individually and through groups spend time sending curses ("negative-prayers"), hexes and spells to destroy people. Missionaries

121

often end up sick with unknown diseases and have to return to their homelands (when leaving and sickness is the curse's purpose), and the witch doctors (who are often paid to do either good or bad) succeed. The missionaries may not even know what hit them. It's not just in foreign countries that curses abound, but also here in the United States. We may find pockets in Louisiana, Florida and New York, but almost everywhere we look deep enough, a voodoo priest, Wicca group, or an evil shaman of some sort can be found.

It is interesting to do a study on curses and blessings in the Bible. We have examples of Jesus cursing a fig tree (Mt. 21:19), the apostle Paul striking a sorcerer blind through cursing (Acts 13:11) and Elisha cursing children with the bears (2 Ki. 2:23,24). We see over 300 references to the "If-Then" cause and effect of curses and blessings. For example, "*If* you do good, *then* you will live and prosper / *If* you turn away from good, *then* you will suffer."

"Whenever we wish evil on others, in the worldview of the Bible, our words may carry not only the human freight of anger and ill-wishing, but a spiritual power to block or hurt people." - *Deliverance from Evil Spirits* by Francis MacNutt (Chosen Books, 1995)

Mona's Curse

"Mona" had been suffering from lower lumbar pain and degeneration for quite some time. Although having a background of hiking activity, yoga exercise and world travel, this still relatively young woman was now in a condition which nearly immobilized her. Her legs moved slowly and with much effort; she had difficulty with walking, and used a cane to get around. She used her arms to accomplish many of her tasks, and could pull herself up off her floor mattress only with great effort. But, she was always in good spirits and dressed herself colorfully, and still found a way to garden in the yard and do the shopping, pushing a cart to walk, when a friend would drive her to town.

On her fourth time to see me at the clinic, I had a revelation for Mona, "this is going to sound crazy, but I see a word spelled out in front of me, and I feel I have to tell it to you." I had my hands on the small of her back, and I was in an undertone of prayer - one ear to the heavens, another to my hands. "I see a muddy yellow background and a word that I have never seen before, 'B*****,' I think there is an 'H' missing. 'Bh****,' I think."

Mona gasped, "Oh my gosh - there was an "H" missing - that is the name of the shaman who told me I would be paralyzed if I left my husband, and it came true! You spelled it out exactly!"

122

My hands still on the small of her back, I said, "It feels odd here, like a bubbling under the skin. Do you think this man put a curse on you?"

"I don't know," she said. "The other meaning of the word is praise - singing Hindu songs of praise. I used to do it everyday, I even spent 40 days getting up at dawn and chanting the sun up." And as she started chanting, I felt the heat stop. Mona wanted to be healed from her problem, but also had a core belief that she *deserved* this curse. As we continued through time, and no more healing was occurring, even though I called upon the name of Jesus, it was clearly evident that she had more faith in the karma of Shiva and curses of men than in the power and authority of the blood of the Lamb. *You need the right tool to get the job done.* We weren't getting anywhere. She had a core belief that she deserved this malady, and nothing I said, and not even a Supernatural event, was going to change that. Even though the Word of Knowledge had been Divinely given, and ascended from the *main point of injury* in her back, *her Free-Will choice had been made.* Mona still gets around as a cripple.

This is a lesson for us. Do we limit the power of God to break our chains? In a very real sense, there are those in spirit and in human bodies who may wish to "paralyze" us, to physically, emotionally or spiritually impede our life's purpose. Are we going to succumb to this and their curses because *we feel we are not worthy to be healed and be free?* This is an example, again, where we see that placing ourselves in the receiving line of Godly love is not about what we've done, but what *we choose to accept.* The law of *grace* takes precedence over the law of *karma.* Remember who you are as a child of God, a ray of light where no darkness can prevail. This is where we find salvation, when we choose the authority of Divine Love in our lives.

How Do We Break a Curse?

You will need to rely on *authority* to break a curse, especially if it is more than simply negative intentions. The persons sending harm to you are probably delving into supernatural power to do so, and usually receive an "exchange" for doing it. Whether it is money or some other thing of value, this exchange forms a "contract." With this commission to send you harm, they have the power of agreement from the authorizing person to do so, and the demonic power of the fallen angels. In the deepest of rituals, blood is always used, hence the sacrifice of animals and worse; and most of the time it is not just you alone being targeted, but everyone and everything you care about - your family and even future generations to come.

Keeping this in mind - how our families can be cursed in the future - how do you know that you don't have a curse on your family from generations before? And where is your

123

authority to break this? You as a mortal human being are vastly overmatched! But, remember, you don't stand alone. Let the Lord fight for you.

"Christ redeemed us from the curse of the law by becoming a curse for us, for it is written: 'Cursed is everyone who is hung on a tree.' He redeemed us in order that the blessing given to Abraham might come to the Gentiles through Christ Jesus, so that by *faith* we might receive the promise of the Spirit." (Gal. 3:13,14) Here is your authority; here is your covenant of blood, scriptural backing and prayer for breaking free.

Say: **"Since Jesus became a curse for me, I now, by the authority vested in me through the shed blood of Jesus Christ, break any curse on me or my descendants back for ten or more generations. I null and void and make invalid through the blood of the Lamb Jesus Christ any hexes, spells, incantations, negative prayer or evil intent of any kind on me or my descendants, going back ten or more generations. I do this with full authority as a redeemed child of Yahweh, God Almighty, with all the power and love of the Father, Son and Holy Spirit. Amen."** Feel the love!

Determine to be a Blessing to All

The typical nature of man is to return injury for injury, and to go further than that. There is a part of us that wants vengeance for our pain, and we may need to *continually* fight that self-destructive desire. Giving in to it will only bring more harm, and could "unplug" us from the Real Source of Blessing.

"Love your enemies, do good to those who hate you, *bless those who curse you,* pray for those who mistreat you…do to others as you would have them do to you." (Lk. 6:27,31)

We are to send blessings back to the ones who mistreat us. Whether you know where the curses came from or not, have the prayerful intention of sending blessings *back along that same line.* This is similar to throwing cold water on a fire. On the other hand, adding more anger to the situation will make the fire only that much hotter, and burn us even more deeply. You must control your mind, and have the "dial" set on spiritual love.

"Those who live according to the sinful nature have their minds set on what that nature desires; but those who live in accordance with the Spirit have their minds set on what the Spirit desires. The mind of sinful man is death, but the mind controlled by the Spirit is life and peace…" (Ro. 8:5,6)

124

"Bless those who persecute you; bless and do not curse…do not repay anyone evil for evil. Be careful to do what is right in the eyes of everybody, if it is possible, as far as it depends on you, live at peace with everyone." (Ro. 12:14, 17-18)

Sanctify Your Home

Is your family constantly plagued by *unexplained* illness, depression, fighting, back-biting, financial difficulties, sounds, coldness, surging lights or equipment failure? Are you moving into a new home or apartment and want to make sure it has no "other occupants?" Have you purchased something, or were given something, and now you can't sleep well at night, have destructive thoughts of self-degradation, or mysterious physical illness? Has your family seemed like it has been under a "curse," or in a seemingly repeated cycle of events that you can't seem to break out of? Do you have nightmares, hear voices, terrifying visions, or are compelled to do things that you would never ordinarily think of doing? It may be you or your home is under unseen attack by wicked forces. And, not just people can have attachments, but so can buildings and various items.

Deliverance is sometimes called the *Fourth Healing:*

(1). Physical
(2). Emotional
(3). Spiritual
(4). Deliverance

There are prayer and sacred rites for sanctifying and purifying your home. Christian de-hauntings (when it is a ghost) and exorcism (when it is a demon) can give your home a peace and security that you have never felt before. Although there are many variables on the ceremony, total reliance on God and absolute faith in His power is the main intention behind the protocol, as is invoking the blood of the Christ, just as in personal deliverance.

Get Rid of What Goes Bump in the Night

How do you consecrate a home back to God? Schedule your team (again, it is nice to work with one or two others) a convenient time to meet with the owner(s) of the home, and have the owner to fill out a questionnaire which asks the history of the home, how long the problem has been occurring, etc. The gift of discernment in used by the team here; and similar to a doctor looking for a tumor, the full diagnosis will only be made when the surgery/rituals are completed. The owner of the home needs to be involved with the team's opening prayers and to read out loud a releasing prayer, granting the

125

team the Free Will ability to work. All of this shows the invisible realm, both the good and bad sides, what the intention is by the owner of the home - of breaking any contracts tied to the home, possessions or family. This Free Will intention includes the owner meeting us at the front door and inviting us in as ministers of God, for the purpose of exorcism for the infestation of the home. This should be spoken out-loud, since we clearly want to make our intentions known, and the demons cannot read our thoughts (isn't that nice!).

When I enter the home, I immediately say the binding prayer (as in deliverance) and cast out any spirit that may be easy to go. Anoint your hands and forehead with oil (frankincense is suggested, blessed olive oil is OK), and do so for the other team members. As I go through the home, I will find anything that has not been easily removed. I stay in an undertone of prayer the entire time, just like I do with a healing. It is important to do the binding prayer quickly when entering, because less damage or no damage at all will occur when dark forces are bound from the beginning. As with all demons, they like to use scare tactics, such as the throwing of objects by an invisible hand, unexplained moaning or shrieking, odd noises from attics, basements or closets, or they may even try to attack the ministers or the householder.

Then, all the doors, cupboards, drawers, etc. the team will ask the owners to open up wide. At that time, we begin a time-honored ceremony of smudging (I use sage); frankincense anointing of doorjambs and windows, and scriptures rolled up and placed in various unseen places of the home (usually one per door or entryway - placed into the encasement if possible). Be sensitive to anything that is unclean spiritually in the room. I also work with a priest who uses a traditional Latin ritual for casting out, along with spritzing of Holy Water in each room. It's good to have a team, to fight things from all different angles. We also do the outside perimeters of the home or property. All during this time, mighty angelic protection from the True Sons are on the home, family and team members, so very little or no destruction takes place.

The Battle Angels

Since the lightning strike, it is natural to see the other side almost as easily as this side - so let me tell you about the battle angels! Different angels have different divisions of purpose, and the ones used to follow through on the words of men in binding demons carry *a lot* of authority! At home infestation occasions, there is always *one* large angel stationed *standing right through the middle of the home,* and they may still tower a good *twenty to thirty feet more above it!* These are mighty, and brilliant with an orange/yellowish gleam in their shimmering. They look like waves of heat shimmering off a golden desert road. These angels are huge! They act as the main guardian and

126

overseer of the process - and they focus some kind of beams of light periodically down through the house, I teasingly call it "rat-zapping, because no demon can hide from it!"

I love a good fight - when I am in battle, there is so much Holy Spirit coursing through my body - I feel like if I wanted to, I could fly! My senses are hyper-observant, and the amount of Energy in my head causes my ears to ring. I don't schedule any healings (or anything else, for that matter) on a "Bless This House" day, since I often find myself sleeping for a good 3 or 4 hours afterward, even in the middle of the afternoon! If you are a new Christian, and really want to know the Power of the Lord up close and personal, volunteer to help in the deliverance and exorcism ministry. What a rush! In fact, this "rush" and enthusiasm is probably the main reason why many churches have tightly maintained that only mature and balanced Christians be involved in this work. Besides needing to speak to the demons with authority, they need to not let the "rush" go to their ego, or go overboard in their handling of affairs. This is understandable. But, every Christian has the authority of the blood of Christ, and God is the One who fights for us, and puts the angels in their positions of authority. So, The Big Guy is our protection and our shield, and we should be allowed to make the decision for ourselves about sanctifying our own homes or not. That is why I have listed the steps here.

Besides the main Battle Angel, there are several smaller ones who speed around very quickly, I usually only see glimpses of them as they quickly whiz on through. I call them the Seekers. These are the ones who cause my attention to become focused on problem areas, so it can be dealt with by Free Will choices of the homeowners. Sometimes we bring home attachments from garage sales, or even family heirlooms that might have negative prayers or curses attached to them. You would be surprised! And usually these things are expensive, which make it more of a problem to dispose of for the homeowner. Sometimes it is even a treasured heirloom, bringing problems to everyone in the family through generations. Just because sweet "Aunt Tilly" gave it to you, doesn't mean it's safe.

I have found some success with praying over the particular afflicted item, dosing it with Holy Water, and rubbing it with anointing oil, to release the effects of curses, hexes and spells. Sometimes wrapping the item in salt and foil will help stop the negative energy from affecting the area until it can be disposed of - but even after unwrapping, I have not seen it come forth "clean." The Holy Spirit will let you know what to do, always keep in prayer. Part of this problem is actually caused by "energy tracings," and ghosts.

The Closing Ritual of Communion and Blessing

The closing ritual will bring back into the ceremony the owners of the home, where we share final prayers and the taking of Communion. The prayers include a filling of the now-empty places and spaces with Love and Light and Bliss. At this time, the team will address its findings, the outcome, and any physical, emotional or spiritual healing of the household members that may be related to the home affliction. A new, free NIV Bible is left with the family on the team's departing, as an anointed gift of God's Word for a continued blessing on the home.

"Heal the sick…drive out demons." (Mt. 10:5-8) Trusting completely on the Lord, by faith we are led to "Walk through the valley of the shadow of death and fear no evil." (Ps. 23:4) We know we have no power in ourselves, but are only willing instruments of the Lord, for the recovering of his children from affliction. As in the case of the healing work, we accept a donation to cover our time so that we can continue to help others and still support our families, ministries and charities. "A worker is worth his wages." (Lk. 10:7) Nonetheless, we do not turn anyone down because of lack of money; or even a trade might happen in this regard. Also, human deliverance or the (rare) need for exorcism may also be prayed for during a house cleansing. As Jesus said, "Love one another, as I have loved you." (Jn. 13:34)

Story of Karen's Home Sanctification

"Karen" called me up in a panic – she had been putting off calling me, but had been advised by a family friend who is a priest, to contact me.

"I don't know, maybe I'm crazy, but I'm scared to stay in this house one more night! It seems like everything is breaking down and going wrong with it, all of us are sick all the time, I just can't bring myself to stay in it any longer! I must be going crazy; do you know what I am talking about? Am I crazy?" Karen asked.

"No, Karen, you are not crazy," I replied. "That is what the other side wants you to think. From what you are telling me, it sounds like you may have an infestation, a demon problem. I won't know for sure until I begin the ceremony, but I think we should do this as soon as possible. I'll contact my teammate, and work out a time when we can see you. Is that OK?"

"Well, I'm not staying here tonight," she said.

"That's fine." I replied. I called the other priest, and quickly confirmed with Karen that we could meet her back at her house the very next morning. Karen's husband, who is also a minister, was in the hospital for an extended time, and they had a very young son. I encouraged her to leave the house as soon as possible, since now that the schedule was set, and the demons heard about it, they may try new scare tactics.

The next morning, Karen met me at the door. She had arrived just a little earlier. She invited me in. "Karen, you must by Free Will invite me in as a minister of God, here to cleanse and sanctify your home from demons," I said out-loud, knowing that I was being listened to from invisible places.

"I by Free Will invite you in as a minister of God, to cleanse my home from demon activity," she said. "Yes, I certainly do! You wouldn't believe what is on the *answering machine* this morning - if I hadn't been afraid before, I would be now! Come and listen to this!"

I followed her in and she replayed the message on the answering machine. A growling, low and unworldly, came from the device.

"Well, just let that erase," I said.

"Do you think it's just from someone with a bad connection?" Karen asked.

I just smiled, not wanting to provide any fuel to the intimidation Satan was trying, and repeated, "it doesn't matter." We waited a bit on "Fr. M," and once he appeared, he began the opening prayers. Then I took my turn. Everything was bound up tight - I didn't think we would be experiencing any resistance. The battle angel was in place. In fact, I thought that it was interesting that I had had an escort of the Seekers that morning, one on each side of the car, about four feet up and over. I felt like I was driving a presidential limo with some very unique flags! They were with me all the way to the house. I had begun my morning prayers calling for help, and what the schedule was for this day. I'm guessing that is when they had been assigned, although I don't know; it might have been set from the conversation of the night before.

As Karen began opening up all the cupboards and drawers, I went from room to room smudging. Sage itself does nothing to oust - prayer does that - but somehow it helps me to see apparitions and manifestations better, and where the vibrations are different in the rooms. Fr. M. was spritzing Holy Water and Latin, and we were well underway. Things were going smoothly. Then, I reached a place of coldness that I had passed through when I came through the front door, it was by the hall closet, which was now open. Since Karen was following me from room to room, and noticed every place I slowed down to consider, she asked me what was wrong.

"It's very cold here." I said. "There is something in this closet."

"This is the place I always feel cold too!" Karen said. "We were given an old guitar, maybe that's it." She pulled out the guitar.

129

"No, that's not it," I said.

"Well, maybe it's this," she said, pulling out something else.

"Nope, not that either. But it's really strong - it doesn't feel like a demon, but it actually feels like a portal, a door that has been used to access the house. There's something down in the corner that's doing it. The portal seems to be in there." I said.

…Now, dear reader, here's the funny part! You know the saying that goes, "I bet he's got a few skeletons in his closet?" Well, how about this…

Karen said, "Well, I do have my mother's ashes in there, *right in that corner…*"

Hmmm. Unfinished business. It was not necessarily because anything was bad about the mother, but it *was* unfinished business needing to be done. This was somehow allowing a contract to an opening for unwanted and undesirable visitors.

"Well, that needs to be taken care of; your mom needs to be buried. Let me say some prayers over this area, and Fr. M, if you could also bless this area, we can close this portal." So we did, and after a while it closed. *The entire feeling of the home changed from that moment on!* I found active tracings of attack in the child's bedroom, and one corner of his sandlot outside, and made the comment that his health and temperament would probably be noticeably improved from now on out.

There were also negative energy tracings attached to a couple of boxes in the bedroom closet. Energy tracings are different than demon or ghost problems. They are caused by people, similar to how curses can occur. An example of energy tracings is when you go into a room where people have just been quarreling - the air seems so thick you can almost cut it with a knife. This is an example of *energy tracings,* or energy dustings. It affects things around it, and it can be directed through distant thought. It is very much like a negative prayer.

Karen gasped in amazement as I pointed at some of the multitude of containers and boxes stacked full in the closet. "You went right to the family silver - there has been nothing but bickering and fighting over this for years! I'm going to give it right back, to everyone who wants any, I'm not going to have anything negative in this house!" she proclaimed.

We closed and Karen was happy. She had been wondering if they needed to sell the house, and Fr. M and I both assured her that it would now feel better than ever - like a brand new, flowery fresh home! She was thankful, and we spoke a while, sharing wonderful and encouraging conversation.

That afternoon, I received a phone call, it was Karen. She had gone to pick up her son from daycare and had an experience to tell me. When she brought him home, he had plopped down on the floor next to the still-open closet. Next, he crawled into it and looked up. "Mommy, look at the stars! There are so many stars Mommy!" he said. She asked him to repeat what he had said, and he did, so happy to look at the beautiful stars. Children are very sensitive, and it was a good validation that this closet would not be a place of evil anymore. Through the mouths of babes! Bright stars in a closet!

What if it's Not Demons; What if it's a Ghost?

Ghosts are folks with unfinished business. Instead of crossing over to God, they are in a "holding pattern." Ghosts are *always* spirits from people who have died. *They do not know any more or any less than when they were alive.* If your aunt was mean when she was here on earth, she will still be mean as a ghost (*spirits* who have gone to God have let go of all that tiresome stuff). If she was the salt of the earth and kind-hearted, that is how she will be as a ghost. So, you do not have to be afraid of them! Let me repeat that, *you do not have to be afraid of ghosts!* They are people who have just shed their physical bodies. They have less power over you now than they ever had.

Ghosts are the easiest to see in all the spirit categories. Often you can tell right off that it is a ghost because of the ability to see all the nuances of his features. For those who are sensitive, you will often see the wrinkles, the color of his eyes, the dryness of his skin. Once, as a waitress I went to pour coffee to one who was just "passing through." Boy, did I feel stupid! When I came within a few feet of the table I saw whom it was, and turned around and came back to the kitchen. There wasn't any one else there yet, except the cook, and did he give me a ribbing. "So, you pour coffee so much it's just a habit of going to tables when there's no one sitting at them, huh?" I smiled, and didn't tell him anything. But, I did go into the backroom and *say a releasing prayer* for the drifting stranger. When I came back out, he had either gone "to the Light of God's Love," as I had prayed, or had just moved on.

When spirits and ghosts are present, there are many tangible things your physical body can notice. Is the hair at the back of your neck or on your arms standing on end? Sometimes, you may see something moving out of the corner of your eye, or flashes of brightness that are gone when you look directly at them. Remember to do the "magic eye blur." Your spirit also has a *knowing* that their spirit is around. You will often feel a coldness, even an icy chill at times. Also, pressure or heat at the base of the skull, or at the center of the forehead, can be a physical sign.

131

A death that was sudden, and came as a shock, will produce the most ghosts. It is as if they keep repeating over and over again the last part of their lives, like a "Ground Hog" day re-run. Sometimes they just can't believe they are dead, and they will go on with the same chores and stresses during their day as if they were still alive. These are the hardest to convince to go home. *They do not believe that the angel God sent as an escort is real* - even if the spirits of loved ones are also there to help welcome them at the moment of death. There are some who will go on like this for hundreds of years without improvement.

Many interesting experiences can come from working with ghosts. If the Lord sees that you are OK with it, he will allow you to help "tidy up" their loose ends and help them get on with their transition. You won't always be successful; after all, they had the Holy Angels who couldn't get them to understand what they should be doing, either. Possibly the one who died thinks the angel is part of a dream, and the reality of death is ignored. Often the humans around them want them to leave more than the ghosts do, hence the "haunting" or "haunted house" feeling. Often, you will not know if it is a demon problem or a ghost problem until you start the ritual. Ghosts cannot be treated like a demon. Ghosts need to be convinced of the reality of their situation, and how much better it is to move on. I am facilitated for this quite a lot, since I can share with them my experience of being before the Presence of the Lord, and how wonderful the warmth of his Love felt. Sometimes unfinished business needs to be attended to first, such as capturing their killer (my other book has the stories, I won't go into it here) or solving a family problem.

When you come across a ghost, treat with love and respect, and kindness. They really are lost souls. They may be bitter, or they may be just confused. It makes me upset that there are so many haunted houses in the United States today that actively encourage people to come visit them, and charge a lot of money to do so. I want to go and free all of them! I have done this without permission of the homeowner before; it's not like breaking a contract, such as with demons, where you need Free Will agreement. Some ministers do not understand the difference between ghosts and demons, and lump them in altogether. One does need to be careful though, since a demon will impersonate the slow vibrational rate and image of a deceased person at times. Again, spiritual discernment and full reliance upon the Lord is what is needed. When you work with ghosts, the original death angel (a releasing angel) for the case is sent back to work with the *both* of you. It really is beautiful when the ghost "gets it" and moves on and upward; such a feeling of relief and joy can be felt! Sometimes others in the room who are not sensitive will also be able to see the heavens open and the ghost leave, the Energy of the room is so charged! This is the same as can happen during the death of a live loved one - a glimpse of heaven at bedside!

132

CHAPTER 6

How to Pray
Ceremonies Used in Activating Godly Power;
Healing Step-by-Step

Divine Healing is better than aspirin and stronger than the most powerful medicine, with no contraindications! Use prayer whenever you want to feel peaceful, loved, strengthened, healed, and want to see a positive change in your life or in the lives of those around you! Realize how powerful an ability you have – with the authority of Divine Love beside you.

USE PRAYER as a Powerful Tool to Curb or Quit Unwanted and Unhealthy Habits (often, with no withdrawal symptoms from drug addictions, and no craving for drink).

USE PRAYER for Pain of All Kinds, Speed Surgery Recuperation, Stress Reduction, to shorten the life-span of Virus and Bacteria, to Abate Nausea from Cancer Chemotherapy, and the Burning of Radiation.

USE PRAYER to Shorten or Abate Diseases and Infection, to Help Balance Blood Sugar and Diabetic Situations, Promote Hormone Balance (including Menopause), Aid in Fertility and Nervous System Problems. Also Ease the Fear and Pain of Childbirth.

USE PRAYER for Immediate Relaxation & Long-lasting Feelings of Well-Being & Peacefulness. Fights Depression, Panic, Anxiety, Severe Mood Swings, Anger.

USE PRAYER with any other Physical or Mental Exercises to Quicken Responses, Aid Visualization, Increase Test Scores, Deepen Concentration and Memory Functions. Increase Intuitiveness, Receptivity, and Sensitivity to God.

USE PRAYER to Enhance any Prescribed Medication, Special Diets, Healing Practices, Medical Treatments, Aid Recovery Time, Lessen Scar Tissue, Sleep Better at Night, Curb "Road Rage", and to Live Your Day Refreshed, Peaceful and Alert.

What Prayer is *Not*

It is *not* wishful thinking, hypnosis, or mind control. It is not the "power of positive thinking," or simply encouraging the spirit within. *It has consistent, measurable results.* Also, as we have seen, *faith* by the sick one is not always the main factor, about whether someone gets healed or not. There are many instances in the scriptures where those *without any faith* were healed. *Faith does not heal - God heals!* (Jn. 5:5-

13) This is why even people without initial trust in God, and babies who cannot make a conscious choice for healing, and agnostics and atheists, receive healings. So do animals!

How to Pray - Manifesting the Invisible through Words

(1). *Talk to God Like You Would a Trusted and Respected Friend.*
You do not need to be in a special place, wearing a special piece of clothing or jewelry, or be in a special mood. We can run into problems if we feel God only hears us from within the confines of a church or at an altar, with lighted candles and incense, etc. We can pray to God anywhere; in our cars, in our bedrooms, our work-places, out in nature, there's no place where he can't hear us. Ritual and ceremony has its place, to be sure - but use it as a vehicle for freedom and consecration to God, *not restriction.* Prayer should never be constricted - God cannot be put in a box of our own choosing.

(2). *Be Humble.*
Humility is of great value in his eyes. If we feel we already know it all, and are just "going through the motions" of prayer, we will gain very little, since we are not open to receiving. Recognize that you are approaching the Maker of All. He has information that you do not have, and the power to do anything he pleases in your behalf. But do not approach out of fear or with trepidation, but with love and a desire to know love more fully.

"O Lord, what are mortals that you should notice us, mere humans that you should care for us?" (Ps. 144:3) New Living Translation

(3). *Show Gratitude and Thanks.*
Show thanksgiving for everything and do not use God as a heavenly "Santa Claus." He wants us to find time to say "Hi" and talk to him, *even* when we don't need things! Like all parents (remember we are made in his character likeness) we don't want our kids coming to see us just when they want something. When we see our dear Tommy only when he wants to borrow money or get the keys to the car, we don't really feel loved. Just used. Maybe we even feel resentful. We might even start occupying ourselves with other things when we see Tommy heading in our direction. It is not that we don't want Tommy to have the things that he desires, but it sure would go a long way if he would just come to talk and visit with us now and then, without having an agenda... so, always be thankful, and "visit" God often, even just to chat. Ending the prayer with acknowledgement of the name of Son and what it stands for, is the utmost realization of thanks.

I want to highlight something very important here - *you will find your own way to*

134

pray, and you will develop your own communication pattern with the Almighty. It's more important to emphasize here, not *How to Pray,* but just *To Pray!*

A Hands-On-Healing Treatment, Step-By-Step

If possible, find a quiet place. Make sure the phones are off, and Fluffy and Junior (your animal and child babies) are not in the room. In fact, it is a good idea to do a healing treatment on them first, they love it - and then they will generally leave you alone! If you have a massage table, a couch or a bed where the person can lie down, that is a good thing. If not, have the person sit in a chair, and be aware of the fact that they may "nod off" or perhaps "Fall in the Spirit," and then you will have to hold them with one hand and work with the other, so they don't fall over. If they go "bump," it will be very embarrassing, and maybe give you more work to do!

Create a Peaceful Atmosphere

It is nice to have a peaceful atmosphere, and if you have a clinic to work out of, so much the better. This would allow you to work with walk-ins off the street, and referrals of doctors, clients and friends, make appointments, and in this way help as many people as possible. But, doing Divine Healing out of your home or the person's home, or meeting at a mutual location or church, can also work. If it's in an environment that you're in control of, muted lighting and soft instrumental music sets a nice tone for relaxing. Please, no incense or perfumed candles, many people have allergic reactions to them, and they are not necessary.

You want people to be as relaxed as possible, because they often do not know what to expect, and are a bit nervous. Also, trying to give them more than just a simple explanation beforehand may be like trying to explain a color to a blind person. They just have to experience it themselves to fully understand!

Take off Glasses, Hearing Aids, Shoes

I ask the person to take off his shoes, glasses, hearing aids, and any pieces of metal. The metal part is up to you - I am also facilitated for the medical intuitiveness, so metal, silver, and certain stones are a distraction for me because they "vibrate" all on their own, and sometimes distract me from the pictures received in my head. Another thing that is up to you is choosing to wear personal jewelry or not. I cannot wear any rings or bracelets, as I was finding tan marks underneath them, showing the metal had gotten hot enough to burn me a bit, from the heat of my hands. Yet wearing a necklace doesn't seem to bother me, and I wear a cross all the time, or a hologram with Jesus imbedded in the glass. I always want to show where the healing is coming from. And personally, I can't wear earrings unless they are studs which would be kept in all the time. This is because I receive a healing when I give one; and evidently having a hole in the ear is not a natural thing - every time I would take out my earrings at night, the next morning the lobes were healed up again! This forced me to have to painfully push back through the skin to put my earrings back in. Soon, as you can imagine, I gave up! Now, what to do with a bunch of earrings? For eyeglasses and other items, try to have a small container available, right beside the door or where you are working, so they are not forgotten by your client on the way out. Please, no disrobing is necessary, or even suggested.

Get in a Comfortable Position

Have the client lie on the table, with a small pillow under his neck, face up. Put another pillow under the knees, to help reduce stress on his lower back. Even if the major complaint is in his back, always start face-up, in this position. This allows you to place a chair for yourself behind him, for your first hand positions to be on his head. But please remember that what I suggest about hand placement is just that - *a suggestion.* Remember, Holy Spirit is like aspirin - it goes to where it's needed! So, even if you're just touching a hand or toe (as in a hospital), healing will happen. And long-distance healing can occur across the bed, the room, the town, the nation, and the world! The hands-on positions are more or less to let you know what is going on, and to let the client know too, which adds to his comfort level.

Tell About the Spectrum of Healing

Before you begin, it is wise to tell about the spectrum of healing, which will let people know what to expect. You need to let people know that there is a *wide range* of what can happen in a healing. At the very least, people will feel calmer and have less stress, experience less pain if they had any, and sleep better at night. At the other end of the spectrum is where the miracles occur and cancer disappears, tumors shrink, eyes see, and the crippled walk! And we never know where in that broad spectrum, that a healing will occur! And, we never know if the healing will be *immediate,* or *gradual* and *over a period of time.*

It is also a good idea to ask the client to *be open to the possibility* of wonderful things happening. They don't have to believe that this works. When you are done, let them see *he who is invisible by the results manifested.* It is all Divine Healing, with Supernatural results. Remember there are three realms to healing - physical, emotional, and spiritual (and the fourth; deliverance) and we never know which single one or combination of healing are best for that person. Just let go and trust, knowing that God

136

knows what is going on, and that it is all for the Highest Good.

How Often Should I Come for a Healing?

This should be left up to the client. I suggest seeing the person at least once more - that way (even if an immediate healing occurred the first time out) you can check the chart you've made for them and see what changes have occurred. The worse the problem, the more you should "hit it on the head" until it is under control. For example, cancer I try to see twice a week, even if the healing time is only ½ hr long. In this way, by the time the Energy starts to leave, the new treatment pumps up the level again, and continues to stimulate recuperation. Remember, Divine Healing is like God's radiation therapy - the longer the malady is in the force-field of his love, the quicker the problem will disappear!

Begin With Out Loud Prayer

Now they are relaxed, mentally receptive, and ready to begin. Let them know you will be starting with an out loud prayer, because it is vital to recognize the Source of the healing, and then let them know that after your prayer, you will be continuing in an undertone of prayer throughout. Encourage them to also be in silent prayer throughout, making Connection, because that way the healing will be much *stronger*.

"For where two or three come together in my name, there am I with them." (Mt. 18:20)

Also, in this way they are also taking responsibility for their own healing. You are sitting in your chair now, facing the client who is face up on the table. Say your out loud prayer. Below is just an *example;* please do not memorize it or repetitively say it just as it is - as in any prayer, it has to be felt from your individual heart, and said in your own words:

"Dear Father, we come before you Lord, by Free Will, for your Spirit to touch ours, for healing. Oh Father, we thank you that you hear us when we are by ourselves, and are all alone in our homes and beds, and you hear us and help us. But we also thank you for giving us opportunity for your kids to come together, to learn to get along, to need each other, and love one another; and your Spirit is there too. Almighty One, we pray for Your Will to Be Done, and we place our trust in you. We know you want your children whole - physically, emotionally, and spiritually - and that you see us in that way. Father, let us see ourselves that way too. You know our DNA, our bones, our sinews, our trauma and everything else about us. We know that what ever happens is all to your Glory, and we are open to an immediate healing, or a gradual one, whatever is best and at the right time for it. Dear Lord, may my hands be *your hands,* my arms *your arms,*

137

my heart - *yours*. I give you my heart as I earnestly seek yours. Without your love, we would never know love. Thank you for loving us! We come before you by the grace of the ransom sacrifice of your Son, Christ Jesus…Amen."

Now, lay your hands gently on the head, fingers together and over the forehead (not down onto the eyes). Feel the Holy Spirit descend upon you like warm honey, starting from the top of your head, down through your feet (which are placed flat on the ground). Bask in the glory of it; a healing will happen here today! Continue in prayer, silently, along with the client.

Placement and Movement of Hands

Again, these are just suggestions, just to give you an idea of flow. And again, you do not need to even be touching the person for love to flow, and prayer to be answered. In those cases, just even pulling a couple of chairs together and praying together is good. Or, if the person is on the table, holding your hands an inch or so away from the body is ok too, if there is concern about touch.

In placement of the hands, moving from head to foot is best, and then (after about ½ hour) having the client roll over and move from head to foot again. All moves are respectful, and without touching any place that would be immodest or crossing any comfort zones. Try to stay in one place long enough to see if your hands are getting hot there - perhaps a minute, or several. If they don't get hot, move on. If there is one particular place God is really working on, stay there with the heat for as much as 10-20 minutes or longer. If you feel the need to check other places in the body, go to them and return to this place later if you can. Remember, The Big Guy doesn't need your hand on it for healing to occur. It is only for your benefit, and that of the client.

On the head, move from the forehead to the top of the head, to the ears (one hand on each), and then to the place under the chin, where the glands are. Perhaps you will want to cup one hand over each eye (one at a time) before you move from the head. Ask permission first before placing your hand over the eyes. The head is the most important place on the body to do healing, *so much* happens from here. It is like a city of its own, including its own electrical system - sparks bouncing from one place to another. It is also one of the places where I receive pictures dealing with emotional items that need to be addressed, cleansed and released. In men, the other places are the heart and the hands - in women, the heart and the solar plexus. And through time, you may be able to "see" the Spirit as it descends down through the body, from the head down the spinal column and dissipating into the tissue and organs all around. In some places you will be able to see it slow down when it comes to a place of damage, and then how that place

138

will start to "glow" with all the Energy building up within it, healing it!

Are There Drugs in the System?

I usually keep in mind what kind of heat I have felt under the neck, and then go to check the liver. The liver is the blood purifier of the body. Everything goes through here, and is a good thermometer of what is going on. Especially are drugs noticed here, and if the liver is working overtime, you will definitely feel it. Then, you may ask, "Are you on any drugs or medications at this time?" And they will answer yes or no. There are some herbal components that also effect heat in the liver, including herbal cleansers. This is not all bad - similar to our running a low-grade fever when we are fighting a cold, we want the body to fight the germs and allow a mark of 101 degrees, but get worried and step in when it reaches 104 or 105. So it is with the liver. It is OK to run a bit hot, to allow it to do its job. We just want to monitor it, and give it some healing prayer to help it on its way.

It took me over a year before I could *speak* to a client and keep in *prayer* at the same time. Even now, I often end up cutting my sentences off mid-way or do a kind of amnesia (what was I saying?)! Keeping in an undertone is keeping one ear to the heavens, and one to what is happening with the client. Listen to *heaven,* listen to *earth.* Remind the client occasionally, especially after you have talked or asked them to roll over, to remain in prayer (unless they fall asleep).

All the Bone Joints

Return to your chair, and now place your hands one on each shoulder. This is a very peaceful position. Now, cup your hands around one shoulder joint, then the elbow, and down to the wrist. Also place their hand cupped between yours, and then slide to the fingers. Do the other side as you did this one. You will find many things in the wrist and hands. Often, the wrists will be at least warm, or hot from overuse (as with someone who has a manual job). Usually you will also be able to know if the person is right or left handed, because there will be more use on that one. Sometimes, the heat will go up to the elbow from the wrist, which can be an indication of "carpal tunnel." Often, places of injury will lead to a weakness that will later be susceptible to arthritis and other conditions. It always amazes me how cells hold on to trauma and for how long. Healing helps stimulate "cell memory" to go back to how they were originally created. Time to fix them up!

Remember, your job is to be a healing to that area, and see it as being healed. You may want to ask (since you are not a medical doctor you cannot diagnose, even if you know what is going on), "there is a lot of work being done here, is this from an injury, or from

139

use?" As you go from area to area, perhaps even finding injuries from 20 or 30 years previously. The client's ability to receive healing will *increase* as their analytical barriers *decrease,* and the Peace of God that excels all thought will fall upon every one in the room, and indeed, even in the whole building (I've even see it happen on entire floors of hospitals)!

"Rejoice in the Lord always. I will say it again; Rejoice! Let your gentleness be evident to all. The Lord is near. Do not be anxious about anything, but in everything, by prayer and petition, with thanksgiving, present your requests to God. And the peace of God, which transcends all understanding, will guard your hearts and your minds in Christ Jesus." (Php.4:4-7)

The Lungs

Standing beside the client, place your hands across the upper chest, to feel where the airways divide between the lungs. Between here and the sinuses on the head, you may get an impression about allergies or asthma. Move slightly lower, and lower again. Is there a difference between the top part of the lungs and the lower? Often, in smokers, the bottom part of the lungs is much hotter than the top; I think it is because they usually breathe shallowly, so the air at the bottom doesn't move much. If you were able to see the lungs of a smoker, the bottom would be dark gray, or even black, and the walls of the lungs do not move much, they are hardened. Often the top is softer, or even with a bit of pink. Healthy lungs are fully pink.

Just a note here - do not put your hands on the breasts. Even if Spirit prompts you to do so, you still ask! Better yet, place your hands in the *air* over the breasts, or not at all - you must be respectful! When you roll the person over and work on the shoulder blade area, there you will be able to sense what is going on in the breasts. Or, if you cannot "sense" it, then possibly have heat there. Directly opposite the breasts, through the back, is just like working on the breasts. Stay until the heat leaves. If there is a "red flag," ask when they did their last mammogram. Do not raise fear. Always be loving and gentle.

If one lung feels hotter than the other, "ask" in prayer to see what is going on (this develops your ability to "hear," and also develops "God sonar"). If you feel a cold spot, it could be a mass or tumor. To me, these areas feel cold under my hands, and the edges blur out into normal warmth. It is the same way with scar tissue. Broken bones have definite lines of cold, without the blurring effect. If you find a cold area, stay over it until the edges start to get warm, and extend inward, until the warmth becomes hot and the cold becomes warm. Allow time for as much healing as will take place. Sometimes over critical areas, a vibration will begin.

Vibration and Heat

Heat is a by-product of work being done. Notice how hot you are after a run, or aerobic work out. It is an expenditure of natural energy. When you are facilitated for a healing, your whole body will heat up, as will that of the client. Sometimes, if your hands are too hot and making the clients uncomfortable, simply raising them or placing a dry cloth between them and you will fix the problem. Most people like the heat; it makes them feel like they're in a spa or Jacuzzi. And indeed, after a healing, that is exactly how I feel! I feel so relaxed and peaceful, it is like being too long in a Jacuzzi, and I feel like softened butter, peaceful, joyful and melting into love.

Vibration is a step above heat. These are visible, physical, involuntary movements of the hands and fingers. I really know "the juice is turned on" when vibration starts to occur. I know that the Lord is really working on that area, and letting me know it. Most of the time, the vibration will occur over the place that needs healing the most; although vibrations can also happen on the head as an access point to another area in the body. If you get vibrations on the head, it is a good idea to reassure the client and let them know about access points; otherwise they may think they have a brain tumor or that something is wrong. The vibrations may scare them. Vibration comes in cycles, or waves. Wait on the area until a *saturation* of Energy occurs. You will see this happening because the vibrations will decrease in intensity and duration. Stay there until there is only heat left. Then stay there until that too, is gone.

How Long Does It Take for a Healing Treatment?

I don't know! No matter how many people I may have, the Holy Spirit just refuses to go by the clock! I normally schedule new people for one hour each. If I have seen them before, I have circled the places of injury on their chart (the chart is a simple outline drawing of the body, front and back, including contact information). Then I don't need to do a full body analysis, and will just work on the places needed; then perhaps a half hour is fine. Having a chart also allows me to see the changes that have occurred since the last time I saw them, have a conversation with them about it, and note the improvements. Sometimes the Spirit will move in 10 minutes, and be done! Then I am left with the quandary of ending the treatment early or spending the allotment of time conversing. Sometimes, however, the Spirit will take much longer, up to two hours! Who am I to tell God what to do? Never may that be so! The interesting thing is, even though it may take me way off schedule for the other people waiting, to this day I have had no complaints or anyone leave in a huff! "Patience is a virtue," we are told. This

141

relates to healings too! Each person knows I will take the full amount of time needed for them too.

The Heart

The heart can have layers of problems that are both physical and emotional. For the beginning person facilitated for healing, it will all feel the same. The healing will occur without your knowing the specifics. If you feel heat, say, "I feel some work being done here. When was the last time you had your heart checked?" I have to do the same, even if I can see that there is a 20% blockage here, a new vessel trying to re-route around an area there. If you're really seeing "red flags" about it, suggest that they go and have it checked; this goes for anything in the body. Have them go get it diagnosed by a medical doctor. It is possible The Big Guy will have already taken care of it, but it is also possible that he gave you those "red flags" for the person to have medical intervention, or for proof that the problem existed before he disposes of it.

In cases where the person continues to ignore your suggestion for medical diagnosis, you have the choice to tell them that you cannot, in all good conscience, continue to work with them until they do so. This shows them how serious you are about it. Only do this if the Lord gives you those red flags. It's all about bringing Glory to him. Sometimes he will allow people to be a miracle in a hospital so that the doctors and nurses will be a witness to his wonderful works. Trust in the Bigger Picture, and that he knows the best timing for everything, and everyone.

Placing your hand on a person's heart is also an emotional center, and may trigger an emotional release. Always have a box of tissues handy! The fellows usually get so embarrassed - "I never cry!" and "I've never cried in front of a woman before!" Let them know that it's OK, that they're safe, and that everything that happens in this room stays in this room. Then let them weep. So much healing is occurring; the Holy Spirit touching deep places that only he can access. Just being there is a comfort to the one releasing; you needn't say a word, just watch the cleansing and healing occur as love embraces.

The Stomach and Intestines

Many people have stomach problems, usually from improper diet or too much stress. This causes an acidity that plays havoc in the system. Often, when I feel the acid / alkaline off balance, I find the valve on the top of the stomach is inflamed, or has been, and has the scar tissue stretch marks to prove it. When this valve gets inflamed, it can't close, and an acid-reflux condition appears, where the stomach juices easily go up the esophagus.

142

In the stomach itself, sometimes I pick up small areas where the stomach lining is thinner in some places than another. These are where ulcers have tried, or are trying, to make problems. The stomach releases into the intestines, and the acid / alkaline imbalance of the stomach reaches here too, as improperly digested food gets sent into the intestinal tract for absorption and nutrient distribution. Sometimes little pockets of pushed out intestine can be felt, which cause problems with elimination; either too much or too little.

When the system is out of balance, the body doesn't get the proper nutrition it needs, even if you may be eating it. Much of it might just pass through. On the way, it may sit in your intestines for a while and putrefy, thus causing gas, painfulness and bloating. Of course, there are other reasons for bloating, and constipation and diarrhea, including colitis. Stress itself will often cause these same problems, and the solar plexus area is one of the places that women put their emotions. Just be a healing. Be in prayer. Share the love. It's an excellent idea to purchase a *detailed anatomical book* or a series of charts so you know where specific organs are. When your hands get hot over these areas, you'll then know what organ, muscle, or bone is involved.

What about Nutrition, Herbs and Medications?

A lot of people ask me for nutrition and herbal advice, and even what conventional medications they should take (sometimes they even bring these with them, for me to "choose"). I am not a nutritionalist, a medical doctor or herbalist. Even if I were, I would choose not to use these things in the same session with Divine Healing. I do not want to be a referral service to something else. That is putting God in a less powerful position than he is! I do what God gives me to do, and see and say what God wants me to say, and that's what I do. That's all I do. That's enough! I don't want people to be confused with what healing is being done by God, and what supplement I give them on the side.

I believe Divine Healing and conventional medicine can and does work very well together - but I will do what I do, and let the experts do what they do in their own field. I am hopeful that my clients will give a bit of time to see the results of the Lord touching them, without trying six or seven new things along with it. They won't know which one worked! Isn't it common sense to try new things one at a time, and then look at the results individually?

The Other Organs and Joints

Continue to move through the rest of the organs, the diaphragm, pancreas, the gall bladder, everything. We will work on the kidneys and adrenals on the backside. For the genitals, this is another private place, and you do not want to place your hands very low on the body so as to cause the client to be uncomfortable. Once again, let me remind you that healing goes to where it is needed. Please also note that I consider this a part of the solar plexus area of the woman (though technically, it is not). A lot of emotions hide buried here. And, in my treatment of thousands of clients now, I can tell you that a good 80% of female problems come from prior abuse situations. Be gentle, and continually use prayer to let emotions release. Remember an unveiling of the memories is going to occur for every one of your clients after they leave your table. There are things that they may need to willfully release on their own, through forgiveness and Connection, in relation to their healing.

Be sure to do the hip sockets, the knees, ankles and feet. These places take a lot of pounding, and even high-school football injuries show up here, years later. Be happy that you are part of helping these old traumas release and heal, under the Gracious hand, so that they will no longer be a weak spot in the body for arthritis and other problems to cling to. If there is already arthritis, keep your hand there and allow healing to occur, as you visualize a great snowball melting on a summer day, and the muddy ground below become strong, smooth and hard. Watch calcium deposits melt, and arthritic joints become pain free and limber. Never put restrictions on what God can do!

Have the Person Roll Over

Remind the person to be in prayer, as you also continue in praise in an undertone, seeing the person well. Sit in your chair again, and place your hands on the back of the head, just above the neck. This is a place of hypersensitivity in many people, and this is a by-product of the many gifts that he gives people, whether they recognize the gifts or not. For example, when I go into a restaurant, I always request to sit in a location where the back of my head faces a wall. Or I might sit in a quiet corner. In this way, I can easily be a barometer of the injuries and illnesses in the room, if I choose to be. I believe I have this sensitivity as a reminder to offer an immediate prayer to help others in need. Other "sensitives" and healers have told me of similar experiences, and that part of their head acts as a reminder for them with their particular gifts.

Having a massage table with a headpiece makes it very convenient for the person to breathe when lying face-down. You don't want to lose anyone through suffocation! Place a clean paper here and poke a hole through it, or a fresh towel with the middle pushed down through. If you have an adjustable headpiece, adjust it slightly down to allow more neck availability. Now move the pillow or bolster under the ankles, elevating them a bit.

The Neck

From the back of the head, go to the side of the person, and gently place your hands over the neck. You are likely to feel heat here. Once again, you can ask the client if this is from an injury or from use, as you are also asking God for his answer on this. Even in a young person, the injury may be from use. Those who have to spend a good part of their day in front of a computer, for example, can have bone degeneration. People who are constantly in high-stress mode typically have this problem. They tense up - almost put into spasm - the neck muscles. As the neck muscles tighten up, they clamp down on the vertebrate and compress the disks. In this condition, we generally continue throughout our day, with bone on bone - over time, degeneration occurs. At this point, there comes a day when we are *not* under any stress yet the neck still hurts, because now our bone structure has changed, and the disks don't fit exactly how they should, as cushions between the bones, so nerves are being pinched. This also creates pain radiating out to the shoulders and upper back.

This is a problem that the client should be made aware of, and his role in it, since he can develop a routine of periodically stretching the neck that will reduce the tightening, and therefore the degeneration. Many people know they unconsciously keep stress in the neck area, but need to be reminded. It will help nip in the bud more complications in the future. Whiplash can be felt here, in the front part of the neck. This is usually from a car accident, although it can happen in other ways too.

The Shoulder Blades, Ribs, Spine, Lower Back

Stand up and place your hands across the upper back, encompassing the shoulder blades. Check for hot places and any tears in the rotator cuffs. Ask yourself if the breasts are in good shape. Stay wherever you feel heat. You may also feel very clearly the lungs here. Now, move your hands progressively down the rib cage, to the small of the back. Then, come back up and focus on the spine, and follow it down. What do you feel? What do you "see?" Is the Lord leading you to any conclusions? Are you feeling any hot spots? Are there any previous cracked ribs (cold lines)? Are there any ruptured disks or curvature of the spine? Is the lower back in need of help? What are you finding there? Remember, being in prayer gives you an ear to God and an ear to the body. Listen to what he says. It takes practice, and the more you hear, the more you will be able to hear, and the more he will be allowed to go into detail with you, including any emotional or spiritual healing he may need you for.

Continue down to the tailbone, and be sure to spend adequate time here and in the lower back. Move as Spirit moves you. See them well! Sometimes, around the tailbone, pinching of the nerves can occur, including the sciatica down the legs. Continue down to the back of the knees, to the ankles again and the feet. If you have time, go back to anything you wanted to spend more time on; if not, leave it for another time, and know the healing process will continue for several more days in the body anyway!

Close the Healing Treatment

I usually close when I am still touching the ankles or feet. It seems to me that people are less dizzy after a healing when I do this. I say out-loud: "OK! Let's both close with a silent prayer of Thanks." And then I do my closing prayer, as the client also does his.

I usually do a simple physical representation of closing the prayer too, a reminder for me that this Divine Healing time is now closed. It is like a subconscious touchstone, a closing of a door. For me, my reminder is putting my hands in prayer position, and then making a sweeping gesture downward, right after my prayer. It's that easy. I then tap the client on the shoulder to let him know I am done.

The Process of Healing Will Continue

Another thing you need to say to the client is this: "The healing does not stop when you get off the table. The process of healing will continue on for an average of another 2 - 3 days." Let them know it is similar to a fan being unplugged from the wall, with the fan blades continuing to spin until they finally slow down and stop. Such it is with the Holy Spirit. They could even feel better tomorrow than today, or even the next day after that, as the healing continues! It is also good to bring up one other point for those three days - the abstinence of alcohol, drugs or heavily oiled or deep-fried foods. Why? I do not know, but it seems to slow the healing down in the system, and we want the Spirit's afterglow to continue as long as possible!

Also, follow good hygiene practices; especially if you are seeing more than one person. Wash your hands between clients. One other thing I want to bring up here. Sometimes, with all the cells being stimulated and all the cleansing and reorganizing going on (remember we are like a dirty glass of water), sometimes the person gets a stomach ache afterward. People tell me that having some steamed vegetables usually does the trick, with yellow squash and zucchini being the favorite picks. Be sure to remind your client to drink *lots* of water. And have water in the healing room so they can drink right away. If the dizziness doesn't go away in a few minutes (the body is not used to having so much Current going through) have them sit or walk around a bit before they drive. They will likely sleep especially well this night, and wake up at peace and deeply rested!

146

An Exchange for Services

People value things more if they have to give something for it. Also, it helps them create good will for themselves, in that they will now be able to better receive in the future. And again, this also aids the clients in becoming willful participants in their own healing.

An exchange for services is important in all relationships. You don't pay for the healing, but for the person's time. Healing belongs to God. The exchange can be anything of value, and should be agreed upon before starting, if possible. It doesn't have to be money; but to be in the full-time healing work, money is a necessity to pay the bills so that you can continue. In very poor places, it may be lunch or just some postage stamps that are given. If you are on your own, and not in a clinic, it is wonderful to just leave it up the client to give a love offering - whatever the Spirit moves them to give; and at times you may find yourself pleasantly surprised to receive a donation of several hundred dollars. I worked for years like this, and never had to worry that my bills wouldn't be paid, because God made sure that what ever I needed, I was provided with. To be full-time in the prayer ministry, the financial donations were necessary to let me be able to continue, to be able to help more and more people and focus on that alone.

Please do not feel you *must* ask for an exchange; be prayerful about it and see what God says to you. Perhaps you are to work for a living, and do Divine Healing on the side. Perhaps you are praying for a friend or relative and you know the exchange has already been made in love and support through the years. This is a delicate point for many who are facilitated for healing - the choice should only come from you, and your communication with your Employer. He will let you know what to do.

Working in Clinics and Offices

Unless you are doing just casual prayer, working out of a clinic is really a good idea. For one, this way people don't know where you live, so you won't have people in need showing up at all hours of the day and night. And sometimes, there are the fanatics who feel that only you have a special connection with God, and think that you are better than sliced bread, and want to spend as much time with you as possible! You need to have a place to rest, and be away from crowds, just like Jesus did through withdrawing by himself up into the mountains.

Working out of a different location, whether it be a medical clinic, a chiropractor's office, or the back room of a health food store or vitamin shop, gives you a central location with parking places, handicap access, and referrals from the owners and

147

workers in the shop. As time goes by, and the people Divine Coincidence has sent to you will be telling others about the work, more and more people will come to see you. It gives you opportunity to schedule, and have days off, and help a lot of people. At home you would be racing around cleaning your house, scuttling off the kids and pets, and trying to arrange prayer around meal times, your husband going to work, etc.

Often in a shop or clinic, a secretary is available, and can schedule appointments for you when people call in. Since I work out of three locations, and do healing in several churches, and also speaking engagements, etc., I use only *my* phone number as the contact. Most of the time, I have my 800 number directed to my cell phone too. I keep a daily schedule book with me at all times, so nothing conflicts, and then call the respective clinic and let the secretary know what times I am booked and on what day. I also ask them to call me whenever they have written someone in that has contacted the clinic directly. This keeps everyone "in the know;" because you will have new people coming into the clinics, and previous ones, who book with the secretaries, without calling you first.

Have a Donation - Only Location Available Too

These locations have overhead to fulfill, and I work out a percentage plan with each one. At the clinics, I charge a flat rate per hour, and per half hour, which is usually comparable to whatever local massage therapists are charging. At the end of each week, I give the clinic a check. Sometimes there will be people who simply cannot pay for a healing. I never withhold a healing from them just because of money. But, it puts too much pressure on the clinics for me to do this there. So, I offer another location where people can go, which is strictly on a donation-only basis, so that everyone can receive from the Lord.

I have a friend who is a Catholic priest, and he graciously allows me to use his family counseling office once a week for healings. He also invites me to do healings after Mass whenever my schedule permits. At this clinic I give a percentage also; to help pay the overhead and keep the lights on, but it is only in reference to what I freely receive from the day.

Twenty dollars to one person can be like $200 to another; having a place for the impoverished lets you help all the people who need it, without restriction. And, it puts the effort in their own lap to get themselves there, which I find is *very* important.

Follow the Law

You may need to get a business license, and other certifications to be able to engage in

Divine Healing outside of your home (and perhaps even in it). Also, there are organizations that you can belong to that will be a covering over you and encourage what you do, including a variety of legal necessities. A good search on the Internet will give you some. Of course, a church covering for what you are called to do is necessary, for fellowship and working within the Body of Christ. There are churches that embrace healing and modern Gifts of the Spirit, and those who don't. You know which one to choose!

Also, it's good advice (and in some places, it's the law) to have a legal disclaimer made, and have it signed by each client, then file it away. Mine is on the same page as the body outline that I use for tracking changes. This may protect you in case of any fraudulent claims made against you. Unfortunately, the evil one will use every method possible to try to dissuade you from pursuing where the Lord leads. Each state has a bit different approach to what they deem necessary in a disclaimer, but one thing they all have is the notice that the session is "not a substitute for medical or psychological diagnosis, and/or treatment." They also all state that the one facilitated for healing "does not diagnose conditions, nor do they prescribe, perform medical treatment, nor prescribe substances nor interfere with the treatment of a licensed medical professional." Find the regulations in *your* state for the particulars that you need.

Other Alternative Medicines

There are other modalities that you can become licensed or certified in, and still do Divine Healing. Reiki and Therapeutic Touch® are some of them, becoming a nurse of some kind is another. There are more. Remember that there are those in these fields who may not use prayer, but you will be using their modality *combined* with prayer. So, you should find a compatible modality that will not go against any of the principles of the God you call upon for Supernatural healing. As you saw from the lightning strike adventure, the Almighty wanted me to have my foot in another door (Reiki), so that more things would be open to me, and make healing more accessible to more people. As in all things, let the Lord lead you, and your spiritual essence and Who you represent will shine brightly, no matter what label you are under!

"One of the most calming and powerful actions you can do to intervene in a stormy world is to stand up and show your soul. Soul on deck shines like gold in dark times. The light of the soul throws sparks, can send up flares, builds signal fires, and causes proper matters to catch fire. To display the lantern of the soul in shadowy times like these - to be fierce and to show mercy toward others, both, are acts of immense bravery and greatest necessity. Struggling souls catch light from other souls who are fully lit and willing to show it…In my uttermost bones I know something, as do you. It is that

149

there can be no despair when you remember why you came to Earth, who you serve, and who sent you here. The good words we say and the good deeds we do are not ours: they are the words and deeds of the One who brought us here. In that spirit, I hope you will write this on your wall: When a great ship is in harbor and moored, it is safe, there can be no doubt. But that is not what great ships are built for." -*Women Who Run With the Wolves* by Clarissa Pinkola Estes, PhD.

Ceremonies Used in Activating Healing Power

There are many scriptures that lead us to believe that there was a ceremony, or an imparting, when it came to people being brought into the work of healing. Ceremony has always played an important part of daily life, in the past and the present. Ritual imparts sacredness to our lives. Birthdays, anniversaries and weddings are some of the wonderful celebrations that give us order; show where we are at the moment, and helps us to focus on where we are going and what our responsibilities are. It lets all onlookers know our intentions too, and can bring others into your support system for helping you accomplish your task. In the case for the healing commission, the onlookers also include the entire realm of angels, both True Sons and the fallen ones.

Today, you may also find various ceremonies used with the healing commission. In Reiki, there are breathing "attunements," and prayers, and even symbols that act like a touch-stone for the healer to focus on to remember different aspects of healing (physical, emotional, and spiritual), similar to tying a ribbon around the finger for remembrance.

But, the most important thing about any ceremony is that you are coming before the God of Heaven himself. For the healing commission, this is a two-way process - *you* need to step up to the plate, and *God* needs to accept you. Remember how he is about Free Will, even if he has placed a calling upon your life; you still need to show your desire to be part of the team. The major focus is about you *presenting yourself freely for the work* – surrendering yourself as a vessel for Holy Spirit to use to the Glory of God and the good of others.

There is sacrifice, to be sure. Your time will not be your own, and your priorities will have to shift. You will be tested as to many things. He will give you many opportunities to live up to your promise, and if you consistently pull back from healing situations he has arranged, he'll see you're not really wanting to be used in this work, and his Spirit may be pulled back. Also, if the powerful healings create problems with your ego, he will pull his Spirit back. Again, *you will be tested as to many things.* He doesn't expect any of us to be perfect. And although he'll give us a training program that allows us to proceed at a good clip, we are not on a dead-line. And, if things *are* moving too fast, just ask, and he will slow them down. There is much to be done.

Along with the added responsibilities come added blessings, and even more blessings will be added with a progressively harder work load. You will be enjoying great closeness with the Almighty, the Christ, and all the angels; several of whom will now be assigned as your invisible partners as you work on the "front lines" of the invisible war. Think of yourself as a nurse in a M.A.S.H. unit, an assistant helping to mend the broken and traumatized. There may be "bombs" bursting all around (remember we do have an enemy who wants to stop us), but we just go in and do our job, and Somehow we stay protected, and everything ends up OK!

We are to Ask for the Greater Gifts

"Which of you fathers, if your son asks for a fish, will give him a snake instead? Or if he asks for an egg, will give him a scorpion? If you then, though you are evil, know how to give good gifts to your children, how much more will your Father in heaven give the Holy Spirit to those who ask him!" (Lk 11:11) "But eagerly desire the greater gifts." (1 Cor. 12:31)

In the early church, those asking for special commissions were brought to the spiritual leaders of the group, and prayer was said, and a laying-on-of-hands. (Acts. 6:6) This was done in the view of others, and was a way to acknowledge that these people were being set apart for special service. Often, Supernatural events occurred during or after the ceremony, showing that the requested gift *was* imparted from God.

Before the Christian era, we see God commanding a hands-on ceremony to the Israelites: "So the LORD said to Moses, "Take Joshua son of Nun, a man in whom is the spirit, and lay your hand on him. Have him stand before Eleazar the priest and the entire assembly and commission him in their presence." (Nu. 27:18,19)

"Now Joshua the son of Nun was filled with the spirit of wisdom because Moses had laid his hands on him. So the Israelites listened to him and did what the LORD had commanded Moses." (De. 34:9)

Jesus uses a Breath Ceremony

After Jesus was resurrected and the disciples locked themselves in a room because of fear, Christ appeared to them and commissioned them for the great work ahead. "Again Jesus said, "Peace be with you! As the father has sent me, I am sending you." And with that *he breathed on them* and said, "Receive the Holy Spirit…" (Jn.20:19-22)

151

The apostle Paul told Timothy: "*Fan into flame the gift of God, which is in you through the laying on of my hands.* For God did not give us a spirit of timidity, but a spirit of power, of love and of self-discipline." (2 Tim. 1:6)

Timothy was not afraid to ask Paul to receive the "gift of God" by his laying-on-of-hands. Do not be afraid to ask others to help you come before the Lord in sacred trust and ceremony. God asks us to take action to show we are serious with our prayers.

Be Bold!

Healing is one of the great commissions, and as believers we are asking God to develop what is already inside us - the authority and power of the Holy Spirit. Some of us may also have specialties that help one disease or problem better than another. Take the opportunities presented to you, even if you are initially shy. Please keep in mind, that if you consistently ignore or refuse his requests, he will call you less and less. He does not want to force you, but he *does* want to encourage you. Think of the spiritual growth and being able to see him do wonderful things through your hands, in front of your own eyes! I pray you will allow this Connection to strengthen!

Think about different ways to present healing to strangers in need; here are a few suggestions: "Hello, may I help you feel better? Prayer always helps me feel better. May I say one with you?" Then place your hand on their shoulder, or their arm. Or perhaps, "I am being trained in the healing arts. May I respectfully place my hands right here (arm, shoulders, or place of injury if it is discreet) and say a prayer with you? It might make you feel better."

Be Persistent!

Don't give up if healing doesn't occur the first time you pray. Perhaps the person needs to move through all three levels of supplication before they will be healed:

(1). Ask. (2). Seek. (3). Knock.

"Ask and it will be given to you; seek and you shall find; knock and the door will be opened to you. For everyone who asks, receives, he who seeks finds; and to him who knocks, the door will be opened." (Mt 7:7,8)

As we have seen, there are the invisible aspects of healing that occur with emotional and spiritual wellness. And, sometimes it is better for the person to deal with the problem for a while and feel the love and support system of friends, family, etc. around him. Also, sometimes a person must be in a complete state of brokenness, when there is nothing else medically that can be done, for the person to surrender to God and allow

152

himself to be healed. These occasions are also a great witness to the medical team and family, as they see miracles unfold.

These are just a few things that might be a reason for the healing to not occur at the present time. There are other barriers to, which we have discussed in the Deliverance chapter. Who knows if God is waiting for us to develop patience and a waiting attitude, and making sure the person is approaching not just for the gifts, but for the Giver? There are so many reasons to be persistent in prayer! Just pray, talk to Dad. Not because of the multitude of words, but to show your open heart condition and desire to yield. (Lk.18:1-8)

Be Available!

There is a saying that I often refer to when I start to consider myself overstretched: "It's not about Ability, or Inability, but *Availability*." How true! We just need to make ourselves available, and we will be facilitated for wondrous things! I am basically a quiet person, and enjoy my time alone; but I make sure to go into places where there are a lot of people, just to make myself available. Invariably, I always come home feeling blessed and happy that I made the effort, because of the good experiences that have happened.

At times, being always available as a vessel for healing can bring a lot of comedy to a schedule, but my children, family and friends have grown accustomed to it, so we have worked out various plans when we are together. For example, if we go to Disneyland or Sea World or any of the amusement parks, we will decide on an "Event" spot. Then, when a seizure, stroke, accident, etc, happens in front of me and I can offer assistance, my family can continue on with their day and know that I will meet them back at our designated place after the "Event." This way, I don't feel rushed, or pressured, I can do what I need to do, and they can have their fun. It works out well!

Sometimes you may feel overwhelmed about all the work to be done. Sister Briege McKenna, a Catholic nun and healer, in her book *Miracles Do Happen,* writes: "I jumped up and said, "Oh, God, how am I going to deal with all these problems, so many people and so many problems?" God replied, "They are not coming to you to solve their problems. They are coming to you because I live in you. If you get up and say, "I have to do it," then you'll forget that I'm the healer and I'm the One who brings peace and heals the sick. All I need you to do is be the instrument. So you just sit down now and *let me go to the door."*

We are just instruments in his symphony orchestra, hoping to stay in tune and interpret the musical arrangements placed in front of us to the best of our ability. He knows that

153

we are imperfect and will make many mistakes; and God forgives us much easier than we forgive ourselves. If we use our gifts for the intended betterment of His Kids (humankind) and His Creation (the earth), then he will keep training us with patience and new opportunities. We can have faith that even in our imperfection our efforts become a beautiful melody of symphonic love, floating gently upward to God, through the power of the Holy Spirit and the grace of our Redeemer Christ Jesus.

Use of Prayer in the Bible

James 5:13 says, "Is any one of you in trouble? He should pray. Is anyone happy? Let him sing songs of praise. Is any one of you sick? He should call the elders of the church to pray over him and anoint him with oil in the name of the Lord. And the prayer offered in faith will make the sick person well; the Lord will raise him up. If he has sinned, he will be forgiven. Therefore confess your sins to each other and pray for each other so that you may be healed. The prayer of a righteous man is powerful and effective."

Jesus is the number one example we have of Living Connection. His entire life was lived in an undertone of prayer, both silent and audible. Whenever we see Jesus under stress - or not - he goes to a quiet place and prays. This also happened on the night that he was given to the soldiers to be taken to Gethsemane: "he fell with his face to the ground and prayed." (Mt. 26:39) He prayed all the time, including speaking to his Father from the cross, "...forgive them, for they know not what they do." (Lk.23:34) And he told the disciples that night to continue to "Pray that you will not fall into temptation." (Lk.22:40) His disciples were chosen through prayer, and all of his disciples were taught to pray, and to teach others to pray also. Jesus taught "The Lord's Prayer" as a good example of how to address priorities in the flow of prayer - the sanctification of God's name and qualities being first. (Mt.6:9-13)

All throughout time, prayer was the link to call upon God. Moses, Abraham, Isaiah, John the Baptizer, and all the folks of old used prayer for communication, besides those in the New Testament. It was their lifeline, and the only way they could fulfill their missions given to them by God. They needed to keep those lines open.

"And when you *pray*, do not be like the hypocrites, for they love to *pray* standing in the synagogues and on the street corners to be seen by men. I tell you the truth, they have received their reward in full. But when you *pray*, go into your room, close the door and *pray* to your Father, who is unseen. Then your Father, who sees what is done in secret, will reward you. And when you *pray*, do not keep on babbling like pagans, for they think they will be heard because of their many words. Do not be like them, for your

Father knows what you need before you ask him." (Mt. 6:5-8)

We are admonished to pray *in behalf of others,* and to ask for their prayers *for us,* too, including prayers for the governmental authorities, (Ezr. 6:10) the peace of towns and cities, (Ps. 122:6) and for those who persecute us. (Mt. 5:44) "Brothers, *pray* for us." (1 Th. 5:25) "I urge you, brothers, by our Lord Jesus Christ and by the love of the Spirit, to join me in my struggle by praying to God for me." (Ro. 15:30) We are also encouraged to pray for *ourselves* (another example from Jesus). Please take the time to read John 17:6-25 where Jesus is in prayer to his Father, and eloquently prays for himself and his followers, with glowing terms of endearment, love and complete trust. This passage here is what many people consider the *real* "Lord's Prayer."

Do Not Doubt

We are told not to doubt, for that shows lack of faith in God's desire or ability to answer us. "But when he asks, he must believe and not doubt, because he who doubts is like a wave of the sea, blown and tossed by the wind. That man should not think he will receive anything from the Lord; he is a double-minded man, unstable in all he does." (James 1:6,7)

Faith is the "assured expectation of things not yet beheld." (Heb. 11:1)

The word "Amen" means "And it shall be," or "So be it." When we end our prayers this way, we are saying that we *know* that we have been heard, and expect a result. It is our natural impulse to speak with authority, for God's word has power. We can have enough faith and knowledge about our Dad that the *Highest Good* for all concerned will be accomplished, at the *perfect time* for it. We need not wonder about it or doubt. Prayer is a gift of God, and by communicating with him everyday he will teach us how to speak, *and how to listen.* But, we must put forth the effort necessary to set aside time everyday for this discipline. We must cooperate with the gift. And he will change us, and open us up, through prayer. "Have faith in God," Jesus answered. "I tell you the truth, if anyone says to this mountain, 'Go, throw yourself into the sea,' and does not doubt in his heart but believes that what he says will happen, it will be done for him. Therefore I tell you, whatever you ask for in prayer, believe that you have received it, and it will be yours." (Mk. 11:22-24)

Often you hear people put a "safety clause" in their prayer. They say "*if* it's your will," which could actually lay blame on God if the prayer is not answered within the time and way the one praying thinks it should. This type of praying is not honest nor effective, and may make people wonder if the God of Love may actually have a desire to *not* have

155

the will to help us. A better way to speak is: "*as* God Wills" or "God's Will be done." (Jas. 4:13-17) We talk, and he listens. He talks, and we listen. Communication!

Be open to no limitations. Even if the outcome is, *different* than what you were expecting! "Let go and let God." See them whole. Here is a healing story that emphasizes that point:

Crippled Hand Revived

When I lived in Tennessee, a man in his 50's came into the restaurant where I worked. As I poured his coffee he pulled out a miniature Bible and started reading it while waiting for his meal. He looked up and smiled, "I can see by the light in your eyes that you have Jesus in your heart."

"Thank you!" I replied, "And I appreciate seeing a person reading the Bible in a public place."

"What church do you and your husband attend?" the man asked.

"I visit many churches," I said, "and I *am* dedicated, not to a man, but to my work with the Lord. I am staying single to do it properly."

"What work is that?" he asked.

"God lets me be there when he heals people." I replied.

"Oh, please! Please!" said the man, "I need a healing. I have a terrible migraine and have been in pain for days!"

"I can't." I said, "I am working right now. But after work I could say prayers with you."

"No, no!" the man said, with a look of despair on his face.

Well, right then I knew I was about to jeopardize my job again for the sake of the Lord, as I was compelled to take one hand, then the other, and say a prayer to God for this man in pain. I touched his shoulders, his head and his chest. He started blubbering and crying out loud. I felt my job would be over - all the other tables were looking strangely at us.

"Why are you crying?" I asked. "Did it hurt?"

"My hand!" he said, as he looked at his left hand curling and uncurling; "My hand! I haven't been able to do that for 24 years! I have arthritis, and look at it stretch out! My

156

headache is gone too, praise the Lord! I don't know what your name is, but I am going to call you Angel, thank you for the healing!"

I leaned over and whispered in his ear, "You do not need to thank me. You know who did the healing, *it was the Lord.* Let this be our secret."

Well, the Holy Spirit knew I had limited time with this man, and facilitated an instantaneous healing within a span of a couple of minutes. And, another miracle - my manager and the other servers didn't seem to have noticed! But it was a good witness to many observing tables. I saw this man several more times, though he never needed another healing. Often he would bring others with him who needed The Great Doctor - and we made plans to heal them *after* hours.

Being open to no limitations applies to knowing miracles are occurring even when you *do not* receive feedback of the immediate outcome. I have found wherever I bring people into prayer - even during public speaking engagements of mixed or non-religious people - miraculous and spontaneous healings will happen; whether I get to spend 30 seconds with personal hands-on time, or even no hands at all. Our invisible God takes every opportunity to manifest visible things on this side to prove once again that he loves us! This story emphasizes that point:

Immediate Healings at Speaking Presentation
(As received by email from Isabelle Bernard)

"Hi Tiffany, We met at the A.R.E. meeting when you gave your presentation and you worked on me because I had a toothache. Well, after your treatment the pain gradually diminished and eventually vanished. Two day later I went to the dentist and he did not see any problem to my gum nor my tooth. Thank you so much for healing me! You also worked on my friend who has had pain in the lower back/hip area. Since you worked on her, she has not felt any more pain. She is especially thankful to you knowing that she's had this pain for *2 years* and her weekly visits to her acupuncturist did not help...on behalf of the two of us, thank you!"

Meditation - Active Listening in the Stillness

"I will sing to the Lord all my life; I will sing praise to my God as long as I live. May my *meditation* be pleasing to him, as I rejoice in the Lord." (Ps. 104:24-34) "I will *meditate* on all your works and consider all your mighty deeds." (Ps. 77:12)

Meditation is a common tool that many cultures use, for people to know themselves and to get close to God. Through meditation, awareness can be nurtured and trained.

Sense the stillness, and the stillness will awaken all your senses. Sister Briege McKenna said: "the discipline of sitting before the Lord is very important. It is only when your spirit is *still* and when the ears of your spirit are *open* that you can really hear the Lord and experience the wisdom and insights that come from the Holy Spirit." *She consistently puts aside three hours every day for this discipline!* It helps fill the "Dixie cup." I try to do 1-2 hours daily, more when I can. This time is precious to me. It allows me to be in the Word, to hear his voice, and just *be*. I get out of balance easily if I don't.

I covered some unusual techniques and methods of meditation and games for making the Connection closer in my previous book *Psychic Gifts in the Christian Life – Tools to Connect,* so I will not go into any here. There are also many good books on different varieties of meditation, just choose them the same way you would an alternative medicine - ask, "Does it make sense? Does it ring true to my spirit? Does it fill me with the light of love? Does it speak the Word of God to my heart?"

Get on a Prayer Chain

These are also called by other names, including "prayer chains." This is basically a list where your name is placed, and/or sometimes your illness, and a multitude of people pray for you. Group intention is important! Besides your church, there are also many churches, including some very big and popular ministries, on the Internet that allow your name to be placed on a message board, to "sign in" to be prayed for, or for you to work as a "prayer warrior" in behalf of another. Why not have a flood of prayers said in your behalf? Bathe in the crystalline waterfall of Divine Love!

The Sacramental Church

In some churches, rituals or sacraments commonly have the same purpose as our four types of healing. Also, celebrating Communion or the Eucharist can be a healing also, no matter what church you belong to. The giving and receiving of the bread and wine (Christ's symbolic flesh and blood) has been linked to miraculous healings in many parts of the world. This God-ordained ceremony seems to have a special anointing on it. In our next chapter, we will look at some other customs and methods of healing that you may find unique to healing in the churches.

"Repentance takes place sacramentally in the sacrament of reconciliation (which used to be called penance); inner healing can also take place in the sacrament of reconciliation; physical healing is meant to take place in the anointing of the sick; and deliverance from demonic oppression or possession takes place in the rite of exorcism." - *Healing* by Francis MacNutt PhD. (Ave Maria Press, 1999)

CHAPTER 7

GROUP HEALING
Power of Agreement; "Slain in the Spirit;"
Church & Conventions

"It is appropriate to encourage many people to pray for the same thing. That is not because there are more fists beating on the heavenly door, but because there are more wills to be aligned with the divine will." - John Polkinghorne

Group Intention - the Power of Agreement

When people are in prayer and have the same Powerful intent, Powerful miracles happen. Prayer is Powerful, and calling upon the Power of the universe is the most Powerful thing a human can do. How many times did I use the word Powerful? Let me emphasize it again - *Powerful!*

I love working with groups of people in one thought. Even at speaking engagements, with people of varying religious or non-religious background, I always make space to have a time of group intent - prayer. I have the audience place their hands upon those areas of the body where they desire healing. Then, we come before the Presence by agreement; I lead with an out loud prayer. On the average, 75-80% of the people will experience *their own hands get hot* over their places of injury! Their eyes light up and sparkle! They think it wouldn't happen to them, or that "the concept" wasn't "for real." Surprise! Once again, God will take every opportunity we provide for him to show he cares for us. All we have to do is make that opportunity!

Drunk in the Spirit

Sometimes after a healing, whether it is one-on-one or in a group, a wonderful thing happens – laughter! I've seen people not be able to stand, not be able to stop laughing, and not being able to stop crying with joy! The Spirit touches people in a variety of ways. Sometimes slurring of speech occurs, or a person may not be in absolute control of his movements. This is what is called in the scriptures, *"drunk in the Spirit."* In Acts 2:15, Peter said to the onlookers about the apostles, "These people are not drunk as you suppose they are." In other words, they were not drunk the way you think (with wine), but *why* did people think the disciples were drunk? *Because they acted like it!*

Falling in the Spirit / Slain in the Spirit

Do we have an example of falling in the Spirit in ancient times? Yes, we do. Here's one: an entire battalion of Roman soldiers were knocked unconscious by the Spirit of God moving upon them. And when they got up, they certainly weren't very coherent! They had to re-ask the question that Jesus had just answered!

"The leading priests and Pharisees had given Judas a battalion of Roman soldiers and Temple guards to accompany him. Now with blazing torches, lanterns, and weapons, they arrived at the olive grove. Jesus fully realized all that was going to happen to him. Stepping forward to meet them, he asked, "Whom are you looking for?" "Jesus of Nazareth," they replied. "I am he," Jesus said. Judas was standing there with them when Jesus identified himself. And as he said, "I am he," *they all fell backward to the ground!* Once more he asked them, "Whom are you searching for?" And again they replied, "Jesus of Nazareth." "I told you that I am he," Jesus said." (John 18:3-8)

The falling under the power of God happens today as has happened throughout time - his Spirit continues to move through the ages. It is a phenomenon that I have not seen outside of Christianity or Christian prayer. Praying through the authority of Jesus' name has great value.

"What Would You Like the Lord to Do for You?"

When the anointing is upon me and I am facilitated by the Spirit to help people, a prayer partner will anoint the forehead of the person who has come up for healing, and ask, "What would you like the Lord to do for you?" Then they will name what they would like to be healed. This, similar to the client following in personal prayer at the clinics, is showing active Free Will participation and reliance upon God. Then, I step forward to touch them, usually on the forehead or on the heart. Sometimes I don't get that far, and as I reach to them they fall down. Often, I find myself making a simple statement, such as, "The Lord loves you," or "Jesus heals you." There are people available to catch them, and to bring them gently to the floor. For the ladies, if they are wearing a dress, it is a good idea for the catchers to place a small covering over their exposed legs, for modesty.

What do I feel? I feel the power surging through me, *and the point of surrender happening in the person,* whether I am touching them or not. I can always tell when faith is in operation, for *faith draws upon the anointing of God.* It is a wonderful feeling to be facilitated for such a powerful work; it always amazes me that he can use simple humans! It's a humbling and powerful experience. The afterglow lasts a long time, up to four hours, and makes electrical interference problems wherever I go, including my cell phone and cash registers at grocery stores. I have to wait to watch TV, because of bands of white going across the picture. It's seems so funny to me!

160

Angelic direction, Holy Spirit and protection continue to follow me. I feel so Blessed! (Lk. 8:48)

When people are slain in the Spirit, they lose consciousness for a period of a few seconds, to an average of several minutes. Some lose consciousness for a much longer time. My choice is to let them lay, and let the Holy Spirit take whatever time he needs with them. Even if people start looking like bales of hay laid here and there, I would rather move down the line and find a new spot for others to rest, then to pick them up too early. It may be the first time in their lives that they have ever experienced this. Let them enjoy! When they are ready and sitting up, the catchers will help them up off the floor.

Sometimes Additional Blessings Happen Too

Sometimes I will have a Word of Knowledge, or one of Prophecy for the person; and I usually get it as I approach them, so can tell them the Word he wants me to convey before they rest. If they go down before I can tell them, in this case I will have the person stood back up again. Also, not everyone falls, and that's OK too. There is no "peer pressure." Falling in the Spirit is a personal thing. Spirit acts differently with different people, and if it's against their Free Will to rest, they will not rest. However, sometimes it simply has to do with the inability to *trust*. And that trust doesn't have anything to do with the "catchers" ability to catch you, but about your own ability to *surrender* to the Spirit of God calling you.

Why Does God Knock Them Out?

At this time, we can't know for sure. There are many possibilities. Perhaps Spirit is just too much for the human body. Perhaps being unconscious it is a way of bypassing all the *blockages* of the analytical brain and all the *questionings* of "what is happening?" or "am I being healed?" etc. Putting them to sleep takes care of that. Remember, the 10% of the brain acts as a bridge or a barrier to spirit. But, as always, he will not go against Free Will.

What Happens When Resting in the Spirit?

While resting in the Spirit, one or more of several things may happen:
- They may commune with God.
- They may see clearly how to deal with pressing problems.
- They may have a vision.
- They may be given words of wisdom or knowledge.

161

- They may be healed, physically, emotionally or spiritual.
- They may be given prophecy
- They may just feel good and don't know why.
- They may wake up "Drunk in the Spirit."

I have been on the *receiving end* of the anointed hand too. At a conference in San Diego I waited in line for Francis and Judith MacNutt (Christian Healing Ministries), and I heard Judith say, "it's OK, Tiffany, just surrender," and Francis reached out his hand, and even before he touched me I felt a wave of Energy that made the world spin, and I woke up on the floor laughing like I'd never laughed before! It was my first experience receiving, and one that I will never forget...! I feel blessed to know now how it feels on both sides of the healing hand.

Anointing and Baptism of the Spirit

Jesus was anointed by *Holy Spirit* and *power* by God. (Acts 10:38) He said the same thing would happen to us: "But you will receive power when the Holy Spirit comes on you." Often, it is called "an anointing" when one has the Spirit of God upon him. Anointing is sign of dedication, and of being chosen for a special task. (Acts 1:8)

Anointing can also come from a holy oil, such as virgin olive, balsam, or frankincense placed as the sign of the cross on the forehead or even just a dab on the back of the hands. Today, there are different "anointing salves" and "anointing oils" freely available in the Christian bookstores. We find the precedent of oil anointing in the scriptures: future kings, altars and utensils for the tabernacle and temples, priests and sons of priests, implements of war, prophets, future kings, the feet of Jesus, etc. (Ex. 29:7,29,36; 1 Ki.1:34, Heb.1:9)

Although some people, especially in a church healing situation, like to do an anointing of the sick person before a healing, it is not necessary to do so. I have seen anointing as an option, since healing will occur without its use. But, anointing is a ritual that comforts many people who choose to do it. When I have a partner helping me in a group situation, I try to have the anointing placed on the people; it seems to help prepare their hearts. But, true anointing comes not from what we can do for each other, but from God's Spirit descending upon us. *This* is the true anointing, the Power of the Spirit!

Not All People or Churches Acknowledge the Healing Gifts

One day a well-meaning relative of mine, a very religious man, casually slipped into our other-topic conversation his view of the work I do, saying, "You know, no more healings have occurred since Jesus left the earth." I smiled and said, "We have different points of view on that," and we continued on the previous topic. But inside I was smiling to myself, "Oh, I guess I'll just have to tell all those people that their healings were all in their imagination!" I knew that only a personal testimony can convince some people, and that it was not going to help to argue the point

There are many people, and *I* was one of them (before the lightning strike), that do not believe in modern day healings. I used to believe that all the gifts died out in the first century, with the apostles and disciples. But how can we read such passages as this, where Jesus said, "I tell you the truth, anyone who has faith in me will do what I have been doing. He will do even greater works than these, because I am going my way to the Father. And I will do whatever you ask in my name, so that the Son may bring glory to the Father. You may ask me for anything in my name, and I will do it." (Jn. 14:12 -14) But scriptural reference for spiritual gifts didn't matter to me, since the outlined time frame was obscure to me; like a needle in a record grove, I could hear it only one way.

I was really the stubborn one. These Spiritual gifts are specific demonstrations of the energy of the Holy Spirit. (1 Cor.12:4-11,31) It took an empirical, first-hand experience for me to change my mind. Scriptural reasoning was not enough. Perfection has not yet come, and we see the gifts are abundant. (1 Cor. 13:8) So I empathize with those who do not believe, but I pray that one day they will! Without being struck by lightning! They are losing out on being witness to, and partakers of, *so much love!*

There are several churches that I am facilitated for healing in. And I also try to be led by the Spirit and drop into various churches to see if the Lord is going to use me there. I have been embraced in the churches for healing, and I have been kicked out for it too! Even in some churches which say they believe in Spiritual Gifts, there are those who do not want an "unknown," and regard anyone with suspicion from outside their church, even if the Spirit clearly shows that one is useful to God. And in other churches, we also see the problem of those in charge wanting the Spirit to move only when *they* schedule him in. All this shows that nothing has really changed in the mind of man in over two thousand years!

If the traveling evangelist Paul, or Peter, or even Jesus himself, showed up at a church today, guess what! I doubt that Jesus would even be given the pulpit to preach from, as was the custom in his day. I doubt that he would "be allowed" to do healings or any other miracles in the church today; any that occurred would be regarded with deep suspicion (this is what happened then, too). It is easy to see that all true Spirit-led men and women of old would be branded in our own time as "heretics" and "independent

163

thinkers" and slandered and ridiculed unless they acted only under the omophor of church authority. In many cases, it would be *more difficult* for the Glory of God to be made know now, than it was at that time. And the modern version of the ancient Sanhedrin (the corrupt and faithless religious governing body at the temple in Jerusalem) would be breathing down the anointed necks at every turn. Jesus "nailed" it when he said they were white-washed graves filled with dead men's bones. (Mt. 23:1-36)

Today's Sanhedrin also discredits any theological education that is not from their own denomination or training facilities. Due to the separation of church and state, the federal government does not mandate what qualifies for religious instruction. So, we see cases where a person may hold a degree, or even a doctorate through one seminary or college, and it may not be worth the paper it is written on to another denomination. It is worthless. "Accreditation" is a slippery road - what is relevant to one may not be to the other. Now, let's bring the example of Jesus, Peter and Paul back in - Paul would possibly be regarded as approved in some sectors because of his religious training. In others, he definitely would not be *because* of that training. But, Jesus, Peter and the uneducated fisherman, sheep herders and the like - would be held accountable for proper certification and theological training too. No matter what Supernatural Signs they were showing! Aren't we glad that Divine knows no such restrictions! "But God chose the foolish things of the world to shame the wise..." (1 Cor. 1:27)

Spontaneous Healing - Kicked Out of Church

We were invited to go with a friend to a new church, and I readily agreed. My daughter and son and I would often visit different churches, of various beliefs and customs. I find it is very similar to finding shimmering jewels on the bare ground. Lifting up one stone and holding it to the light, turning it this way and that way to look at the glistening facets, one can see the beauty of each precious one, without judging it in comparison to the others. Big or small, with different shapes and different colors, and found in various locations, the rubies, diamonds and emeralds will far outweigh the accidental pieces of clay and sandstone you may pick up. If our eyes be clear, the individual perfection of that stone will be clearly revealed when held up to God's love light of truth.

"Do not judge, or you too will be judged. For in the same way you judge others, you will be judged, and with the measure you use, it will be measured out to you. Why do you look at the speck of sawdust in your brother's eye and pay no attention to the plank in your own eye? How can you say to your brother, 'Let me take the speck out of your eye,' when all the time there is a plank in your own eye? You hypocrite, first take the

164

plank out of your own eye, and then you will see clearly to remove the speck from your brother's eye." (Mt. 7:1-5)

This large Christian church had a wonderful service and joyful praise! With heartfelt desire they were calling upon God to bless their congregation, calling upon the Holy Spirit to descend, and Jesus to guide their hearts and minds. My hands were getting hot just sitting there - I knew that the Spirit was willing! I wondered what would happen, and how he would communicate with his people that *he was certainly here.*

On this particular day most of the brothers were absent, having gone to a retreat. The wives of the ministers and servants were taking care of the service, and I offered myself to one of the wives to help when the call went out for those who would like to be prayed for. There would be about four or five sisters helping. The minister's wife thought that it would be fine, and I stood beside her at the end of the service so as to respect her position of authority, as people started walking up.

A woman in her 50's came up, and started pouring out her heart to the minister's wife. She was having problems at work, and also had diabetes. She felt hemmed in on all sides. The minister's wife started praying for her, and anointed her with oil. I was standing by and listening. The Spirit chose the mid-part of the prayer for me to put my hand on the woman's heart…and she fainted dead away! She locked her knees and fell flat backwards to the floor, bumping her head with a "crack" sound as she went! She had been "slain in the Spirit." This was my very first time to be used by the Holy Spirit to facilitate this.

It startled me - I looked at the minister's wife and said, "I'm sorry!" (I promise not to apologize for the Holy Spirit ever again - it was just my first human reaction). The wife was just staring - I dropped to my knees and started praying over the woman's body, keeping my hands lifted a few inches away. A crowd gathered, and I praised God, and blessed him for hearing the cries of his people. Four or five minutes later, the woman finally came to, and started *laughing joyously,* without restraint. She was just lying there, laughing, and not moving a muscle anywhere else! I whispered in her ear, "God has heard your pleas, he loves you. You are never alone - spend the rest of your day praising him!"

She finally sat up, and was helped to stand, where I led her to a chair and talked to her about God's love and guidance in our lives, and how everything that happens to us can be an opportunity to shape ourselves more into his likeness. Her face was as innocent and glowing as a newborn child. I knew the Lord had removed her illnesses, and I simply told her that her stomach would also be feeling better.

165

I could tell that I needed to disappear now. This had evidently not happened here before, and it seemed to cause quite a commotion. I would like to have stayed to see what else the Spirit would do, but felt compelled to leave. I did not want to be a side-show or cause attention to myself. I was here to worship God and focus attention on him. As I was walking away, I saw the minister's wife go over to the woman, and I heard the woman say, "She knew that my stomach hurt, and God has healed me!" I rejoiced for the joy in her heart. This had been a powerful witness to the All Mighty and Powerful God!

I took my children to a local park and sat on a large rock, feeling the comfort and connectedness all around me. How my heart was pounding with joy! I felt like I had completed twenty healing sessions - so much power had shot through me! What bliss and exhilaration I was experiencing! Looking around me, I could see everything keenly that had the blood of life rushing through its veins - the birds in the trees; the squirrels in their burrows, even the fish I could sense under their spot in the water. Nothing could hide from me. It was "medical intuitiveness" in a unique way - a "life-force intuitiveness," if you will. I praised God for this opportunity to be used in the church for his will. I asked forgiveness for any undue attention that it gave me, wishing only to be a reflection of his love.

Two days later, I received a phone call at lunch from the minister's wife. I asked her if I could call her back, that I was at a restaurant about to eat a meal with my family. She then proceeded to verbally attack me, calling me a wolf in sheep's clothing, saying also "*by whose authority* do you do this? Who are you associated with?" She ripped into me from all angles, saying I can't be going to the churches to heal, and that I was not submissive to the headship in their church; but that possibly…if I am repentant and come under their authority, I might be used later on, "under close supervision."

I answered her with scriptures the best I could, and let her angry words, prompted by fear, wash over me like water off a duck's back. I had expected a welcome to come back, and to hear a kind word of praise for the Lord who chooses to work with vessels of clay. Instead she repeated, "Do you understand what I am saying? You cannot come back here! Do you understand? You cannot come back!"

I was laughing to myself as the Lord brought these words to mind: "Blessed are you when people insult you, persecute you and falsely say all kinds of evil against you because of me. Rejoice and be glad, because great is your reward in heaven, for in the same way they persecuted the prophets who were before you." (Mt. 5:11,12) I rejoiced that I was being persecuted with almost the *exact same words* uttered by the chief priests and teachers of the law almost two thousand years ago against Jesus, when they

166

said, "Tell us by what authority you are doing these things," and "Who gave you this authority?" (Lk. 20:2; Mt. 21:23; Mr. 11:28)

It also reminded me of when Jesus had healed a demon-possessed man who was blind and mute: "But when the Pharisees heard this, they said, "It is only by Beelzebub, the prince of demons, that this fellow drives out demons." Jesus knew their thoughts and said to them, "Every kingdom divided against itself will be ruined, and every city or household divided against itself will not stand. If Satan drives out Satan, he is divided against himself. How then can his kingdom stand? And if I drive out demons by Beelzebub, by whom do your people drive them out? So then, they will be your judges. But if I drive out demons by the Spirit of God, then the kingdom of God has come upon you." (Mt. 12:22-28)

My children were upset when I relayed the information that we would not be returning, and why. Being in their teenage years, their sense of right and wrong created an immediate flare of indignation over injustice. I told them to laugh it off - that the conversation had just been prompted by fear of that which cannot be controlled (how to control the Holy Spirit?).

The church had prayed for the Will of God. His Holy Spirit fell out on a believer, and when they saw it occur, it scared them and they denounced it! It is so sad when God is put in a "box" as if to control him to conform to a church's programs and level of understanding. That is not how he works! He does what he wants! The sacred secret is…he often does what *we* want, too. Hence the old adage: "Be careful what you pray for."

Although I felt glorious for being put in the same category as these wondrous souls in the past, I also felt very sorry that the woman and all the people who were joyful witnesses at the church would now be *confused* at what they saw. Also, it proved to be a temporary stumbling for my friend who had invited me, and she stepped down from her position at the church, saying: "How can they say one thing and do another; and to tell a daughter of God she can't come back to the church - and over the phone instead of in person!" I agreed with her, but also reminded her that people are very fearful, and that God still has to use imperfect people to do his will. Just look at me for an example of that! But perfect love drives all fear aside. We need to keep such ones in our prayers.

But in some places that a person would not think it, healing is requested and appreciated, for example, in one place I am regularly facilitated for healing after Catholic mass - even though I am not a Catholic, and for many it may be a new idea. The Lord opens the hearts of the people who have an open mind toward him.

In Another Church, Joy

The primary church that my covering is under is very open to Spiritual Gifts. And, the Holy Spirit is *never* put on restriction. He can break out wherever and whenever he wishes, and often does! Gifts of prophecy abound, and the healings are well attended, with several being anointed with his Spirit to heal. It is very similar to a 1st Century church, and includes having traveling ministers speak, and a monthly group of 5 or 6 other congregations meeting together under one roof. The worship team is talented and varies from week to week, and the singing is loud and joyous. It is not a large church, and it resonates with my soul.

It is also nondenominational, and is tolerant and respectful of other religions. It holds retreats often, and every night of the week some kind of ministry is going on. This is the kind of congregation I wish you to find, so God can work freely in it, and with you, in relationship with others who are going through the same things as you. "And let us consider how we may spur one another on toward love and good deeds. Let us not give up meeting together, as some are in the habit of doing, but let us encourage one another…" (Heb. 10:24, 25)

Pieces of Paper on the Wall, or Human Hearts?

As we have seen, some people and places need paper on the wall to prove worldly qualifications, and do not take the time to see how the Spirit qualifies people. It is enough for the love in your heart and the signs that God freely moves you as a surrendered vessel. Let that be the "proof in the pudding" as they say. What do the end results of your day show as to your qualifications to be a worker for The Big Guy? Do your qualifications only shine on *parched paper* under a 9 x 11 piece of glass? Rather, aren't your true qualifications the *humans* that your life has been led to touch? To me, the answer seems obvious.

At one point in my life, due to pressures for conformity and false reasoning that I could help more people if I "played the game" and had the paperwork; I did gather all my credentials and certifications that would in any way apply to the work. I had agreed to be a guest speaker at a healing convention, and the convener was very excited about asking me to partake in it. Others were not; and even though I had completed the six-month training course they offered, I was still not "one of them." There are always those who will be jealous, suspicious, and be soaked in legalism. The paperwork I gave for qualifications, even those from some large organizations, were not recognized by them and their organization. So, in this instance I was not able to speak, but I was "cautiously" allowed to help with the healing afterwards.

168

At the healing part of the convention, much to the surprise of many, people were lying on the floor, laughing and crying - the Holy Spirit overflowing and healing them! Many were taken aback. This was new to most of the people there; so much so that people needed to be instructed in "catching," and even after all this the people still stood there, not being sure of what they were witnessing. The main speaker had seen Spirit before, and was openly pleased to see the Lord move through me as an anointed vessel. I felt Blessed, as always, to be facilitated by Spirit; and healings and "Words of Knowledge and Prophecy" were also occurring.

Perhaps, today the minds of a few would be stretched, only God knows the ripple effects and the Bigger Picture of it all. I, for my part, felt I had gone through this test well, and it *was* a test for me. My ability to do my best to reach hearts, through words, scripture, and testimony, had been greatly reduced by not being able to also *teach*. Now, I did have the Free Will choice to not participate at all after the co-speaker opportunity was yanked away; I could have elected to bow out of the whole thing. Yet, in this case the Lord answered my prayer stating I should continue, so I humbled myself under this restrictive hand, and *God himself* spoke up for me! He showed that *his* Mighty Hand is not a restrictive one, and he Powerfully qualified me! Everyone could see the Signs that God works good for all those who love him, and this night they could see it by just "looking in the pudding!"

"Be still before the Lord and wait patiently for him; do not fret when men succeed in their ways, when they carry out their wicked schemes. Commit your way to the Lord; trust in him and he will do this: he will make your righteousness shine like the dawn, the justice of your cause like the noonday sun." (Ps. 37:5-7)

Do All Things for God's Love and to His Glory

In cases like these, make sure you are doing everything for the right reason - as I said, I could have gotten in a huff when I was not allowed to speak, and walked away from the whole thing. This would have showed pride and ego on my behalf. And, the suppositions against me would have been believed. Instead, I submitted to whatever position I was put in, and the Lord used it all for his glory - he showed up in a Mighty way and was my testimony. Let God be *your* defender, and do not do anything that would be a bad reflection on him.

Paul is considered the greatest of all the apostles, and yet he was also spoken against. "I ought to have been commended by you, for though I am a nobody, there is not a thing these arch-apostles have that I do not have as well. You have seen done among you all the signs that mark the true apostle, unfailingly produced: the signs, the marvels, the

169

miracles - with great perseverance." (2 Cor. 12:11,12).

Sometimes we just have to *be who we are,* be who we were created by God to be. No matter what anyone else thinks, your candle is lit and you are going to stand out in this dark world! You don't have to please everybody. Once you make the right choice about *who* you want to please the most – all else will fall into Divine place! But be careful, there will always be people who want the glory and authority over you that rightfully belong to God alone. As a well-known actor used to say, "Who loves you, baby?" Well…I am loved by God and am one of his kids…and, s*o are you!* We are the *same!* We are *all* his kids. And you'll see when you crawl up onto your Father's lap that there's plenty of room for everyone - no need to push anyone else out! But, while you are up there, see if you can also lean over and look down, why are there some of his kids who are on the floor crawling *away* from Dad? Hmmmm…

CHAPTER 8

Keeping Your Healing
Barriers to Healing; Power of Disbelief; Peer Pressure

Not everyone wants to be healed. Not all who come up, wanting to be healed, will be. Sometimes the person who walks in *without* faith will be healed. Sometimes the devoted, faithful prayer warrior *won't be*. Such is the mystery of Divine Healing. God is in control, the Great Weaver of Tapestry. He knows what threads go where, in what pattern, and why. We may get a glimmer now and then - perhaps a blink into the greater musical occurring behind the scenes, or the words between the written lines. Then what do we do? Most of the time we then read into it *more* than we are supposed to! Impatience and personal interpretation can be a deadly combination when we think we know all the answers! Now, saying that, let's pluck at some simple threads related to healing; and understand why "keeping your healing" is a topic full of controversy and conjecture.

Some people believe that everyone who asks should be healed. Some believe insufficient faith or unconfessed sin is holding them back. While this should be explored, it is not always the case, and could go beyond it. Prayer will often let us know what barriers to healing are in our way. Be open to the whispers of God - his wisdom might come as the remembrance of a former sin, unforgiven memory or new problem that he "pops up" in your mind. Be consistent in prayer, and keep asking until you understand the whispers clearly.

Not everyone is open even to the *possibility* of being healed. Some people feel Supernatural Intervention just doesn't exist anymore. Many do believe in it, as we have addressed, but simply feel that it will happen for someone else, and not for them. Then, there are other barriers to healing.

We All Have Imperfections

We see that even the faithful of Biblical times were left with a few problems to deal with. The apostle Paul had healed many people, and even resurrected a couple, yet he had a "thorn in the flesh" which was persistent, and he was never healed from. What was Paul's attitude about this? He felt it kept him from getting conceited about the work he was facilitated for, and accepted it by saying, "I will boast all the more gladly about my weaknesses, so that Christ's power may rest on me...for when I am weak, then I am strong." (2 Cor. 12:7-10)

We also see that Paul told Timothy to stop drinking only water, and to drink a little wine for his stomach troubles and frequent cases of illness. (1 Tim. 5:23) So, why do we feel that those used for even extraordinary healings must be without any problems of their own, if these faithful men weren't? Yes, we receive a healing every time we give one, but we also must deal with imperfections. I have known people who will not go up for God to heal them, because the one he is facilitating wears glasses! I'm sure that Timothy and Paul, and probably also the congregations they visited, had prayed for *Supernatural* healing for Timothy's troubles many times. Now, the next step was to look to the *natural things* that God had placed upon the planet as a healing in behalf of mankind, in his case, wine (which aids digestion, among other things).

The Power of Unbelief

Similar to the people who die prematurely "because they do not love," in this scripture we see that the power of unbelief was even *greater* than even Jesus' power to *heal!* "Jesus left there and went to his hometown, accompanied by his disciples. When the Sabbath came, he began to teach in the synagogue, and many who heard him were amazed. "Where did this man get these things?" they asked. "What's this wisdom that has been given him, that he even does miracles! Isn't this the carpenter's son? Isn't this Mary's son and the brother of James, Joseph, Judas and Simon? Aren't his sisters here with us?" And they took offense at him. Jesus said to them, "Only in his hometown, among his relatives and in his own house is a prophet without honor." *He could not do any miracles there,* except lay his hands on a few sick people and heal them." (Mark 6:1-5)

Even though some people in that area *did* see miracles performed, they still did *not* believe. The *power of unbelief* can prevent us from many wonderful things in our lives. For example, do you believe that your mate really loves you? *Really?* Or do you disbelieve it way down in your soul? That kind of unbelief is destructive to relationships. No matter how much caring, nurturing and attention lavished upon you, there will be a hesitancy to respond as well and openly as you could, and there will be a slight unnaturalness to your affection. This can be felt by the other, no matter how much you may try to deny it or place the fault on distraction, having a lot on your mind, business, etc. This unbelief ultimately undoes the *entire structure* of the relationship, because the underlying foundation was crumbly. Unbelief restricts the flow of love. *How many things are you going to let it destroy for you?* It's your Free Will choice, and *you* are the one in charge of changing this. It may feel like a risk to trust. But, *not risking* is *not truly living.* Have faith! Enjoy Life!

Unbelief is *different* from doubt, because unbelief refuses to accept the evidence;

whereas doubt just needs more information before the brain can process and accept the evidence as true.

Faith is the Ability to Take Risk

"As John Wimber used to say, "Faith is spelled 'R-I-S-K.' Like Abraham we set out for an unknown promised land. The faith lies in setting out on the journey, not in being sure of exactly where we are going. We believe that God is faithful, provided we do what is in our power - and that is to pray for the sick. Discovering this reality was liberating: to know that faith is simply obedience and the willingness to risk; not an absolute certainty about what is going to happen on the journey!" - *Healing* by Francis MacNutt, PhD. (Ave Maria Press, 1999)

We need to have faith, not in our own inadequate application of faith, but in that which is *beyond* our inadequacies. Don't have faith *in your own faith* - have faith *in God.*

Faith is also about being open to many different styles of Divine Healing, knowing that God can use many touch-stones to access him. There is no certain script to follow, no special words to repeat, that "cause" a healing to happen every time. Although there are guidelines and examples related here in this book, it is not meant to put God in a box and limit how the Spirit guides. There are many evangelists who have caused great harm to the healing ministry because of proclaiming "only one correct way" to do things. Because of this, some people have "thrown the baby out with the bath water;" throwing out God because the religious methods supposedly representing him. Let us not be so narrow-minded, and choose to see the fruitage of the tree before we chop it down. It might be a tree that God himself has planted, and could bear outrageous quantities of delicious fruit!

"Now faith is being sure of what we hope for and certain of what we do not see…and without faith it is impossible to please God, because anyone who comes to him must believe that he exists and that he rewards those who earnestly seek him." (Heb. 11:1,6)

Do We Know All the Factors About this Healing? No!

When I see someone blind or lame, I see the possibility of their being miraculously touched by God and being made whole. Seeing this as a *possibility* instead of a *certainty* does not mean I lack faith in God's promise to heal. It means I realize I do not know all the extenuating circumstances related to the process and the outcome of the healing. Faith is trust, and letting go of the end result. Our job is to pray, and let The Big Guy do what is best, without personal ego attached. *Perhaps* the best *is* an immediate healing! *Perhaps* it is a miracle at a *later time,* or with *someone else*

173

brought into their lives to pray. *Perhaps* the miracle will *begin* with this single prayer, and healing will *continue* from there. We do not know all the *"perhaps."* That reminds us that *we* are not in control; and if we have done our best to pray, and have done what we are led to do for emotional, physical, spiritual, or deliverance healing (or a combination of the four), we have done all that was required. Spirit is the worker – let him do his job without interference! Now sit back and bask in the glow of love, accomplishment, and trust. It's just like that - it's that easy! Let go and let God. He's the One in charge!

Even in Jesus' life, if he had healed *everyone* with whom he came in contact, do you think there would have been so much excitement and amazement about every healing that happened? His healings were not commonplace, and as we have seen, not all locations received him well. There were underlying circumstances. *Perhaps* a few could be healed here, or there, *and perhaps many, many more!*

Fear is a Barrier to Healing

Some people are afraid to try anything new. Others are afraid because they don't really want to heal - they can't see their lives beyond their illness. They identify with it too much. In these cases, it is often because they have dealt with it for so long, that they don't know anything else. Change is a stress, even if it is for our own good. It goes back to those things that we feel comfortable with, our developed habits. We need to pray for emotional healing in such cases, so that we can look beyond and see ourselves whole and happy with new, healthy habits.

We need to look at our core belief systems too. Sometimes people feel it's God's Will for them to suffer, to do penance as it were. While it is true that an illness often leads to our spiritual growth, it is also true that illness is an enemy and that we do not need to suffer for our sins - they have been already nailed upon the tree for us. *We do not need to be a martyr.* That, my friend, is actually denying the ransom sacrifice! Also, taking illness upon our own body does not prevent illness from coming upon our family - again, we are not asked to be the sacrificial lamb in any way.

"He himself bore our sins in his body on the tree, so that we might die to sins and live for righteousness; by his wounds you have been healed." (1 Pe. 2:24) Instead, we are admonished to be well, and to be whole.

Brain Tumor Shrinks

Not all healings end with the expected results. We must always remember that each person is on his own path, and will make his own choices, for good and for bad, along

174

the way. The Lord never retrieves his outstretched hand, but so often we take our own away from him. This is what happened with "Rachel:"

Rachel had an inoperable brain tumor and was on several medications. I didn't know when I was called to help her that there was a tumor involved - I knew that she was sick and couldn't keep her balance when she got up from the couch. She fell down a lot. I knew that she had a lot of pain and had a lead weight in her eyelid to keep it down. I also knew that her kids and grandchildren came over all the time to take care of her and see how she was doing.

When I started the prayers and put both of my hands over her ears is when I noticed the tumor deep in her brain. I told her something needed to be checked there - hoping she already knew about the problem. I was relieved when she verified it. This is what was messing with her balance, and with her eyesight. She said this was her second time. The first tumor had been in a place where they could remove it with laser surgery. This one, they couldn't. I drew a picture of it on a piece of paper, showing two lobes and a web of tentacles around it. She verified the size and shape to be what the doctors had shown to her.

I visited Rachel at her home every week for four weeks, twice a week. Under the power of the Holy Spirit I felt the tumor reduce in size, pull back its tentacles from one side, and "turn color" in my mind's eye from beige-orange to light brown. It became like melted bubble gum! Her ability to walk and keep her balance improved. Her eyesight became better, her skin tone more balanced. She had other things wrong with her too, and the Energy from God was taking care of it in its own time. Her hands and knees were almost pain free and her mobility had greatly increased.

Rachel told me how much better she felt; and how she had been talking to her neurologist and how he wanted to meet me, which was not what she had expected. He had been her surgeon for over six years, and had seen Rachel go through a lot. The doctor said there were signs that the tumor was better; and that he was tremendously impressed with the mobility she was having. He scheduled new tests. He encouraged her to *"keep doing whatever you are doing."* Rachel invited me to come to her next tumor support group meeting, held monthly. She also said that she had been getting out more and able to do some things with her husband.

She also expressed that her daughter and grandkids weren't coming around as much anymore, now that she was getting better.

At the next appointment, I showed up and no one was home, and with no note. Later I talked to Rachel on the phone, and she said it was OK if I stopped coming over because

175

they really couldn't afford to pay a love offering (donation) anymore. I suggested that if they just covered my gas, it would be enough. I said I wasn't going to let money keep me from being facilitated to heal her, and expressed the desire to continue on a regular schedule, until the Lord said, "it is enough."

But, it seemed *I* wanted to heal her more than *she* wanted the healing. I found I couldn't win - she identified with the tumor too much. And, *I wanted My Will to be done.* My ego was now tied up with beating this thing. During our conversations she would say things such as: "I wonder if the grandkids will still come over if I am well?" "I have the tumor because I am taking upon my own body anything that might hurt the grandkids – it's better me than them." She had a core belief that she held deep inside; that she was keeping her kids and grandkids healthy in *"having"* their diseases. She also felt that they would *ignore her* if she weren't dying!

When I went to the next appointment, no one answered the door. I once again called her on the phone, and we had a nice conversation. I spoke to her in plain terms. I told her Christ was the martyr for us - we don't need to carry sin or illness on our own body for anyone else - we are denying the sacrifice of Christ by doing so. I pointed out that her ego was getting in the way, and that she was afraid of getting well because she would lose the attention that she received by being in her weakened state. I quoted scriptures and promised that her family would enjoy being around her *even more if she were well!* I asked her to think of all the things they could do together! But, I was hitting my head against a wall. She had retrieved her hand, and the Lord would not heal her against her will, or, for *my* will. Nothing was going to change her mind.

I felt flattened for a few days. I had a lesson to learn the hard way. I don't know how the patience of our Lord, who is so long-suffering, can endure us! My ego was involved, and I had to let it go.

When I next heard of Rachel's condition, I was told that she had taken a turn for the worse and was in bed again, unable to stand and barely able to see. I was sure the tumor had come back with a vengeance. Jesus had been healing her…but she didn't want him to anymore. Situations like this still make me want to cry inside. But, it is her Free Will choice, and God won't *force* her to be well. *Spiritual freedom* does not mean accepting life's inadequacies - it means being exonerated from them! "Beloved, I wish above all things that thou mayest *prosper* and be in *health,* even as thy soul prospereth." (3 Jn.2) *King James Version*

Feeling Unworthy

We have covered this already, but I wanted to emphasize it again, since it is a real

176

barrier to healing, "God couldn't love me," "healing will happen for them, but not for me." God doesn't make unworthy things - or in the vernacular - "God don't make no junk!" When you say or think these dark things, it is hurting his Spirit, and your own. All of creation is beautiful, has a purpose, and is loved! Including you! Let him *embrace* you in love, and *receive* his gift of love; the healing of your ills, inside and out.

In nature, we see all things progress to a state of ripeness and beauty. The flower grows from seed and bulb to bud, to full blossom, to producing more seeds and bulbs. The tree grows strong to reach the sky, is a shelter to animals and birds, and produces more seeds. Animals grow to maturity and abundance too. This is the way God intended us - to grow strong and reach maturity and abundance, and progress to a state of beauty and produce fruit (spiritually and physically). This is the order of the natural world, the things of the earth that were lovingly created and put into being by his hands. Why would mankind, "made in his likeness," expect anything less? Feel the blessing of Spirit upon you, and recognize your worth!

Peer Pressure

Once in a while, a wonderful healing occurs (or even a miracle), with the person being relieved and overjoyed when they leave the clinic or healing function. They are praising the Lord in their hearts, and my heart overflows with gladness for them! *Then,* I hear later that the problem has returned, and the person isn't even sure if the former healing had been real. In most of these cases, I come to find out it's because they succumbed to peer pressure from misinformed friends. The client goes home, spilling over about the wonderful way the Divine hand has touched them and how good they feel. Instead of being joyous with them, friends, relatives, workmates or suspicious religions will start attacking them, attacking the healing work or attacking me. And as the client starts to replace their joy and love with fear and suspicion, they stop praising God for the healing, and by a conscious or subconscious choice of Free Will, they deny the healing, so it is lost. How sad when this happens! Don't let this happen to you! Don't pull your hand out of the Divine Hand!

Fear is one of Satan's most formidable weapons, and one that he often uses against people. If Satan tries to use fear as a weapon against you to steal your miracle, remember, identify your enemy and resist him.

"Submit therefore to God. Resist the devil and He will flee from you." (James 4:7)

He is a powerful active force, and though he and his fallen angels are in the invisible sphere to us (as are the True Sons of God), they nevertheless manipulate heavily behind the scenes. And since they are not allowed to materialize physical bodies for themselves anymore, they use humans as their mouthpieces and tools to harm.

As we have shared, if you have ever heard a destructive voice in your head that encouraged you to steal, hurt yourself or another, commit suicide, harm animals, rape, etc., then you have heard the demons trying to manipulate you. Intentionally or not, this is what he is doing with your misinformed friends. But, it is your choice to go along with them or not. Be strong! Keep your healing!

"And we know that in all things God works for the *good* of those who love him..." (Ro. 8:28)

Cancerous Tumor on Throat

A man and woman from a local church came to the clinic with a problem. The woman had a large tumor on the side of her throat. Previously, she had undergone radiation for a cancerous lump on her arm, and it had disappeared, but the couple had chosen not to do radiation for the new lump on the throat, since they were of the opinion that the previous cancer had spread because of the radiation. I began with my out-loud prayer, and in agreement both the husband and wife joined me in silent prayer for the duration of the treatment. It was a glorious hour, and the Spirit moved freely. The woman got up from the table feeling blessed and happy, and I assured them to "look for big changes to occur." They thanked me profusely, picked up a few brochures to pass out to friends, and left. That was the last time I saw them.

A few weeks went by. Then, I heard from my friend, "Julie," a pastor's wife, who had recently spoken to the couple. The large tumor had broken into several smaller ones, and had dissolved and totally disappeared! I was joyous at the news! But - there was more. When they had shared their joy with others at the church, they were attacked, as well as my reputation, mostly because of the fear of the unknown term "Reiki." So, the healing was snatched away by the evil one. And, in its place came the tumor back, in full force. How sad! Also, perhaps to make the healing more unacceptable in her mind, the woman told Julie, "And I felt something dark in that room." "Well, if you did, it didn't come from Tiffany!" Julie explained. "God uses her for mighty works - and even for healing my husband of *lung cancer!*" That was the last I heard about her and her husband, but they are still in my book of prayers, as are all the people God has brought into my life for healing. We need to continue to send them love

"For this people's heart has become calloused; they hardly hear with their ears, and they have closed their eyes. Otherwise they might see with their eyes, hear with their ears, understand with their hearts and turn, *and I would heal them.*" (Mt 13:15)

Sometimes We are the Barrier

This is a parable that speaks about the different kinds of "soil" that our hearts might be. Sometimes it is our own stubbornness and lack of "root" (bending to pressure), and worry ("will the illness come back?") that chokes the healing. But, it is because we are working against evil forces sent against us that the good is then "snatched away."

"When anyone hears the message about the kingdom and does not understand it, *the evil one comes and snatches away what was sown in his heart.* This is the seed sown along the path. The one who received the seed that fell on rocky places is the man who hears the word and at once received it with joy. But since he has no root, he lasts only a short time. When trouble or persecution comes because of the work, he quickly falls away. The one who received the seed that fell among the thorns is the man who hears the word, but the worries of this life and the deceitfulness of wealth choke it, making it unfruitful. But the one who received the seed that fell on good soil is the man who hears the word and understands it. He produces a crop, yielding a hundred, sixty or thirty times what was sown." (Mt. 13:19-23)

The enemy wants to steal the healing from us *before* it can become firmly rooted. Only seed firmly rooted can produce a harvest. The devil doesn't want God's love to be made manifest, or people to look into his healing Word, the scriptures. So he tries to cut things off and root it out when it is *new and vulnerable.* But our Dad is bigger and tougher than this neighbor bully. Hold fast!

"...and Jesus went about doing good, and healing all who were oppressed by the devil; for God was with Him." (Acts 10:38)

Throughout this book we have looked at different barriers to healing that we may come across in different aspects of healing physically, emotionally, and spiritually. These are the barriers we have looked at: the desire to hold onto addictions; not being open to conventional medicine, herbs or other opportunities that Spirit presents for healing; timing; lack of faith and unbelief; peer pressure and spiritual pride; keeping the sickness to prevent others from "getting" it; the false piety of desiring personal suffering; unforgiveness of ourselves and others (sin); and demonic interference. Whatever stronghold you are facing, remember that love, trust and faith breaks down all barriers.

Keeping in Balance as a Healer

Spiritual and emotional balance is essential for one facilitated in the healing work. As we have seen, sometimes physical problems will plague the body, but should not be an indication that God is using that person or not. Prayer time, meditation and study, and quiet time outside in the creation, is all necessary to stay in balance. So is proper nutrition and sleep. Find a church that can support you and be a covering for your work. Scheduling time off (and sticking to it) is a must. Even a lot of emergency calls can usually be rerouted or rescheduled for the next day. You need a day to catch up on your chores, *and* a day to just rest (two separate days). If you start getting out of balance, you may start feeling resentful, fatigued, and burned-out. Then the love can't flow, and the Spirit cannot work freely.

Remember to stay "grounded." Imagine your legs as mighty oak roots going down through the earth and encircling the molten core itself. See the Holy Spirit as a waterfall washing downward from the heavens through the top of your head and through your body. Try to spend time in the outdoors or at the sea. It really helps me to swim in the ocean; I feel holy and pure, physically, emotionally and spiritually.

Jesus would often withdraw alone to a quiet place. That is a good example for us. So is looking at him as a Man. He sat where people sat. He did most of his sermons not in a temple, but among the masses, *wherever* they were. He placed himself in the village streets, in the homes, in the towns, out of towns, on the roadways, in the country, *wherever he was* and *saw there was a need.* Likewise, we should be compassionate and willing to help people with whatever their need is, wherever *we* go. Listen to Spirit's guidance and be a reflection of his healing love. Meet people where the people are, at their point of need.

Wholeness is a birth rite for us as the children of God! Receiving it is like receiving bread and food at our Father's table. We, as his children, do not need to beg for it or just expect a few crumbs on our plate. We need to *surrender* to his love, receive it, and reflect it, in all the various forms that Spirit allows. Develop trust, grow in faith, and remain steadfast, and God will free you from physical, emotional, spiritual and demonic dis-ease. BE HEALED! Be whole and balanced physically, emotionally and spiritually. See and experience "Signs and Wonders," and ask to be gifted with the opportunity to be a facilitated vessel for MIRACLES by his Hand! *All things are possible when you just add prayer.* Keep your ears open to the whispers of God, be vigilant with your Connection, and delight in the Divine spark within yourself, and in others. And you will be blessed, healthy, and happy, forever! May you continue to be blessed with gifts and the courage to live them out!

Much Health to You; Love One Another!

"Pay attention, my child,
to what I say. Listen carefully.
Don't lose sight of my words.
Let them penetrate deep within your heart,
for they bring *life*
and *radiant health*
to anyone who discovers their meaning.
Above all else,
guard your *heart,*
for it affects everything you do."
(Pr. 4:20-23)

CHAPTER 9

Healing Scriptures, Poems & Prayers
Inspiration from Mystics, Prophets, Saints, Everyday People & God Himself

This chapter is filled with a variety of verse that may stimulate your own expression of love in song, poetry, or prayers. The spirit in us yearns to express itself, and the truest fulfillment of that is to express it to our Creator with all the unique abilities and gifts he individually made within us. Perhaps you'll resonant with some of the heart-felt expressions here as if they were your very own. Be joyful!

Scriptures

"…for I am the Lord, who heals you." (Ex. 15:26)

"I trust in God, so why should I be afraid? What can mere mortals do to me?" (Ps 56:11)

"And the prayer offered in faith will make the sick person well; the Lord will raise him up. If he has sinned, he will be forgiven. Therefore confess your sins to each other and pray for each other so that you may be healed. The prayer of a righteous man is powerful and effective."(James 5:14)

"Look at the birds. They don't need to plant or harvest or put food in barns because your heavenly Father feeds them. And you are far more valuable to him than they are. Can all your worries add a single moment to your life? Of course not. And why worry about your clothes? Look at the lilies and how they grow. They don't work or make their clothing, yet Solomon in all his glory was not dressed as beautifully as they are. And if God cares so wonderfully for flowers that are here today and gone tomorrow, won't he more surely care for you?" (Mt. 6:26-29)

"Now faith is being sure of what we hope for and certain of what we do not see." (Heb.11:1)

"And we know that in all things God works for the good of those who love him…" (Ro. 8:28)

"Blessed is the man who does not walk in the counsel of the wicked or stand in the way of sinner or sit in the seat of mockers. But his delight is in the law of the Lord, and on his law he meditates day and night. He is like a tree planted by streams of water, which yields its fruit in season and whose leaf does not wither. Whatever he does prospers." (Ps. 1:1-3)

"You will keep in perfect peace him whose mind is steadfast, because he trusts in you." (Isaiah 26:3)

"Have faith in God," Jesus answered. "I tell you the truth, if anyone says to this mountain, 'Go, throw yourself into the sea,' and does not doubt in his heart but believes that what he says will happen, it will be done for him. Therefore I tell you, whatever you ask for in prayer, believe that you have received it, and it will be yours." (Mk. 11:22-24)

"Then they cried to the Lord in their trouble, and he saved them from their distress. He sent forth his word and healed them; he rescued them from the grave. Let them give thanks to the Lord for his unfailing love and his wonderful deeds for men." (Ps. 107:19-21)

"But we have this treasure in jars of clay to show that this all-surpassing power is from God and not from us. We are hard pressed on every side, but not crushed; perplexed, but not in despair; persecuted, but not abandoned; struck down, but not destroyed." (2 Cor.4:7-9)

"When Jesus landed and saw a large crowd, he had compassion on them and healed their sick." (Mt. 14:14)

"He himself bore our sins in his body on the tree, so that we might die to sins and live for righteousness; by his wounds you have been healed." (1 Pe. 2:24)

"Surely he took up our infirmities and carried our sorrows, yet we considered him stricken by God, smitten by him, and afflicted. But he was pierced for our transgressions, he was crushed for our iniquities; the punishment that brought us peace was upon him, and by his wounds we are healed." (Is. 53:4,5)

"When evening came, many who were demon-possessed were brought to him, and he drove out the spirits with a word and healed all the sick. This was to fulfill what was spoken through the prophet Isaiah: "He took up our infirmities and carried our diseases." (Mt. 8:16,17)

"Worship the Lord your God, and his blessing will be on your food and water. I will take away sickness form among you, and none will miscarry or be barren in your land. I will give you a full life span." (Ex. 23:25)

184

"Are not five sparrows sold for two pennies? Yet not one of them is forgotten by God. Indeed, the very hairs of your head are all numbered. Don't be afraid you are worth more than many sparrows." (Lk. 12:6,7)

"The apostles performed many miraculous signs and wonders among the people...as a result, people brought the sick into the streets and laid them on beds and mats...crowds gathered also from the towns around Jerusalem, bringing their sick and those tormented by evil spirits, and all of them were healed." (Ac 5: 12-16)

"This is the confidence we have in approaching God: that if we ask anything according to his will, he hears us. And if we know that he hears us - whatever we ask - we know that we have what we asked of him." (1 John 5:14)

"The Spirit helps us in our weakness. We do not know what we ought to pray for, but the Spirit intercedes for us with groans that words cannot express." (Romans 8:26)

"Then Jesus said, "Come to me, all of you who are weary and carry heavy burdens, and I will give you rest." (Mt.11:28)

"And we know that in all things God works for the good of those who love him, who have been called according to his purpose. If God is for us, who can be against us? He who did not spare his own Son, but gave him up for us all - how will he not also, along with him, graciously give us all things? Who shall separate us from the love of Christ? Shall trouble or hardship or persecution or famine or nakedness or danger or sword? No, in all these things we are more than conquerors through him who loved us. For I am convinced that neither death nor life, neither angels nor demons, neither the present nor the future, not any powers, neither height nor depth, not anything else in all creation, will be able to separate us from the love of God that is in Christ Jesus our Lord." (Romans 8: 28)

"The Lord is close to the brokenhearted; he rescues those who are crushed in spirit." (Ps.34:18)

"If I speak in the tongues of men and of angels, but have not love, I am only a resounding gong or a clanging cymbal. If I have the gift of prophecy and can fathom all mysteries and all knowledge, and if I have a faith that can move mountains, but have not love, I am nothing. If I give all I possess to the poor and surrender my body to the flames, but have not love, I gain nothing. Love is patient, love is kind, it does not envy, it does not boast, it is not proud, it is not rude, it is not self-seeking, it is not easily angered, it keeps no record of wrongs. Love does not delight in evil but rejoices with the truth. It always protects, always trusts, always hopes, always perseveres. Love

185

never fails…And now these three remain, faith, hope and love. But the greatest of these is love." (1 Cor.13)

"Suddenly, a man with leprosy approached Jesus. He knelt before him, worshiping. "Lord," the man said, "if you want to, you can make me well again." Jesus touched him. "I want to," he said. "Be healed" And instantly the leprosy disappeared." (Mt 8:2,3)

"Submit therefore to God. Resist the devil and He will flee from you." (James 4:7)

"He rescues and saves his people; he performs miraculous signs and wonders in the heavens and on earth. He has rescued Daniel from the power of the lions." (Daniel 6:27)

"Who can forget the wonders he performs? How gracious and merciful is our Lord!" (Ps.111:4)

"Praise the Lord, I tell myself, and never forget the good things he does for me. He forgives all my sins and heals all my diseases. He ransoms me from death and surrounds me with love and tender mercies. He fills my life with good things. My youth is renewed like the eagle's!" (Ps. 103 2-5)

"Then Jesus said, "Come to me, all of you who are weary and carry heavy burdens, and I will give you rest." (Mt.11:28)

"He gives strength to the weary and increases the power of the weak. Even youths grow tired and weary, and young men stumble and fall; but those who hope in the Lord will renew their strength. They will soar on wings like eagles, they will run and not grow faint." (Is. 40:29-31)

"Even when I walk through the dark valley of death, I will not be afraid, for you are close beside me." (Ps. 23:4)

"The Lord is close to the brokenhearted; he rescues those who are crushed in spirit." (Ps.34:18)

"He heals the brokenhearted, binding up their wounds." (Ps. 147: 3)

"I waited patiently for the Lord to help me, and he turned to me and heard my cry. He lifted me out of the pit of despair, out of the mud and the mire. He set my feet on solid ground and steadied me as I walked along. He has given me a new song to sing, a hymn of praise to our God. Many will see what he has done and be astounded. They will put their trust in the Lord."(Ps. 40:1-3)

Prayers

Thanks for the Earth

We give you thanks, most gracious God, for the beauty of earth and sky and sea; for the richness of mountains, plains, and rivers; for the songs of birds and the loveliness of flowers. We praise you for these good gifts and pray that we may safeguard them for our posterity. Grant that we may continue to grow in our grateful enjoyment of your abundant creation, to the honor and glory of your name, now and forever. Amen.
- Book of Common Prayer

Worry

Teach me, good Lord:
Not to murmur at the multitude of business and the shortness of time.
Not to magnify undertaken duties by seeming to suffer under them,
but to treat them all as liberties.
Not to call attention to crowded work, or petty fatigues.
Not to gather encouragement from appreciation by others,
lest this should interfere with the purity of my motives.
Not to seek praise, respect, gratitude, or regard from others.
Not to let myself be placed in favorable contrast with another.
- Edward White Benson (1829 -1896)

Sickness

Lord, teach me the art of patience while I am well, and give me the use of it when I am sick. In that day either lighten my burden or strengthen my back. Make me, who so often in my health have discovered my weakness presuming on my own strength, to be strong in my sickness when I solely rely on your assistance.
- Thomas Fuller (1608 -1661)

Dear Father, I thank you for loving us. Thank you for desiring to touch us, and bringing out of the invisible realms the tangible manifestations of signs and wonders, and healing us physically, emotionally and spiritually. May we constantly live in an undertone of prayer as we continue to desperately seek your face. Help us to hear Jesus' message of love and gratitude, and seek the kingdom constantly, as we come before you by grace. Remind us always that the true miracle is that of salvation, and the body is but a temporary vessel that you have given us to be used in accord with your will of

loving you, loving ourselves, and loving one another on this spiritual journey. Thank you Yahweh, Jehovah, Almighty Father, our Alpha and Omega, for loving us, when we didn't even know how to love ourselves; help us to be a reflection of your love, and strive to light the candles of others or to fan their flames if they are growing dim. I give my heart to you, as I desperately seek yours; may my hands be your hands, my life yours, to guide forever and ever. With the covering of the Blood of Jesus I pray. Amen.
- Tiffany Snow (1962 -?)

Come creator Spirit, visit the souls of your people; fill with the grace of heaven the hearts that you have made. You who are called friend to us, gift of the most high God, the spring of life, of fire, of love, the anointing of the soul…Kindle your light for our senses, pour love into our hearts, make strong our bodies' weakness with your unfailing strength…Through you may we know God our Father and learn to know his Son; and you, the Spirit of them both, may we believe always.
- Veni Creator Spiritus, Saint Benedict's Prayer Book

Family Wholeness

Father, grant to us true family love, that we may belong more entirely to those whom you have given us, understanding each other, day by day, more instinctively, forbearing each other, day by day, more patiently, growing, day by day, more closely into oneness with each other. - Anonymous

Peace

Lord, make me an instrument of your peace, where there is hatred, let me plant love; where there is injury, pardon; where there is doubt, faith; where there is despair, hope; where there is darkness, light; where there is sadness, joy. Oh, Divine Master, may I not so much seek to be consoled as to console; to be understood as to understand; to be loved as to love. For, it is in giving that we receive; it is in pardoning that we are pardoned; it is in dying that we are born to eternal life.
- St. Francis of Assisi (1182 - 1226)

I embrace God's establishment in my heart and soul. I willingly subject myself to the wisdom and will of God for the individual and collective flourishing of our world.
- Lucy Elizabeth Larson

Guidance & Protection

Help me today to realize that you will be speaking to me through the events of the day, through people, through things, and through creation. Give me ears, eyes and heart to

perceive you, however veiled your presence may be. Give me insight to see through the exterior of things to the interior truth. Give me you Spirit of discernment. O Lord, you know how busy I must be this day. If I forget you, do not forget me.
- *God's Presence in My World* by Jacob Astley (1579-1652)

Bless all who worship you, from the rising of the sun unto the going down of the same. Of your goodness, give us; with your love, inspire us; by your Spirit, guide us; by your power, protect us; in your mercy, receive us now and always. - Anonymous

Grant me, O Lord, to know that which is worth knowing, to love that which is worth loving, to praise that which pleases you most, and to esteem highly that which is precious to you. Amen.
- Thomas Kempis (1379 -1471)

Grant us, we pray, almighty and most merciful God, fervently to desire, wisely to search out, and perfectly to fulfill all that is well-pleasing to you this day. Order our worldly condition to the glory of your Name; and, of all that you require us to do, grant us the knowledge, the desire, and the ability, that we may so fulfill it as we ought; and may our path to you, we pray, be safe, straightforward, and perfect to the end.
- Thomas Aquinas (1225 -1274)

Humility

Teach me, good Lord: Not to murmur at the multitude of business and the shortness of time. Not to magnify undertaken duties by seeming to suffer under them, but to treat them all as liberties. Not to call attention to crowded work, or petty fatigues. Not to gather encouragement from appreciation by others, lest this should interfere with the purity of my motives. Not to seek praise, respect, gratitude, or regard from others. Not to let myself be placed in favorable contrast with another.
- Edward White Benson (1829 -1896)

Almighty God, you have made all things for us, and us for your glory. Sanctify our body and soul, our thoughts and our intentions, our words and actions, that whatsoever we shall think, or speak, or do, may by us be designed for the glorification of your name. And let no pride or self-seeking, no impure motive or unworthy praise, no little ends or low imagination stain our spirit, or profane any of our words and actions. But let our body be a servant to our spirit, and both body and spirit servants of Jesus Christ.
- Thomas Kempis (1380 -1471)

Self-Worth

O eternal and most glorious God, you who assure us that precious in your sight is the death of your saints, enable us in life and death, seriously to consider the value, the price of a soul. It is precious, O Lord, because your image is stamped and imprinted upon it; precious, because the blood of your Son was paid for it; precious, because your blessed Spirit, the Holy Ghost, works upon it and tests it by his various fires; and precious, because it is entered into your revenue and made part of your treasure.
- John Donne (1572 -1631)

Wisdom

Grant me, O Lord, to know that which is worth knowing, to love that which is worth loving, to praise that which pleases you most, and to esteem highly that which is precious to you. Amen.
- Thomas Kempis (1379 -1471)

O God, our great Companion, you are the light of minds that know you, the life of souls that love you, and the strength of wills that serve you: Help us so to know you that we may truly love you, so to love you that we may fully serve you, who to serve is perfect freedom; through Jesus Christ our Lord. Amen.
- Forward Movement

Seeking God

O Lord my God, teach my heart this day where and how to see you, where and how to find you. You have made me and remade me, and you have bestowed on me all the good things I possess, and still I do not know you. I have not yet done that for which I was made. Teach me to seek you, for I cannot seek you unless you teach me, or find you unless you show yourself to me. Let me seek you in my desire, let me desire you in my seeking. Let me find you by loving you, let me love you when I find you.
- Saint Anselm (1022 -1109)

O Lord, help us to turn and seek you; for you have not forsaken your creatures as we have forsaken you, our Creator. Let us turn and seek you, for we know you are here in our heart when we confess to you, when we cast ourselves upon you and weep in your bosom after all our rugged ways; and you gently wipe away our tears, and we weep more for joy; for you, Lord, who made us, do remake and comfort us.
- Saint Augustine (354 - 430)

O God, before whose face the generations rise and pass away: Age after age the living seek you and find that there is no end to your faithfulness. Our forbears in their pilgrimages walked by your guidance and rested on your compassion. To their children you were the cloud by day and the pillar by night. Where but in you have we shelter from the storm and shadow, from the heat of life? Take now the veil from every heart, and join us in one communion with your prophets and saints who have trusted in you and were not ashamed. Not because we merit it, but because of your mercy, hear our prayer. - Anonymous Traditional Prayer

Faith

O Almighty God, when our vision fails and our understanding is darkened, when the ways of life seem hard and brightness of life is gone, grant to us the wisdom that deepens faith and enlarges trust. And whenever the ways in nature or in the soul are hard to understand, then may our quiet confidence, our patient trust, our living faith in you be great...May we with a quiet mind at all times put our trust in you. Amen.
- Harold Vincent Milligan

Give me, O Lord, a steadfast heart which no unworthy thought can drag downwards; an unconquered hear which no tribulation can wear out; an upright heart which no unworthy purpose may tempt aside. Give me also, O Lord my God, understanding to know you, diligence to seek you, wisdom to find you, and a faithfulness that may finally embrace you through Jesus Christ, our Lord.
- Saint Thomas Aquinas (1225-1274)

Joy

As the hand is made for holding and the eye for seeing, you have fashioned me for joy. Share with me the vision that shall find it everywhere: in the wild violet's beauty; in the lark's melody; in the face of a steadfast man; in a child's smile; in a mother's love; in the purity of Jesus.
- Gaelic prayer

Lord, make me an instrument of your peace: where there is hatred let me sow peace, where there is injury let me sow pardon, where there is doubt let me sow faith, where there is despair let me give hope, where there is sadness let me give joy. O Divine Master, grant that I may not try to be comforted but to comfort, not try to understood but to understand, not try to be loved but to love. Because it is in giving that we receive, it is in forgiving that we are forgiven, and it is in dying that we are born to eternal life.
- Saint Francis of Assisi (1182-1226)

191

Stress

O God, my God, give me a heart to thank you. Lift up my heart above myself, to you and your eternal throne. Let it not linger here among the hardships and turmoil of this lower world. Let it not be oppressed by any earth-born clouds of care or anxiety or fear or suspicion. Bind my heart wholly to you and to your love. Give me eyes to see your love in all things and your grace in all that surrounds me. Help me to thank you for your love and your grace to all and in all. Give me wings of love that I may soar up to you, cling to you, adore you, and praise you more and more, until I am prepared to enter into the joys of your everlasting love. Amen.
- Edward Pusey (1800 -1882)

Patience

We resign into your hands our sleeping bodies, our cold hearths, and open doors. Give us to awaken with smiles; give us to labor smiling. As the sun returns in the east, so let our patience be renewed with dawn; as the sun lightens the world, so let our loving-kindness make bright this house of our habitation. Amen.
- Robert Louis Stevenson (1850 -1894)

I need you to teach me day by day, according to each day's opportunities and needs. Give me, O my Lord, that purity of conscience which alone can receive, which alone can improve your inspiration. My ears are dull, so that I cannot hear your voice. My eyes are dim, so that I cannot see your gifts. You alone can quicken my hearing, and purge my sight, and cleanse and renew my heart. Teach me to sit at your feet and to hear your Word. Amen.
- John Henry Newman (1801-1890)

Fighting Dark Forces

God, of your goodness, give me yourself, for you are enough for me. I can ask for nothing less that is completely to your honor, and if I do ask anything less, I shall always be in want, only in you I have all.
- Juliana of Norwich (c.1342 - c.1413)

A Sinner's Prayer

Lord Jesus, I'm tired of trusting in myself. My Free Will desire is to trust in you. I am a sinner, and I know that I have sinned. I am sorry for all my sins. Please forgive me. I ask you to come into my life and live within me, and be my guidance forever. I recognize the Blood of the Lamb, and how it was poured out as a ransom sacrifice for

my sins. You are my Lord and Savior. Give me eyes and discernment to recognize and turn away from everything sinful. Help me to hear and obey you for the rest of my life. Father, I know and have faith that now all my sins are forgotten and forgiven, they have been nailed to the cross, and you have accepted me as your son/daughter. Thank you for loving me. Thank you Jesus. Amen.
- Tiffany Snow (1962 - ?)

Worship

God, you are with me and you can help me. You were with me when I was taken, and you are with me now. You strengthen me. The God I serve is everywhere - in heaven and earth and the sea, but he is above them all, for all live in him: All were created by him, and by him only do they remain. I will worship only the true God; you will I carry in my heart; no one on earth shall be able to separate me from you.
- Quirinius of Siscia (d. 308)

Purity

Almighty God, you have made all things for us, and us for your glory. Sanctify our body and soul, our thoughts and our intentions, our words and actions, that whatsoever we shall think, or speak, or do, may by us be designed for the glorification of your name. And let no pride or self-seeking, no impure motive or unworthy praise, no little ends or low imagination stain our spirit, or profane any of our words and actions. But let our body be a servant to our spirit, and both body and spirit servants of Jesus Christ.
-Thomas Kempis (1380 -1471)

Humility

Lord, forgive me that when life's circumstances lift me to the crest of the wave, I tend to forget Thee. Yet, like an errant child, I have blamed Thee with my every failure, even as I credit myself with every success. When my fears evaporate like the morning mist, then vainly I imagine that I am sufficient unto myself, that material resources and human resources are enough. I need Thee when the sun shines, lest I forget the storm and the dark. I need Thee when I am popular, when my friends and those who work beside me approve and compliment me. I need Thee more then, lest my head begin to swell. O God, forgive me for my stupidity, my blindness in success, my lack of trust in Thee. Be Thou now my Savior in success. Save me from conceit. Save me from pettiness. Save me from myself! And take this success, I pray, and use it for Thy glory. In Thy strength, I pray. Amen.
- Peter Marshall (1902 -1949)

Confidence

Give us, O Lord, a steadfast heart, which no unworthy affection may drag downward; give us an unconquered heart, which no tribulation can wear out; give us an upright heart, which no unworthy purpose may tempt aside. Bestow upon us also, O Lord our God, understanding to know you, diligence to seek you, wisdom to find you, and a faithfulness that may finally embrace you; through Jesus Christ our Lord. Amen.
- Thomas Aquinas (1225 -1274)

Offering Your Own Expressions of Love through Songs, Poems and Prayers

Writing *songs, poems and prayers* to God is a good way to express your love, abundant gratitude and desire for his Spirit in your life. It does not matter if you feel you are "any good at it" or not – however you are moved to express your gifts of love will make the Father smile. The outpouring of our hearts is like sweet-smelling incense gathered up to the nostrils of our Lord. Especially in times of trauma, we need to continue to keep the lines of communication open, so we may hear the whispers of God amidst the noisy turmoil. Here are a few that I have written that have helped me along the way, simple trust and love is all he asks from us. That alone is an inspiration to put words on paper, and in the air! Whatever your personal gifts are, use them in expressing the uniqueness of you! Everything you dedicate to God or in his service to mankind is praise and glory to his name; whether it is a garden, artwork, or a simple flower arrangement. Be Creative! Be Blessed!

Daily Prayer for Praise & Protection

Dear Father, I ask you to protect me and each of my family members
from sickness, from all harm and from accidents.
If any of us has been subjected to any curses, hexes,
or spells, null and void them in the name of your son Jesus Christ.
As your humble worker in the forefront of battle,
I pray for Supernatural physical, emotional and spiritual Strength
to Fight the fine fight of the Faith, ever listening to Your commands.

Listen - oh evil spirits sent against us - to the authority
granted Christians by Holy Spirit.
I decommission and bind you in the Name of Jesus
and I send you to the Presence of God,
to deal with as He sees fit. You have no authority over me.

Jehovah Rophe (my healer), I ask You to send Your Holy Angels
as my constant Impenetrable Shield,
to give me the peace I need to accomplish Your Will.
Fill all empty places around me and in me,
with Your All-Encompassing and Powerful Love.

May Your Name be lifted up above all others,
may Your Kingdom come upon the earth, as it is in heaven.
You are Jehovah Jireh (my provider), Thank You
for giving me what I need each day for maintaining life,
and forgive me where I have failed You and My True Self,
as I strive to understand and implement my lessons of Total Forgiveness for others.

Guide, protect, cleanse and deliver me
from the machinations of the rebellious one and his fallen angels.
Give me Faith Beyond Reason, and Divine Ability to be a clean channel
for Your Healing Love, so others may recognize Your True Nature,
and Glorify You.
I choose by Free Will to walk hand-in-hand with You,
in fulfilling Your Will for my life.

I ask to clearly hear, see, and feel when You
or your True Messengers connect with me.
Give me Boldness Without Restraint to speak the words you place in my mouth.
Sanctify me, cleanse me, train me, and choose me, for the Mighty Work to be done.
My hands are Your Hands, my arms Your Arms, my heart Your Heart
- I give it to You -
as I forever seek in desperate passion with deep longing, Your Own Heart.

I Love You, Abba Almighty, Thank You for Loving Me.
With all honor and respect, I recognize the name and sacrifice

of your Son Jesus Christ who opened the Way of Grace and
Enlightenment for mankind.
May Your Name be Praised throughout all Creation,
May Your Will Be Done Forever Without End.
For all of Eternity, I will know You as the One True Lover of my Soul.
So Be It,
Amen.

POEM

You Brought Me to the Desert
(so my roots could grow deeper)
Written in New Mexico while Healing in the Isleta Pueblo Reservation

The valley entered my heart with a vision - "understand what you know."
The petroglyphts entered my mind with urgency - "this is the language you know."
The people entered my soul with overflowing thanks
for God to touch their minds, spirit and bodies.
The yearning to help is strong - my eyes cry with their pain, and I call out to God.
I want to fix it all. This is not God's will. He knows what is best.
"Abba, Father, Help Me to Understand."

This person he helps, this person he does not.
This work is his. This work he directs.
This is *not* a work whose main focus is the outside body.
This work is for healing of the spirit *first.*
Everything has a season - a seed cannot be forced to grow faster.
The Great One will shine his warmth and moisten the earth in turn,
Each at its own time, the time that is right.
As the small plant uncurls its first leaves, and then its second, and its third -
the kind of plant it will be is made known.

Some will be flowers, other wheat, others weeds.
Everything has a purpose - will we succeed in rocky soil?
Yes, if our roots go deep enough.
Down through the crevice, down through the sand,
the search is hard, but the water is there.

The water is a Promise.
The Promise is his Power and Enduring Love.
I drink freely, and he replenishes me.
I share the cup with all who come, and the cup overflows.
He makes new all things, as the dry leaves uncurl.
To some it will be just cool water,
to others a vibration of life that quenches to the toes.
Sometimes healing the memories.
Sometimes healing the body.
Always fulfilling his purpose.

196

And I wait on him, and the roots grow deeper, anchoring me to the stone.
And the wind will blow, and the sun will parch, but his Promise stays true.
And the refreshing water is always there, just under the surface. *Always there.*

"Understand what I know," the vision unfolding, see the seasons of God.
"Understand the language," the tongue a soothing salve, bringing the heart to God.
The soul overflowing, "thank you, thank you, thank you Great Father."
You brought me to the desert so my roots could reach deeper.
I praise you in the dry wind. I give you my life.
The vision becomes clear and strong.
The dust flies away.
And You are what I see.

POEM

Like a Little Child
Who does not know
What is right to do,
We'll grow up straight
In your Holy Place
By paying attention
To You!

POEM

I will not shake with fear
When I feel pain is near,
I will not doubt
God's will to heal.
I will not turn aside
Lower my head and hide
For I know I abide
With the God that's real.

197

POEM

I am a moon
He is the sun,
I just reflect his light
My universe revolves around him.

SONGS

*Here are a few songs that help me become more in a mindset for receiving love
and for giving love and gratitude back in praise and worship. I invite you to write
your own poems, songs and prayers too.*

*As David said in the Psalms:
"I will Praise God's name in song
and glorify him with thanksgiving." (69:30)*

Be Healed!
Tiffany Snow ® 2004 SnowCat Music

(1). It's only in the darkness that we dream,
Seek out His guiding light,
believe in things unseen.
It's only when we're broken that we yield,
then He reaches out to save us,
and Be Healed, Be Healed!

(C). "Be Healed!" Our Father calls to us!
"Be Healed, and let me lift you up!
Trust in me, and faithfully yield -
and I will touch you,
and I will keep you,
and I will love you,
and you'll Be Healed…Be Healed!"

(2). God can heal us everywhere it hurts,
He pours out fresh water,
and cleans up all the dirt.
Painful weeds grow with us in the field,

but He reaches out to save us,
and Be Healed, Be Healed!
Be Healed, Be Healed! (C)

All Divine Grace
Tiffany Snow ® 2004 SnowCat Music

(1).You who knows my soul
Who's seen me out of control,
whose precious things I stole…from You.
You who knows my heart
and all my stops and starts,
the times I depart…from You.

(C). Thank You, Thank You!
The Blood of the Lamb
cleans up my hands,
washes the sin off my face -
Beside me you stand, the Great "I AM,"
Father of ALL DIVINE GRACE!
Thank You, Thank You!
Father of ALL DIVINE GRACE!

(2).You who know my dreams,
nothing more than schemes,
and the things I never seem…to do.
You who knows I love,
then fearfully turn from,
who says I will, then won't…to You. (C)

Closer
Tiffany Snow ® 2004 SnowCat Music

(1). Yesterday was worlds away,
from far away I'm come, Closer.
In His hand, at His command,
from far away I'm come, Closer.
By Grace, He forgives.
And every day we'll live - Closer!

199

(2).Mighty God knows the very hour,
to heal and empower, Come Closer.
Give prayer, sacred song and praise,
at night, and all thru the day, Come Closer.
Letting go, He forgives.
Every day to live - Closer!

(C). Closer, Closer, Closer, Here I Am!
Closer, Closer, Closer, Here You Are!

(4).Yesterday was worlds away,
Never far away, You've Come - Closer.
In Your hand, at Your command,
Never far away, You've Come - Closer.
Letting go, I am His.
Eternity to live - so much Closer! (C)

Love, Love, Love

Tiffany Snow ® 2004 SnowCat Music

(1). An eagle perched high believes in grace,
She leaps off the cliffs to the wind's embrace.
No fear in believing what can't be seen,
No black or white questions, no gray in-between.

(C). Have you never heard the voice inside you,
Have you never felt an angel beside you,
Have you never seen God's hand guide you?
The God of Love is singing to your heart!
And He sings; "Love, Love - Love each other,
Love, Love - all men are brothers.
Love, Love - love one another,
Just as I Have Always Loved You."

(3). Breezes dance by, so fresh and cool,
It laughs with the aspen, it ripples the pool.
Though we can't see Him, like gravity and air,
The Love that He shows can be felt everywhere. (C)

My Soul Loving You!

Tiffany Snow ® 2004 SnowCat Music

(1). For so long I was forsaken,
driven by the dark.
Now I'm a new creation
inside salvation's ark!

(C). Oh Dear Lord, look what you've done to me!
With fainting bliss, I'm down on my knees.
Heart overflows, my eyes do too.
I feel Your Spirit inside - My Soul Loving You!
I feel Your Spirit inside - My Soul Loving You!

(2).My friends all think I'm crazy,
and I know it's true!
And I'm the one who's praying
They'll be Blessed this "crazy" too!
Now my heart is open, my soul believes!
No longer torn in confusion, or deceived! (C)

Spirit Come, Spirit Flow!

Tiffany Snow ® 2004 SnowCat Music

(1). Spirit Come, Spirit Flow!
Spirit never, never go.
Like warm honey on my soul,
let it flow, let it flow!

(2). Spirit Come, Spirit Flow!
Spirit never, never go.
Your healing makes me whole,
let it flow, let it flow!

(3). Spirit Come, Spirit Flow!
Spirit never, never go.
Your love, I well know,
let it flow, let it flow! (repeat all)

When I Pray

Tiffany Snow ® 2004 SnowCat Music

(1). When I Pray with my eyes closed,
I can almost see your face.
I feel the warmth of your embrace, when I Pray.

(2). When I Pray and I'm alone,
my fears you all replace.
You bring me to a peaceful place, when I Pray.

(C) When I Pray, When I Pray,
When I Pray you hear me.
Oh my Lord, what can compare
to the Holy gift of prayer?
Your ears are everywhere and you hear me…When I Pray!

(3).When I Pray and I'm not well,
I can feel my strength regain.
I have hope and joy again, when I Pray.

(4). When I Pray to clearly see,
your perfect path and will for me.
Your answer comes so easily,
When I Pray. (C)

And the Lord said,
"Until now you have not asked
for anything in my name.
Ask and you will receive,
and your joy
will be complete."
(Jn.16:24)

CHAPTER 10

Questions & Answers
What You Always Wanted to Know,
But Didn't Know How to Ask!

What is the Difference between Spiritual & Divine Healing?

Spiritual healing can be Reiki, Therapeutic Touch®, Qigong, Quantum Healing, etc. Spiritual healing has come to mean a variety of methods which may employ some sort of spiritual aspect with the healing, but may or may not include prayer. Also, the person healing may or may not be including his *own* energy in with the healing. *Divine Healing always* includes prayer, cannot activate without it, and healing is *never* done by including any of the person's own energy. It often includes some version of hands-on-healing or "laying-on-of-hands."

A person may, such as I, be certified as a Reiki Practitioner, yet do Divine Healing. I always include Connection in prayer before I begin, cannot do a healing without it, and then I proceed to get myself out of the way so the Big Guy can work. Reiki allows me to easily work in the clinics under CAM, and prayer allows me to facilitate the best healings possible. These Supernatural healings tap into Power beyond our own capabilities, and are far beyond just speeding up the body's own natural recuperation times, as may be seen typically in spiritual healing. *Miracles* can and do occur. The invisible may become manifest in our physical world, beyond the scope of our known perception of reality. The difference might be compared to using a battery with stored energy, as compared to live current. AC versus DC. Both use energy; either their own or Someone else's. But which is more powerful? Which one would you choose to work on you?

Will the Healings Be Immediate or Gradual?

Both can happen. Do not limit what may occur. Also, be persistent! *Orare est laborare, laborare est orare* – "to pray is to work, to work is to pray" (ancient motto of the Benedictine order). In most cases, healings will happen over a period of time, sometimes beginning with a single prayer, and more often with a course of several over a period of days or weeks. Over all, it seems that healing is like Divine radiation therapy - the longer the sickness is held in the force-field of God's love, the more it shrinks, until it finally disappears! And, just because improvement seems to be slow at one time, does not mean it will be that way the next. And as I said before, always be open for immediate healings to occur. Remember one of my favorite sayings? Be

Realistic...*Expect Miracles*!

Can Only Christians Pray for Healing?

No. But, in my experience, it certainly helps. We as humans are made in the likeness of God and are *all born* with an amount of ability to heal. And through the years I have noticed that there are many people who have stimulated this small amount of natural ability into a larger_amount - many of these have spent years focusing love through their hands in one matter or another; whether as a musician, artist, florist, animal handler, surgeon, massage therapist, etc. They have widened the natural channels we were *all* created with. *Natural* healing is Love. Divine healing is *Supernatural* Love, complete with a vast amount of miracles and immediate healings. *There is a difference in the results.* I have only seen "falling down in the Spirit" in the Christian churches, with Christ-centered prayer. But, keep in mind that God is Love, (1 Jn. 4:8) and prayer is love, so *any* prayer that is prayed in love will have God's Power in it, *no matter what the spiritual view!*

How Does this Work?

Once, I had a physicist on the table, who felt he knew how this Connection works. He said, "Everything in nature wants to remain whole; even at a cellular level - if one cell doesn't have what it needs, it takes from its neighbor so that it itself, can be complete. Somehow, I think in what you do, you create the ability for this to happen, for the cells to take what they need to be whole." It seems to me that the Holy Spirit bathes all the individual cells with a "cosmic energy soup," stimulating recuperation time and promoting "cell memory" of how the original cell structure was made. There certainly are a lot of changes that happen. Who can know exactly how the process occurs? I'm just glad, as are thousands of other people...that it does! "For I know the plans I have for you," declares the Lord, "plans to prosper you and not to harm you, plans to give you hope and a future." (Jer. 29:11)

Why Do Your Hands Get Hot, Why the Vibration?

Heat is a by-product of work being done, and I may stay in one place for three minutes, or 20, depending on the need. My hands will cool down when the spot is done, and it is time to move on to another. In my case, I also have "God-sonar" or what is often called "medical intuitiveness," which lets me "see" even deeper into what is going on. And often, a vibration will occur over a more difficult injury, or over a place that seems to be a good access point to another place that needs healing in the body. When a vibration occurs - which means I'm "really plugged in to the 220," I know that the deepest healing is occurring, and I keep my hands there until all the vibration is gone. It comes in waves, or oscillations, and I stay there until the vibration slows down and stops, the heat also leaves, and the place cools down. If I have a place that does not want to cool down, I may leave it to see what else is going on in other places of the body, and then return to it later. By using heat, The Big Guy can also let a person know where to go, and when to move on, without medical intuitiveness being necessary at all.

What Does A Hands-On-Healing Feel Like?

A hands-on-healing treatment feels like a wonderful glowing radiance that flows through and around you, similar to warm honey flowing from the top of your head down through your legs to your feet. The clients will be asked to slip off their shoes, and be invited to lie down on the table, face up. I suggest leaving jewelry at home, and to take off any metal objects (belt buckles, bracelets, etc) since it can disrupt the energy around that area, making it harder for me to sense what is going on there (gold seems to be the exception, it conducts Energy very well – its just a distraction to the medical intuitiveness). I place a bolster under the knees, to help relieve strain on the lower back. *There is no disrobing of any kind.*

Before I begin, I explain a bit about the process, including the hot hands and possible vibrations. I answer any questions, and give the option for the client to state why they came. If they elect not to (as is sometimes the case in emotional healing), no worries! The healing will occur just the same, whether I know about it or not. The Holy Spirit is like aspirin; it goes to where it's needed! Also, the Big Guy will probably let me see anyway, especially if it is something he needs me to address; for example, an issue or blockage on some level that will aid in healing so full wholeness can occur.

Does the Process of Healing Continue After I Leave?

Yes, after the healing is initially finished, the Spirit's energy is still in the body for several days, *continuing the process of healing.* It is similar to unplugging a fan out of the wall; just like fan blades which continue to spin, taking them a while to slow down and stop. I always encourage drinking a lot of water through this time - there is a lot of cleansing out and changing at a cellular level, and the body needs to flush it out. Also, I suggest for this duration, to avoid alcohol, and deep-fried or heavily oiled foods. It seems to slow the Spirit down in the body. People often feel very peaceful and relaxed, as all the Wonderful Energy of God touching them leaves a lovely residual effect! If they are dizzy, I have them walk around a bit before driving home. They usually report sleeping very well that night, and awakening refreshed, lighter, and feeling better in many ways.

205

Why Do I Fall Asleep on the Table?

Sometimes clients will immediately fall asleep on the table - another way for Holy Spirit to move without restriction beyond the "I wonder if this is working" phase. Sometimes it happens so fast that I know it's the same thing that I see when healing in the churches, an action of "falling by the Spirit" or "slain in the Spirit," where The Big Guy knocks people out so he can heal them quickly and without interference, bypassing the analytical brain. At other times, the sleep appears to be just a progressive slumber that occurs from being in a comfortable setting, a natural sleep. Either way, the circuits being bypassed allows for the best possible healing to occur.

How Does the One Facilitated for Healing Feel?

The one facilitated for the healing will also feel the Glow - for me it starts at the top of the head, a feeling of effervescent warmth and sparkle, then slowly descends down through the rest of my body. It is always accompanied by a feeling of peace and bliss – it's that feeling of communion that I live for! I find that if even a couple of days go by and I haven't yet been utilized for a healing, that I'll become anxious. I need my "fix!" Working for the Supreme One is the best addiction in the world! The healings make me feel peaceful, calm, and as warm as stepping out of a hot Jacuzzi. I also receive a healing too, every time, and feel totally embraced by love. Who wouldn't want that 24-7!

Another of the many "perks" of working so closely with the Almighty is a *feeling of being connected to all living things* - I seem to know where every bird and squirrel is in the trees, where every bunny is under the bushes! Colors themselves seem to be brighter, and hearing and smelling more intense. A sense of *well-being* and *peace beyond words* descends upon me, and at night, *truly blissful sleep* comes from knowing that I am fulfilling the true purpose for my life, in service to others. And I know it makes The Big Guy smile.

How Do I Feel the Love Necessary for Healing Complete Strangers?

There will be a time in your life, if you choose to spiritually progress, that this *will not* be a problem, and you will genuinely feel deep love for *every* person you meet, always seeing the Divine Spark within, and the great possibilities ahead for them. Even the most hardened of criminals will feel like your own son! In the meantime, you might try this: remember a deeply moving incident in your life that made you feel great joy and love, and use that memory as the catalyst, then spread that love to others.

Why Does God Need A Mediator for Healing?

He doesn't. We know *he can go direct* by Divine Prayer, without any "middle man," and he *often* does! We see that whenever we approach him when we are by ourselves in our room, our car, or outside. He doesn't need a mass of flesh and bones to yield himself to him as His Hands to work on others. So why does he use "healers?" Simply because of this - he is a good, loving father who wants all of his kids to *work together, love each other and to learn to get along!* It's the same as when he decided that male and female should come together to create a child. He actively wants us to *interact together* for the common good and to help and encourage one another. He doesn't *need* to use us at all, but he does, because he just wants to, it's for the Highest Good of humankind, and a visible touch-stone to faith.

But I'm No One Great, How Do I Feel Worthy Enough to Pray?

Moses was a murderer and a stutterer, yet God forgave him, refined him, and used him to free the Israelites from Egypt. He did this through many miracles and manifestations of power, including numerous plagues and parting the Red Sea. King David was an adulterer and murderer, yet he was forgiven and anointed by God to be a great King, ancestor of Jesus, and the writer of one of the most popular books of the Old Testament - *Psalms* has inspired poets and writers throughout time. "But God chose the foolish things of the world to shame the wise; God chose the weak things of the world to shame the strong. He chose the lowly things of this world and the despised things - and the things that are not - to nullify the things that are, so that no one may boast before him." (1 Cor. 1:27) He always amazes me! So remember this when you think, "I am not good enough to pray." It's not about *us* being good - we can't *earn* any of this – it's about *him* being good. Very Good!

Why Do I Feel Guilty for Getting Sick?

Sometimes people have the belief that an illness is always a physical reflection of a spiritual imbalance. If they get cancer, they wonder what they did to "deserve" it. *Trees* get cancer, as do animals. Do we blame and criticize trees and animals for their illness? No! We give them love, understanding and support. Yes, some things we bring upon ourselves because of emotional and spiritual imbalances. But, we also need to acknowledge many other factors including, but not limited to: genetics, environmental pollutants, addictions (parental addiction while in the womb), working conditions, childhood nutrition, etc. Now, can you blame yourself for all these things? No! You are bombarded by many factors. Take note that also, sometimes the cells in our body *simply malfunction*. We are a long way from the Garden of Eden and perfect bodies.

So, *stop feeding off the guilt platter* and decide from this day forward to use your energy to fix the problems, instead of all the energy it requires for placing blame!

How Do I Relieve Stress?

The dictionary describes stress as "mental, emotional, or physical tension; strain, distress." The world we live in is fast-paced and competitive, and causes stress in our lives. Changing schedules, budget concerns, credit card bills, car repairs, mortgage, relationship problems, children difficulties, endless appointments, etc. - it all requires *a lot* of energy. A *depletion* of energy means a need for *replacing* energy. Again, the law of cause and effect comes into play. Rest, exercise, trips to the beach or to the mountains, a bubble bath, a babysitter and a dinner out, a massage, a drive in the country, a picnic at the park, solitude, a movie - all these things can help relieve stress. But sooner or later, you have to face those things that created the stress. How do you restore a weary heart, build courage, or hope for things to get better? This *only* comes from filling the spiritual need. We were created with an empty "God-Spot."
Just like a car can only work well feeding on gasoline, our spirit can only work well feeding on Spirit.

Most people wait until their "stress balloons" keep growing bigger and bigger, until one day, they "pop!" Then they lose control and go off in all directions - they leave their job, their family, the country, find a lover, etc. Everything breaks down, falls apart, and crumbles – often like dominos leaning against each other, everything tumbles down. There is another alternative! Instead of "breaking," all it takes is *one step at a time,* a progressive letting air out of the stem of the balloon, releasing its pressure *gradually* until it is safely deflated. It can then remain resting there whole and unbroken. Learning to see opportunities in many situations develops character and confidence.

Why Should I Make Time for a Spiritual Life?

Take a step back and look at your life. Are you happy, no matter what life is giving you? If your answer is no, they you must *buy out the time. Buying* means we have to exchange something for it. That is what we normally do for things of *value.* What happens when you buy out time for spiritual growth? You will find peace, understanding, answers for many of life's questions (big and small), endurance, strength, and love. What else occurs when you make time to look for God? You find him! "You will seek me and find me when you seek me with all your heart. I will be found by you," declares the Lord." (Jer. 29:13,14)

"Examine your priorities and ask the tough questions. Are the things you're investing your time in, things that will last? Will you have anything to show for your hard work and frantic pace when you come to the end of your life? If you're too busy for God, then you're too busy." - *Stress* by Melanie Jongsma (The Bible League, 1992)

How Do I Know if it's Me Talking, or God?

God gives us a knowing, and a discernment to know his voice over a counterfeit one. Test it out! God would never tell us to hurt ourselves, or others, or to be an extremist. It will not contradict anything that we know about his character of love, his teachings of wisdom (being familiar with his Word lets you know the difference – the personality of God, the history of how he deals with mankind), the undefiled conscience, or the commonsense he created us with. See if what you are hearing resonates in your bones, and makes you feel happy, peaceful, balanced and confident. If it doesn't, it's not True Source.

As for knowing if it is your own intuition, or your own spirit talking, that can also be answered. Ask him to make it clear! This is what I did (remember the freedom we have through Free Will, we have to ask for things first!), and now when the Lord speaks to me, there is a definite distinction. He uses my voice, *but* it's more punctuated, has no language contractions, is slower, in colonial English, and has a definite "Old World" flavor to it - I can't mistake it now!

Does the Person Receiving Healing Have to Believe in It?

No, we are not limited to healing through first lifting the understanding of the client into the deeper meaning of God's love. The results of the healing itself, the empirical experience, will often get the person wondering about a Greater Force. As they hear us say our beginning prayer, they hear more about who that One is. Some may also wonder if it's right to pray in the power of Jesus' name for one who is not willing to accept Christ. Let's look at this from a simple point of reason, and not argue theology.

In a hospital, would a patient preparing for surgery ask to look over the doctor's tools, and then disdainfully forbid the surgeon to use the ones he personally doesn't care for? If the doctor is prevented from using the implements he knows and has had much success with, the patient would be harming himself by being so judgmental - perhaps to a disastrous outcome. The same would be true of a mechanic being limited to the tools he needs to work on your car; the plumber's wrenches, etc. Sometimes it's worth a try to be quietly tolerant, and wait for the final outcome to see if proof of competency is there, to see if those tools actually fix the problems presented to it.

How Often Should I Come for a Healing?

This should be left up to the client. I suggest seeing the person at least once more – that way (even if an immediate healing occurred the first time out) you can check on the chart you've made for them and see what changes have occurred. The worse the problem, the more you should "hit it on the head" until it is under control. For example, cancer I try to see twice a week, even if the healing time is only ½ hr long. In this way, by the time the Energy starts to leave, the new treatment pumps up the level again, and continues to stimulate recuperation. A Remember, a Divine Healing is like God's radiation therapy - the longer the malady is in the force-field of his love, the quicker the problem will disappear!

Why Do I Feel Dizzy After a Healing?

Sometimes, in this agitating and cleaning-out process, the physical and emotional bodies may need a couple of days to detoxify, since so many changes are taking place at the same time, and at an incredible rate of speed. At times, this may cause dizziness, or an upset stomach, or other symptoms of detox, which seems to be lessened by eating some steamed vegetables and getting more rest. Think of yourself as having just completed a long-distance run - the body needs time to recuperate, and rest and nutrition helps it do its job. Light-headedness after a healing is a common side effect of the Spirit working in the body. It seems the average human being is not used to so much "current" going through it. It is a pleasing feeling, and is accompanied by a feeling of joy, calm and peacefulness. Drinking some water and walking around takes care of the dizziness – and please be sure to wait before driving home when you feel this way!

But I Have Prayed Many Times, and Nothing Happens, Why?

If you have prayed about the problem many times and don't think anything has changed, don't feel hopeless - that is why God allows mediators, and *intercessory* prayer. If you feel God doesn't love you anymore and your candle of faith is burning low, let the faith required come from the one praying in your behalf. If you are moved to, unburden yourself upon the one helping you, and as before, feel all the emotions there are to feel. You can do this with someone you feel safe with, who has an *active* prayer life. You can also go back to one who is facilitated for Divine Healing, planning to spend at least an hour, so that Spirit can flow naturally, in a private setting. As his kids, we have one another other for a reason. When one is down, the other can lift him up, we are meant to need each other and get along. "He comforts us in all our troubles so that we can comfort others. When others are troubled, we will be able to give them the same comfort God has given us." (2 Cor.1: 4)

210

We also need to be persistent, and know there is right timing for everything. He does love us. He does hear us. He does communicate with us; perhaps you are just not seeing it clearly at the moment. And, making sure what we are praying for is not about ego or excess, we learn to wait in expectation with love and obedience. Then look for the results: "Devote yourselves to prayer, being watchful and thankful." (Col. 4:2)

What's that on Your Wall?

If we don't transform it, we transmit it. That is why the exercise about what our last conversations are about, *are so telling* about how we truly look at life through our own hurt. We must forgive, not only others, but ourselves. We must show love to others, to God, and to ourselves. Here is one way to transform negative feelings from bad experiences, an example mostly taken from a speaking engagement I attended with Colin Tipping, the author of *Radical Forgiveness: Making way for the Miracle*:

"Imagine a wall hanging a friend gives you, they tell you to hang it on your wall because it is growing in value and will be worth a lot one day. You look at it, and all you see is a ugly mix-match of chaotic colors woven here and there with no random pattern, and loose threads and knots. You can't imagine what he is talking about, but you take it home and hang it on your wall. One day you notice some brown paper hanging down off one corner; the backing is torn so you turn it around to mend it. Underneath this torn backing you notice something usual, so curiosity gets the better of you, and you tear the entire backing off. There in front of you is an exquisite woven tapestry! A landscape so beautiful, with all the most inviting colors and fine craftsmanship imaginable! And then you smile to yourself, because now you understand that every piece of colored yarn and every place where the chaotic colors where, and every knot was *exactly where it was supposed to be!* Everything was as it should be, you were just not aware of it! Such it is with your life. You just aren't seeing the bigger picture yet." So it is with our own chaotic life. We are the weavers of yarn, each working on a different place, at a different time, on a different scenic tapestry, in our spiritual journey toward God.

How Can I See Angels?

When you sense these feelings, try to lift your own vibrational level up as far as you can – go into prayer and meditation, and breathe very deeply, even physical activity and aerobics help. Do a healing on yourself or someone else, thereby bringing Holy Spirit further into play. Now, cross your eyes slightly (as if you were looking at a "magic eye" puzzle of the 1980's) and be open, open, open without fear, asking to see God's messenger. The angel also has to *choose* to let you see him, and to slow down his energy to make it possible. Remember that True Sons do not want glory for themselves, so will only appear if it is in the best interest for the job they have been sent for. Be prepared to see angels in a much different way than Hollywood portrays! They can be so very huge – I've seen an angel almost 40 feet tall, standing head and shoulders over a house that had just been spiritually purified (exorcised). They can also be very small, less than three feet high!

How Long Does It Take for a Healing Treatment?

I don't know! No matter how many people I may have, the Holy Spirit just refuses to go by the clock! I normally schedule people for one hour each. If I have seen them before, I have circled the places of injury on their chart (the chart is a simple outline drawing of the body, front and back, including contact information). Then I don't need to do a full body analysis, and will just work on the places needed. Then perhaps a half hour is fine. Having a chart also allows for me to see the changes that have occurred since the last time I saw them, have a conversation about it, and note the improvements. Sometimes the Spirit will move in 10 minutes, and be done! Then I am left with the quandary of ending the treatment early (which can make a client feel uncomfortable), or just spending the allotment of time conversing. Sometimes, the Spirit will take much longer, up to two hours. Who am I to tell God what to do? Never may that be so! The interesting thing is, even though it may make me way off schedule for the other people waiting, to this day I have had no complaints or anyone leave in a huff! "Patience is a virtue," we are told. This relates to healings too!

What Results Can I Expect?

There is a wide spectrum of what might happen in a healing. At the very least, there will be a sense of peace, stress relief, less pain and better sleep at night. At the other end of the spectrum - cancer cells, heart disease and chronic pain disappear, brain tumors shrink and legs straighten! One never knows where in this spectrum a healing will fall. Personally, I have immediate, spontaneous healings in about 10 -12% of my cases, which is considered very high! I have learned to never place limits on what might occur - including *miracles* - and I feel this percentage will grow over time, as *my* conduit of faith strengthens, and as *others open* to the fact of Divine Healing.

What is Reiki?

Reiki is a Japanese term for a "hands-on-healing" modality which is recognized by the American Medical Association as a Complementary Alternative Medicine (CAM). It is used in many hospitals by trained nurses and doctors as a complement to normal health care needs. It has consistent and measurable results. There are more and more studies (including double-blind studies by NIH) and more research is being conducted. This form of hands-on-healing is easily accessible, and more and more accepted by the public. Reiki is also a healing modality that allows me to submit legally appropriate insurance claims for integrative healthcare interventions using ABC codes (this is not available for "Healing Prayer" at this time). This ability to bill insurance makes Hands-On-Healing more available for those who really need it, and legitimate as a recognized tool in healthcare.

Create a Peaceful Atmosphere

It is nice to have a peaceful atmosphere, and if you have a clinic to work out of, so much the better. This would allow you to work with walk-ins off the street, and referrals of doctors, clients and friends, make appointments, and in this way help as many people as possible. But, doing Divine Healing out of your home or the person's home, or meeting at a mutual location or church, can also work. If it's in an environment that you're in control of, muted lighting and soft instrumental music sets a nice tone for relaxing. Please, no incense or perfumed candles, many people have allergic reactions to them, and they are not necessary.

How Do I Pray?

Approach the Almighty Father as a dear respected friend. Know that you can talk to him casually, without any fancy words and in any setting. People often feel that they can manipulate God into doing whatever they want him to do, if they find the "magic formula" of words to say, then they drone on and on, all within ear-shot of other people. Did that work to manipulate your earthly father at home? I doubt it! It doesn't work with your Heavenly Father either! A lot of people use God like a Santa Claus, just begging for things. Don't use all your time trying to convince God into making deals! He knows what you need before you even ask for it. Spend time in praise and common thought and ring him up through "prayer phone." His cell phone is never out of range, never has a low battery, or even a busy signal! Picture that every time you pray, you are making a deposit in your grace bank account. You do not have to even pay a nickel for this cell phone. In fact, you receive the benefit. Become a millionaire!
"If the only prayer you said in your whole life was "Thank You," that would suffice." - Meister Eckhart (c.1260 - c.1327)

What is *Healing of the Memories?*

As long as three weeks after a healing treatment, different memories may come up that were thought to be long forgotten; such as memories of trauma, physical and emotional abuse, and unforgiveness and destructive thoughts. Often we think that these are things

213

we had *already* gotten rid of, when we had merely suppressed them. Remember how we are like the glass of water with dirt in the bottom. These hidden, unhealthy emotions are part of what Divine Healing stirs up and brings to the surface, to be given another opportunity for release out of our systems. So, when this unfolding happens, one thing I suggest is that you allow yourself to *totally feel all the emotions* of the experience, and not to push them back down into suppression. Then, see the memory as simply an experience that you moved through, and that it is over now, and done. You are not the victim anymore. You must forgive the situation, the other people, and yourself. What we *receive in forgiveness* will be in *direct relation* to that which we *give.*

Why Must I Forgive?

Frankly, it doesn't matter what happens to you, it matters *how you deal with it.* It's the *re*action to the action. *Not being able to forgive is pride.* It is a matter of trust to be able to let go, even of the bigger things, and in this way surrender to our next stage of spiritual development where we can *quickly* and *easily* forgive. Surrender is not a one-time occurrence. It is a constant and long-term process that occurs in stages. Scripture says that God will *not listen* to the prayers of those who continue to hold unforgiveness in their heart. It's considered a sin, grave imperfection, to do that. That's how important it is! "Love your enemies, do good to those who hate you, bless those who curse you, pray for those who mistreat you." (Lk. 6:27) Forgiveness is essential to healing.

"Forgiveness is a complex act of consciousness that frees the psyche from the need for vengeance or retribution. Energetically and biologically forgiveness heals. Let go of all angry thoughts. Holding anger in your being hurts you." - *Reiki, A Way Of Life* by Patricia Rose Upczak (Synchronicity Publishing, 1999)

How Do I find the True Purpose for My Life?

God speaks through our natural abilities. He created us with certain skills and desires, and each of us is unique in doing these things, and they "come easy" to us. We gain pleasure in doing them. What are you good at? What do you like to do? Pursue your natural talents and find a way to use it to enrich the lives of people around you, then watch for God to bless your efforts. If you spend your life doing the things you hate to do, having a job that you hate to go to, and live in a place that you hate, why are you still there and doing these things?

Yes, it is a scary step to change our mindset on this. So much responsibility weighs on our shoulders. But, perhaps you can adjust slowly, create a business on the side, and test the waters. Pray about it. If grace is *not present,* there will be a continuing struggle, and you will need to look at your other creative assets. If grace *is present,* doors will

214

open and opportunities will appear! Now this is important - if your passion and Free Will are *not* engaged in what you are doing, you cannot create anything dynamic in your life, because there is nothing to Bless. *Nothing to Bless!*

How Can I Pray over the Phone?

Praying with someone over the phone is a good and simple form of long-distance healing. The person is awake and paying attention, and has the choice to come together in agreement with you. It's a good idea to request that the person being prayed for also says an out-loud prayer of his own afterwards; this strengthens their commitment to fully receive the manifestations of the mutual prayer. Even over the phone, healing in this matter can be instantaneous or gradual, and it's possible you might be gifted with an impression or even prophecy that the Big Guy wants you to share. Have the caller place their own hands on their body where they want to be physically healed. For emotional healing, have the men place their hand over their heart; and the women on their solar plexus (belly); this is where the larger seat of their emotions dwell. Say a short out-loud prayer of blessing, knowing that God knows what is needed, and knows where these people are.

You may be surprised to hear Words of Knowledge or Prophecy occur at these times too. When this happens, know that you must speak, boldly, the words in your heart; but at the same time, that the whole world is listening! It is a delicate balance; personal privacy and teaching a group - but if you are in Spirit, what needs to be said and done, will be. "The Lord said to me, "the telephone is a means of communication. People talk to each other on it. I can also use it. You use the phone. People will hear you, but experience me." I don't have to see them, just unite with them before Jesus." - *Miracles Do Happen* by Sister Briege McKenna

What is the Difference between Deliverance & Exorcism?

It is rare that a person is actually *possessed* (thus requiring a solemn *exorcism, by qualified clergy*). Possession is *absolute* demonic control of the person. More often it is an evil attachment/affliction that is occurring *(simple deliverance)*. It is demonic *oppression,* where the good and normal nature of the person is attacked. This is very common. Most people have just attracted evil to themselves from past bad decisions (sin), so it has an actual right to be there, a contract as it were, and it just won't let go.

Free Will acts like a protective armor around us - through *lapses of Free Will,* such as drunkenness or drug abuse, we may have received "holes" in our armor, places of weakness where we have been attacked. If your Free Will was usurped by another through rape or other abuse, you may have holes. If you have willfully played games

215

(such as using the Ouija board) that opened a door to inviting in evil, you may have holes. By breaking the contracts and cleaning out the holes, and then filling them up again with solid, strong material, your armor can be restored to gleaming perfection and you will live healthy and well, physically, emotionally, and spiritually. You may even be wearing armor that is full of holes that were passed down to you by your relatives. Isn't it time to repair the armor?

When would I Need the Prayer of Deliverance?

When you feel that evil is attached to you in some way and you are constantly thinking evil thoughts, are confused, or want to harm yourself or others, and can't seem to shake it, you may need a prayer of deliverance. If you have compulsions that drive you to distraction, suicidal tendencies, desire to inflict damage on objects and animals, sexual addictions, dark thoughts that "come out of nowhere," and you bristle or anger for no apparent reason (especially around spiritual people), you may need a prayer of deliverance. If your family seems to have "bad luck" following it (even through generations), or you have mysterious physical pain or undiagnosed disease that may even baffle the doctors, you may need a prayer of deliverance.

Why is My Life so Full of Repetitive Cycles?

"You have made your way around this hill country long enough." (De. 2:3) This comes from a place in the scriptures where the Israelites had been wandering in the wilderness for 40 years, as a way for them to learn to develop spiritually and rely on God. They would go around and around, seeing the same rock outcroppings, the same valleys and hills, and still they weren't allowed to go to the land "flowing with milk and honey." They weren't ready yet. Then, one day it came! The repetitive cycle was broken. Now progress happened very quickly, and soon they entered and settled in the "Promised Land" and became a mighty nation for hundreds of years. Sometimes we get stuck in repetitive cycles too, and wonder why we are being presented with the same problems over and over again, in only a slightly different manner. It is usually because we haven't learned what we need to from it yet - we keep making the *wrong turn* that *will not* break the cycle.

If you are seeing repetitive cycles in your life, search your heart, and feed the loving, compassionate choice, the one that benefits *others* as well as yourself. The choice that leaves selfishness and ego out of the way, and allows you to become the true potential that you already are. Choose differently, through spiritual eyes. You will be surprised how quickly freedom will come, and how quickly progress will then be made. The repetitive cycle will be broken. You may see patterns that have surfaced throughout

216

your life for many years, and even why you chose the way you did, and the outcomes of those decisions.

Are There Drugs in the Body System?

The liver is the blood purifier of the body. Everything goes through here, and is a good thermometer of what is going on. Especially are drugs noticed here, and if the liver is working overtime, you will definitely feel it. Then, you may ask, "Are you on any drugs or medications at this time?" And they will answer yes or no. There are some herbal components that also effect heat in the liver, including herbal cleansers. This is not all bad - similar to our running a low-grade fever when we are fighting a cold, we want the body to fight the germs and allow a mark of 101 degrees, but get worried and step in when it reaches 103 or 104. So it is with the liver. It is OK to run a bit hot, to allow it to do its job. We just want to monitor it, and give it some healing prayer to help it on its way.

What about Nutrition, Herbs and Medications?

A lot of people ask me for nutrition and herbal advice, and even what conventional medications they should take (sometimes they even bring these with them, for me to "choose"). I am not a nutritionalist, a medical doctor or herbalist. Even if I were, I would choose not to use these things in the same session with Divine Healing. I do not want to be a referral service to something else. That is putting God in a less powerful position than he is! I do what God gives me to do, and see and say what God wants me to say, and that's what I do. That's all I do. That's enough! I don't want people to be confused with what healing is being done by God, and what supplement I give them on the side.

How Long will Healing Continue after a Treatment?

Another thing you need to say to the client is this: "The healing does not stop when you get off the table. The process of healing will continue on for an average of another 2 - 3 days." Let them know it is similar to a fan being unplugged from the wall, with the fan blades continuing to spin until they finally slow down and stop. Such it is with the Holy Spirit. They could even feel better tomorrow than today, or even the next day after that, as the healing continues! It is also good to bring up one other point for those three days - the abstinence of alcohol, drugs or heavily oiled or deep-fried foods. Why? I do not know, but it seems to slow the healing down in the system, and we want the Spirit's afterglow to continue as long as possible!

217

What is Meditation?

Meditation is a common tool that many cultures use, for people to know themselves and to get close to God. Through meditation, awareness can be nurtured and trained. *Sense the stillness, and the stillness will awaken all your senses.* Sister Briege McKenna said: "the discipline of sitting before the Lord is very important. It is only when your spirit is *still* and when the ears of your spirit are *open* that you can really hear the Lord and experience the wisdom and insights that come from the Holy Spirit." *She consistently puts aside three hours every day for this discipline!* It helps fill the "Dixie cup." I try to do 1-2 hours daily, more when I can. This time is precious to me. It allows me to be in the Word, to hear his voice, and just *be.* I get out of balance easily if I don't.

What is a Prayer Chain?

These are also called by other names, including "prayer chains." This is basically a list where your name is placed, and/or sometimes your illness, and a multitude of people pray for you. Group intention is important! Besides your church, there are also many churches, including some very big and popular ministries, on the Internet that allow your name to be placed on a message board, to "sign in" to be prayed for, or to work as a "prayer warrior" in behalf of another. Why not have a flood of prayers said in your behalf? Bathe in the crystalline waterfall of Divine Love!

Why Does God Sometimes Knock Them Out during a Healing?

At this time, we can't know for sure. There are many possibilities. Perhaps Spirit is just too much for the human body. Perhaps being unconscious it is a way of bypassing all the *blockages* of the analytical brain and all the *questionings* of "what is happening?" or "am I being healed?" etc. Putting them to sleep takes care of that. Remember, the 10% of the brain acts as a bridge or a barrier to spirit. But, as always, he will not go against Free Will.

What Happens When Resting in the Spirit?

While resting in the Spirit, one or more of several things may happen:

- They may commune with God.
- They may see clearly how to deal with pressing problems.
- They may have a vision.
- They may be given words of wisdom or knowledge.

218

- They may be healed, physically, emotionally or spiritual.
- They may be given a prophecy
- They may just feel good and don't know why.
- They may wake up "Drunk in the Spirit."

How Could Fear be a Barrier to Healing?

Some people are afraid to try anything new. Others are afraid because they don't really want to heal - they can't see their lives beyond their illness. They identify with it too much. In these cases, it is often because they have dealt with it for so long, that they don't know anything else. Change is a stress, even if it is for our own good. It goes back to those things that we feel comfortable with, our developed habits. We need to pray for emotional healing in such cases, so that we can look beyond and see ourselves whole and happy with new, healthy habits.

We need to look at our core belief systems too. Sometimes people feel it's God's will for them to suffer, to do penance as it were. While it is true that an illness often leads to our spiritual growth, it is also true that illness is an enemy and that we do not need to suffer for our sins - they have been already nailed upon the tree for us. We do not need to be a martyr. That, my friend, is actually denying the ransom sacrifice! Also, taking illness upon our own body does not prevent illness from coming upon our family - again, we are not asked to be the sacrificial lamb in any way. "He himself bore our sins in his body on the tree, so that we might die to sins and live for righteousness; by his wounds you have been healed." (1 Pe. 2:24) Instead, we are admonished to be well, and to be whole.

What Religion is God?

In the great majority of cases, about 98% of the time your religion is cast by where in the world you were born. If someone is born in Egypt to Muslim parents, that person will very likely be a Muslim. If born to Buddhist parents in Burma, a Buddhist. To a Hindu parent in India, a Hindu - if to a Christian parent in the United States, a Christian. In all of these cases, the person may be fully committed to his faith, or merely affiliated with it. All of them have very different belief systems and customs to help facilitate the person's faith. In some of the religions, such as Christianity and Judaism, belief systems and customs are much further broken down into hundreds of branches and myriad versions of dogma. Yet, all profess to have the corner on God; with their method of worship culturally deemed the best.

So, how does a God-Seeker go about finding the right religion? *How about from the top down?* We may never make the journey if we trace out every path and follow it until we find ourselves lost. We will probably get scared of the complexity, run out of time, and consider it useless. Then we "throw the baby out with the bathwater." Sometimes we forget about the destination of God when we get twisted, dizzy and disheartened by the path, and others we meet alongside the road who seem beat up by it. *But* if we look at it simply…*what religion is God?* Starting at the top should help us get the idea of what the end of the journey should look like, especially if we are unsure of the particular path we may find ourselves on at this time.

Why Visit a Variety of Churches?

The hungry Spirit has a spiritual need. If you don't have people who can encourage you, believe in Divine Healing and Gifts of the Spirit, share the Word, and see the beauty of individuality alongside the oneness of love, you are missing out on a very joyful and helpful experience. Even if you are happy in your home church, it is a good exercise to see the family of God in many places. There are many journeys of the soul; and seeing God break out in a multitude of various homes keeps us as humble children, never believing that we can keep God in a box of our own choosing.

What about Healing Animals?

Animals, just like small children, have no barriers to accepting healing. The Energy courses through quickly, and when the "spark" fly from your hands to the animal, the initial surprise of it might startle them, and they may move away. But, give them just a few seconds, and they will be back again, wanting more! They love to feel the Glow, and healing for animals is such a Godly and wonderful thing to do - after all, we were originally created to fully care for them and the earth. Since animals in pain cannot tell us where they hurt, Divine Healing can be a miracle for them; your hands will get hot and healing will flow to where ever it is needed. Just touch where they will let you - you do not need to be right over the spot. The healings will be much quicker than on humans. The "hot-spots" may be an aid to diagnosing the area where tests or x-rays need to be done, thus helping save cost and vet time. Your hands may stay cold on an animal that is about to die – they will not receive Spirit. Or, they may only get warm, as if only enough healing is happening to lessen any pain. No matter what the reason for an animal to be brought into your path, know you are given the gift of healing to help all of God's creatures, great and small.

What if I Have More Questions?

Contact me at:

Spirit Journey Books
P.O. Box 61
San Marcos, CA 92079

Or via: emailtiffanysnow@aol.com

Or through my website at www.TiffanySnow.com

And I will try to personally answer your questions, often within one week.

Perhaps the question you have will be included in a new book!

"And we have the word of the prophets
made more certain,
and you will do well to pay attention to it,
as to a light shining in a dark place,
until the day dawns
and the morning star rises in your hearts."
(2 Pe. 1:19)

QUICK ORDER FORM

The Power of Divine: A Healer's Guide
Tapping into the Miracle

ISBN:0-9729623-3-6 SPIRITJOURNEYBOOKS.COM

For orders via mail, please send this form along with check or money order
Written to: Spirit Journey Books

Spirit Journey Books
P.O. Box 61
San Marcos, CA 92079
1-800-535-5474

For expedited orders, please order via credit card through our websites at:
www.SpiritJourneyBooks.com
www.TiffanySnow.com

Name:_____

Address:_____

City:_____State:_____Zip:_____

Email or phone number:_____

Amount for Book is: $18.95

CA. Sales Tax: (7.75% If applicable)

Book	**$18.95**
(Quantity) x (	**)**
+CA. Tax (	)
+Shipping (	)
TOTAL=	_____

Shipping: Please add $3.00 for first book, and $1.00 each additional book.
Tax: Please add 7.75% for books shipped to California addresses.
For wholesale or library discounts, please call 1 (800) 535-5474

I would like Free Information Regarding Workshops, Seminars and Book Signings:
(circle one)   YES   /   NO

I would like to receive Tiffany Snow's monthly email newsletter:
(circle one)   YES   /   NO   Email address:_____

223

Also by Tiffany Snow

PSYCHIC GIFTS IN THE CHRISTIAN LIFE –
TOOLS TO CONNECT

ISBN:0-9729623-0-1 SPIRITJOURNEYBOOKS.COM

ACTIVATE SPIRITUAL GIFTS IN YOUR DAILY LIFE!

"Tiffany Snow's *PSYCHIC GIFTS IN THE CHRISTIAN LIFE – TOOLS TO CONNECT* is the book you've been waiting for. It is a "self-help" manual that will show you how to manifest and use your Supernatural Gifts. Step-by-step learn how to tap into the Divine Connection and your own natural-born intuitive abilities. Each reading of this amazing book will lead you to a new level of understanding, ability and insight for enhancing your self and God awareness and for the betterment of the world."
- Ivy Helstein, Psychotherapist and Author of *INFINITE ABILITIES: Living Your Life On Purpose*

FINALLY! A book that bridges the gap and speaks frankly about God's Supernatural Gifts as a NATURAL AND NORMAL PART OF SPIRITUAL LIFE!

"Thank you, Tiffany, for being in the world and for helping it to be a better place for all of us to be. God bless...I am proud of the work you are so diligently doing in service to enlightenment. Keep it up, Girlfriend. The world is a much better place due to the loving efforts of shining souls such as yourself." **- Dannion Brinkley, International Best-Selling Author of *Saved By the Light, At Peace in the Light,* and Founder of Compassion in Action**

"Through Tiffany's sharing of her amazing journey, she is a pioneer in bridging religion with spirituality, reminding us all that life is about our own experience and expression of the powerful love of God in our everyday life. It is a must read for all people on all paths of life."**- Joan Grinzi, RN, President of Holistic Health Resources/***Alternative Paths to Healing***

"Tiffany Snow has written a remarkably lucid presentation of how to make the Spirit and spiritual gifts each of us possess become activated in our daily lives. Besides being a "How-To-Book" it is more importantly an invitation, a clarion call to "why not you?"
– Rev. Francis J. Marcolongo, S.T.L., S.S.L., Ph.D., MFT

"Tiffany Snow is as gifted a writer as she is a healer. Her book, "Psychic Gifts in the Christian Life: Tools To Connect," is filled with wisdom, insight and a pure spiritual joy that is infectious. She is truly an inspiration; a bright light in a world so often filled

225

with darkness." **- Rev. Marie D. Jones, Author** *of Looking For God In All The Wrong Places*

From the Author: Tiffany says: "From the very beginning, God has demonstrated that his Spirit is Supernatural, and has given us gifts to keep in contact with him. So many of us have special abilities that are shut down as children, from well-meaning friends or misinformed religions. But God has always used Supernatural ways to connect with his kids, and still does today. Become the potential you already are! In my book, GOD IS OUT OF THE BOX! And, for those who are Christian, throughout the book you will find cited scriptural backing for understanding your gifts without fear. No one has to be struck by *lightning* to have this Connection – my hope is that this book will be *your* defining moment. We ALL have gifts!" From a sumptuous buffet laid before you, you will be able to choose from many tools to learn how to use and develop the natural gifts we were all created with, and the Supernatural ones that we can tap into. Games will activate your God-Spots becoming more intuitive and sensitive. Some Topics: Channeling Holy Spirit; Finding Missing Children through Prayer Power, Helping FBI, our God-Spots.

QUICK ORDER FORM

Psychic Gifts in the Christian Life – Tools to Connect

ISBN:0-9729623-0-1 SPIRITJOURNEYBOOKS.COM

For orders via mail, please send this form along with check or money order
Written to: Spirit Journey Books

Spirit Journey Books
P.O. Box 61
San Marcos, CA 92079
1-800-535-5474

For expedited orders, please order via credit card through our websites at:
www.SpiritJourneyBooks.com
www.TiffanySnow.com

Name:_____

Address:_____

City:_____State:_____Zip:_____

Email or phone number:_____

Amount for Book is: $24.95

CA. Sales Tax: (7.75% If applicable)

Book	**$24.95**
(Quantity) x (	**)**
+CA. Tax (	)
+Shipping (	)
TOTAL= _____	

Shipping: Please add $3.00 for first book, and $1.00 each additional book.
Tax: Please add 7.75% for books shipped to California addresses.
For wholesale or library discounts, please call 1(800) 535-5474

I would like Free Information Regarding Workshops, Seminars and Book Signings:
(circle one)   YES   /   NO

I would like to receive Tiffany Snow's monthly email newsletter:
(circle one)   YES   /   NO   Email address:_____

Printed in the United States
19909LVS00003B/233